# Other Books and Series by Jeff Bowen

*Applications for Enrollment of Chickasaw Newborn Act of 1905*
*Volumes I thru VII*

*Cherokee Intermarried White 1906 Volume I thru X*

*Applications for Enrollment of Creek Newborn Act of 1905*
*Volumes I thru XIV*

*Applications for Enrollment of Choctaw Newborn Act of 1905*
*Volume I, II, III, IV, V, VI, VII, VIII, IX, X, XI, XII, XIII, XIV, XV, XVI & XVII,*

Visit our website at **www.nativestudy.com** to learn more about these and other books and series by Jeff Bowen

# APPLICATIONS FOR ENROLLMENT OF CHOCTAW NEWBORN ACT OF 1905

## VOLUME XVIII

### TRANSCRIBED BY
## JEFF BOWEN

NATIVE STUDY
Gallipolis, Ohio
USA

# Other Books and Series by Jeff Bowen

*1901-1907 Native American Census Seneca, Eastern Shawnee, Miami, Modoc, Ottawa, Peoria, Quapaw, and Wyandotte Indians (Under Seneca School, Indian Territory)*

*1932 Census of The Standing Rock Sioux Reservation with Births And Deaths 1924-1932*

*Census of The Blackfeet, Montana, 1897- 1901 Expanded Edition*

*Eastern Cherokee by Blood, 1906-1910, Volumes I thru XIII*

*Choctaw of Mississippi Indian Census 1929-1932 with Births and Deaths 1924-1931   Volume I*
*Choctaw of Mississippi Indian Census 1933, 1934 & 1937, Supplemental Rolls to 1934 & 1935 with Births and Deaths 1932-1938, and Marriages 1936-1938 Volume II*

*Eastern Cherokee Census Cherokee, North Carolina 1930-1939 Census 1930-1931 with Births And Deaths 1924-1931 Taken By Agent L. W. Page Volume I*
*Eastern Cherokee Census Cherokee, North Carolina 1930-1939 Census 1932-1933 with Births And Deaths 1930-1932 Taken By Agent R. L. Spalsbury   Volume II*
*Eastern Cherokee Census Cherokee, North Carolina 1930-1939 Census 1934-1937 with Births and Deaths 1925-1938 and Marriages 1936 & 1938 Taken by Agents R. L. Spalsbury And Harold W. Foght Volume III*

*Seminole of Florida Indian Census, 1930-1940 with Birth and Death Records, 1930-1938*

*Texas Cherokees 1820-1839 A Document For Litigation 1921*

*Choctaw By Blood Enrollment Cards 1898-1914 Volumes I thru XVII*

*Starr Roll 1894  (Cherokee Payment Rolls) Districts: Canadian, Cooweescoowee, and Delaware  Volume One*
*Starr Roll 1894 (Cherokee Payment Rolls) Districts: Flint, Going Snake, and Illinois   Volume Two*
*Starr Roll 1894 (Cherokee Payment Rolls) Districts: Saline, Sequoyah, and Tahlequah; Including Orphan Roll  Volume Three*

*Cherokee Intruder Cases  Dockets of Hearings 1901-1909  Volumes I & II*

*Indian Wills, 1911-1921  Records of the Bureau of Indian Affairs Books One thru Seven;*
*Native American Wills & Probate Records 1911-1921*

# Other Books and Series by Jeff Bowen

*Turtle Mountain Reservation Chippewa Indians 1932 Census with Births & Deaths, 1924-1932*

*Chickasaw By Blood Enrollment Cards 1898-1914 Volume I thru V*

*Cherokee Descendants East An Index to the Guion Miller Applications Volume I*
*Cherokee Descendants West An Index to the Guion Miller Applications Volume II (A-M)*
*Cherokee Descendants West An Index to the Guion Miller Applications Volume III (N-Z)*

*Applications for Enrollment of Seminole Newborn Freedmen, Act of 1905*

*Eastern Cherokee Census, Cherokee, North Carolina, 1915-1922, Taken by Agent James E. Henderson    Volume I (1915-1916)*
*Volume II (1917-1918)*
*Volume III (1919-1920)*
*Volume IV (1921-1922)*

*Complete Delaware Roll of 1898*

*Eastern Cherokee Census, Cherokee, North Carolina, 1923-1929, Taken by Agent James E. Henderson    Volume I (1923-1924)*
*Volume II (1925-1926)*
*Volume III (1927-1929)*

*Applications for Enrollment of Seminole Newborn Act of 1905 Volumes I & II*

*North Carolina Eastern Cherokee Indian Census 1898-1899, 1904, 1906, 1909-1912, 1914 Revised and Expanded Edition*

*1932 Hopi and Navajo Native American Census with Birth & Death Rolls (1925-1931) Volume 1 - Hopi*
*1932 Hopi and Navajo Native American Census with Birth & Death Rolls (1930-1932) Volume 2 - Navajo*

*Western Navajo Reservation Navajo, Hopi and Paiute 1933 Census with Birth & Death Rolls 1925-1933*

*Cherokee Citizenship Commission Dockets 1880-1884 and 1887-1889 Volumes I thru V*

Copyright © 2013
by Jeff Bowen

ALL RIGHTS RESERVED
No part of this publication may be reproduced
or used in any form or manner whatsoever
without previous written permission from the
copyright holder or publisher.

Originally published:
Baltimore, Maryland
2013

Reprinted by:

Native Study LLC
Gallipolis, OH
www.nativestudy.com
2020

Library of Congress Control Number: 2020918113

ISBN: 978-1-64968-111-9

*Made in the United States of America.*

**This series is dedicated to the descendants of the Choctaw newborn listed in these applications.**

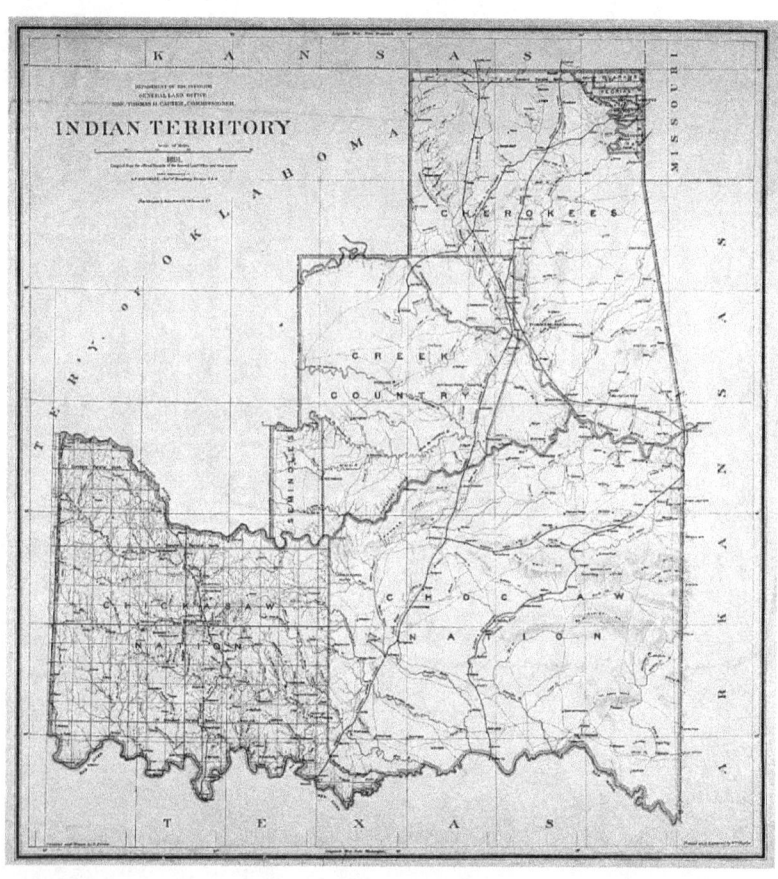

This map of Indian Territory shows how large the Choctaw and Chickasaw Nations' land base was that contained huge deposits of asphalt and coal. Just the size and territory involved was flooded with the "Grafters".

DEPARTMENT OF THE INTERIOR.
Commissioner to the Five Civilized Tribes.

# NOTICE.

## Opening of Land Office at Wewoka,
### IN THE SEMINOLE NATION, INDIAN TERRITORY.

Notice is hereby given that on Monday, September 4, 1905, the Commissioner to the Five Civilized Tribes will establish a land office at Wewoka, in the Seminole Nation, Indian Territory, for the purpose of allowing citizens and freedmen of the Seminole Nation to select allotments of land for their minor children enrolled under the Act of Congress approved March 3, 1905 (33 Stat. L 1060), and for the further purpose of allowing citizens and freedmen of the Seminole Nation, whose allotments are incomplete, to select additional land in order to bring the value of their allotments up to the standard of $309.09, as nearly as may be practicable.

Each child whose enrollment in accordance with the Act of March 3, 1905, has been duly approved by the Secretary of the Interior, is entitled to receive an allotment of forty acres without regard to the character or value of the land selected.

Selection of allotments for minor children must be made by their citizen or freedmen parents or by a duly appointed guardian, or curator, or by a duly appointed administrator.

TAMS BIXBY,
Commissioner.

Muskogee, Indian Territory,
July 29, 1905.

*This particular notice for the Seminole and Creek Newborn makes mention of the Act of 1905. It is likely that a similar notice was posted in the Choctaw and Chickasaw Nations for the registration of newborn children.*

# DEPARTMENT OF THE INTERIOR,
## Commission to the Five Civilized Tribes.

### Rules and Regulations Governing the Selection of Allotments and the Designation of Homesteads in the Choctaw and Chickasaw Nations.

1. Selections of allotments and designations of homesteads for adult citizens and selections of allotments for adult freedmen must be made in person except as herein otherwise provided.
2. Applications to have land set apart and homesteads designated for duly identified Mississippi Choctaws must be made personally before the Commission to the Five Civilized Tribes. Fathers may apply for their minor children and if the father be dead the mother may apply. Husbands may apply for wives. Applications for orphans, insane persons and persons of unsound mind may be made by duly appointed guardian or curator, and for aged and infirm persons and prisoners by agents duly authorized thereunto by power of attorney, in the discretion of said Commission.
3. At the time of the selection of allotment each citizen and duly identified Mississippi Choctaw shall designate as a homestead out of said selection land equal in value to one hundred and sixty acres of the average allottable land of the Choctaw and Chickasaw Nations, as nearly as may be.
4. Each Choctaw and Chickasaw freedman, at the time of selection shall designate as his or her allotment of the lands of the Choctaw and Chickasaw Nations, land equal in value to forty acres of the average allottable land of the Choctaw and Chickasaw Nations.
5. Citizens, freedmen and identified Mississippi Choctaws who are married, whether they have attained their majority or not, will be regarded as of age for the purpose of making selections.
6. Selections may be made by citizen and freedman parents for unmarried male children under twenty-one years of age and for unmarried female children under eighteen years of age, and a male citizen or freedman may make selection for his wife, if she is entitled to make selection, unless she shall, at the time or previously thereto, protest in writing.
7. Where the father of an unmarried minor citizen, freedman or identified Mississippi Choctaw is a non-citizen, the citizen, freedman or identified Mississippi Choctaw mother of such children must make selection in person in behalf of said children.
8. Selections of allotments and designations of homesteads for minor citizens and selections of allotments for minor freedmen may be made by the citizen father or freedman father or mother, as the case may be, or by a guardian, curator, or an administrator having charge of their estate, in the order named.
9. Selections of allotments and designations of homesteads for citizen, and selections of allotment for freedmen, prisoners, convicts, aged and infirm persons and soldiers and sailors of the United States on duty outside of Indian Territory, may be made by duly appointed agents under power of attorney, and for incompetents by guardians, curators, or other suitable person akin to them.
10. Selections may be made and homesteads designated by duly identified Mississippi Choctaws, who have, within one year after the date of their identification as such, made satisfactory proof of bona fide settlement within the Choctaw-Chickasaw country, at any time within six months after the date of their said identification.
11. Persons authorized to make selections by power of attorney, as provided in rules 2 and 9 hereof, must be the husband or wife, or a relative not further removed than a cousin of the first degree of the person for whom such selection is made.
12. It shall be the duty of the Commission to the Five Civilized Tribes to see that selections of allotments and designations of homesteads for the classes of persons mentioned in rules 2, 6, 7, 8 and 9 hereof, are made for the best interests of such persons.
13. Selections of allotments for citizens, freedmen and identified Mississippi Choctaws who have died subsequent to September 25, 1902, and before making a selection of allotment, shall be made by a duly appointed administrator or executor. If, however, such administrator or executor be not duly and expeditiously appointed, or fails to act promptly when appointed, or for any other cause such selections be not so made within a reasonable and practicable time, the Commission to the Five Civilized Tribes shall designate the lands thus to be allotted.
14. In determining the value of a selection the appraised value of the land selected shall be increased by the appraised value of such pine timber on such land as has heretofore been estimated by the Commission to the Five Civilized Tribes.
15. Selections of allotments may be made only by citizens and freedmen whose enrollment has been approved by the Secretary of the Interior, and by persons duly identified by the Commission to the Five Civilized Tribes as Mississippi Choctaws, and by none others.
16. When a selection of land has been made by a citizen, freedman or identified Mississippi Choctaw, and the land so selected is claimed by a person whose rights as a citizen or freedman have not been finally determined, contest for the land so selected may be instituted by the person claiming the land, formal application for the land being first made as is required by the Rules of Practice in Choctaw and Chickasaw allotment contest cases.

THE COMMISSION TO THE FIVE CIVILIZED TRIBES.
TAMS BIXBY, Chairman.

Muskogee, Indian Territory, March 24, 1903.

---

The above statement published prior to 1905, was established for what was supposed to be a set of guidelines when it came to allotments. But with supplemental agreements and Congressional legislation, time frames as well as rules and regulations often changed and were not the same for every tribe.

# INTRODUCTION

The *Applications for Enrollment of Choctaw Newborn Act of 1905*, National Archive film M-1301, Rolls 50-57, are found under the heading of Applications for Enrollment of the Commission to the Five Civilized Tribes. For this series, I have transcribed the application forms filled out by individuals applying for enrollment in the Five Civilized Tribes under the Dawes Commission. These applications contain considerably more information than stated on the census cards found in series M-1186. M-1301 possesses its own numerical sequence, separate from M-1186. To find each party's roll number you would have to reference M-1186.

The Choctaw as well as the Chickasaw allotments were likely some of the most sought after properties in Indian Territory. There was supposed to be a 25-year restriction on the sale or lease of any Indian lands so as to insure that the owners wouldn't be swindled, but that isn't what happened. This fact is borne out in the Dawes Commission General Allotment Act, of February 8, 1887, Section 5, which "Provides that after an Indian person is allotted land, the United States will hold the land 'in trust [1] for the sole use and benefit of the Indian' (or his heirs if the Indian landowner dies) for a period of 25 years. (Land held in trust by the United States government cannot be sold or in anyway alienated by the Indian landowner, since the United States government considers the underlying ownership of the land held by itself and not the tribe. After the period of trust ends, the Indian landowner is free to sell the land and is free from any encumbrance from the United States.)"[1] Instead, Native Americans were exploited by the devious. The Choctaw and Chickasaw Districts both had huge asphalt and coal deposits, so there was pressure from outsiders to acquire them from the minute they were discovered. After repeated attacks throughout the years and many legislative changes, President "Roosevelt finally signed the Five Tribes Bill at noon on April 26, 1906, the forces seeking to end all restrictions were disappointed. Section 19 removed restrictions from the sale of all inherited land but directed that no full-bloods could sell their land for twenty-five years. The Act also prohibited leases for more than one year without the approval of the Secretary of the Interior."[2]

Angie Debo described the opportunists that wanted these Native American allotments as, "Grafters". The parents of the newborns enumerated within this series would no sooner receive the approval for their child's allotment than there would be someone there with cash in hand holding a new deed or lease for the parents to sign their child's birthright away. Angie Debo said it best, "As the business incapacity of the allottees became apparent, a horde of despoilers fastened themselves upon their property." According to Debo, "The term 'grafter' was applied as a matter of course to dealers in Indian land, and was frankly accepted by them. The speculative fever also affected Government employees so that it was almost impossible to prevent them from making personal investments."[3]

---

[1] General Allotment Act, Act of Feb. 8, 1887 (24 Stat. 388, ch. 119, 25 USCA 331)
[2] The Dawes Commission and the Allotment of the Five Civilized Tribes, 1893-1914 by Kent Carter, pg. 173
[3] And Still the Waters Run, Angie Debo, p. 92.

# INTRODUCTION

According to the Department of Interior in 1905, "It is estimated that there will be added to the final rolls of the citizens and freedmen of the Choctaw and Chickasaw nations the names of 2,000 persons, including 1,500 new-born children to be enrolled under the provisions of the act of Congress approved March 3, 1905."[4]

The quote below explains, in detail, the requirements for qualifying as a newborn Choctaw, "By the act of Congress approved March 3, 1905 (H.R. 17474), entitled 'An act making appropriations for the current and contingent expenses of the Indian Department and for fulfilling treaty stipulations with various Indian tribes for the fiscal year ending June 30, 1906, and for other purposes,' it was provided as follows:

'That the Commission to the Five Civilized Tribes is hereby authorized for sixty days after the date of the approval of this act to receive and consider applications for enrollment of infant children born prior to September twenty-fifth, nineteen hundred and two, and who were living on said date, to citizens by blood of the Choctaw and Chickasaw tribes of Indians whose enrollment has been approved by the Secretary of the Interior prior to the date of the approval of this act; and to enroll and make allotments to such children.'

'That the Commission to the Five Civilized Tribes is authorized for sixty days after the date of the approval of this act to receive and consider applications for enrollment of children born subsequent to September twenty-fifth, nineteen hundred and two, and prior to March fourth, nineteen hundred and five, and who were living on said latter date, to citizens by blood of the Choctaw and Chickasaw tribes of Indians whose enrollment has been approved by the Secretary of the Interior prior to the date of the approval of this act; and to enroll and make allotments to such children.'

"Notice is hereby given that the Commission to the Five Civilized Tribes will, up to and inclusive of midnight, May 2, 1905, receive applications for the enrollment of infant children born prior to September 25, 1902, and who were living on said date, to citizens by blood of the Choctaw and Chickasaw tribes of Indians whose enrollment has been approved by the Secretary of the Interior prior to March 3, 1905."[5]

Following is the scope of these transcriptions: Besides the applications themselves, researchers will find the identities of other individuals within these applications -- doctors, lawyers, mid-wives, and other relatives -- that may help with you genealogical research.

Jeff Bowen
Gallipolis, Ohio
*NativeStudy.com*

---

[4] Annual Reports of the Department of the Interior For the Fiscal Year Ended June 30, 1905, p. 609.
[5] Annual Reports of the Department of the Interior For the Fiscal Year Ended June 30, 1905, p. 593.

## Applications for Enrollment of Choctaw Newborn
## Act of 1905   Volume XVIII

Choc New Born 1327
    Martin A. James
    (Born Feb. 28, 1904)

**NEW-BORN AFFIDAVIT.**

Number..............

### ...Choctaw Enrolling Commission...

IN THE MATTER OF THE APPLICATION FOR ENROLLMENT, as a citizen of the Choctaw Nation, of Martin A. James

born on the 28 day of __Fauary[sic]__ 190 4

Name of father   Allen W James   a citizen of   Choctaw Nation final enrollment No.   5950
Name of mother   Vicey Fobb   a citizen of   Choctaw Nation final enrollment No.   2567

                          Postoffice   Smithville Ind Ter

**AFFIDAVIT OF MOTHER.**

UNITED STATES OF AMERICA
INDIAN TERRITORY
    Central   DISTRICT

    I   Vicey Fobb   , on oath state that I am 21 years of age and a citizen by Blood of the Choctaw Nation, and as such have been placed upon the final roll of the Choctaw Nation, by the Honorable Secretary of the Interior my final enrollment number being 2567 ; that I am the lawful wife of Allen W. James , who is a citizen of the Choctaw Nation, and as such has been placed upon the final roll of said Nation by the Honorable Secretary of the Interior, his final enrollment number being 5950 and that a Male child was born to me on the 28 day of Feb 190 4; that said child has been named Martin A. James , and is now living.

                                      Vicey Fobb

Witnesseth.
    Must be two
    Witnesses who   } Laisen Gibson
    are Citizens.      Harrison McGee

## Applications for Enrollment of Choctaw Newborn
## Act of 1905 Volume XVIII

Subscribed and sworn to before me this 17 day of January 190 5

B.H. Barton NP
Notary Public.

My commission expires: Aug 12-1905

---

## AFFIDAVIT OF ATTENDING PHYSICIAN OR MIDWIFE

UNITED STATES OF AMERICA
INDIAN TERRITORY
Central    DISTRICT

I, Sisey McGee       a       citizen on oath state that I attended on Mrs. Vicey Fobb wife of Allen W James on the 28 day of Feb, 190 4, that there was born to her on said date a male child, that said child is now living, and is said to have been named Sisey x McGee
(her mark)

Subscribed and sworn to before me this, the 17 day of January 190 5

WITNESSETH:                              B.H. Barton    Notary Public.

Must be two witnesses who are citizens { Laisen Gibson

Harrison M{c}Gee

We hereby certify that we are well acquainted with_____
a_____ and know _____ to be reputable and of good standing in the community.

Laisen Gibson                              _____

Harrison McGee                             _____

---

BIRTH AFFIDAVIT.

## DEPARTMENT OF THE INTERIOR.
## COMMISSION TO THE FIVE CIVILIZED TRIBES.

IN RE APPLICATION FOR ENROLLMENT, as a citizen of the Choctaw Nation, of Martin A James, born on the 28th day of February, 1904

Name of Father: Allen James         a citizen of the Choctaw Nation.
Name of Mother: Vicey Fobb          a citizen of the Choctaw Nation.

Postoffice   Smithville, Ind. Ter.

# Applications for Enrollment of Choctaw Newborn
## Act of 1905   Volume XVIII

### AFFIDAVIT OF MOTHER.

UNITED STATES OF AMERICA, Indian Territory, }
    Central                    DISTRICT.

    I,    Vicey Fobb    , on oath state that I am  21   years of age and a citizen by blood   , of the   Choctaw   Nation; that I am the lawful wife of    Allen James   , who is a citizen, by blood   of the   Choctaw   Nation; that a   male   child was born to me on   28$^{th}$   day of   February   , 1904; that said child has been named   Martin A James   , and was living March 4, 1905.

                                      Vicey Fobb

Witnesses To Mark:
  { Harrison McGee
    *(Name Illegible)*

    Subscribed and sworn to before me this  26   day of      June     , 1905

                                      A.W. James
                                      Notary Public.

---

### AFFIDAVIT OF ATTENDING PHYSICIAN OR MID-WIFE.

UNITED STATES OF AMERICA, Indian Territory, }
    Central                    DISTRICT.

    I,    Sisey M$^c$Gee    , a   midwife   , on oath state that I attended on Mrs.   Vicey Fobb   , wife of   Allen James   on the 28$^{th}$   day of   February   , 1904; that there was born to her on said date a   male   child; that said child was living March 4, 1905, and is said to have been named   Martin A James

                                      Sisey M$^c$Gee

Witnesses To Mark:
  { Harrison McGee
    *(Name Illegible)*

    Subscribed and sworn to before me this  26   day of      June     , 1905

                                      A.W. James
                                      Notary Public.

## Applications for Enrollment of Choctaw Newborn
## Act of 1905   Volume XVIII

BIRTH AFFIDAVIT.          7 NB 1327

### DEPARTMENT OF THE INTERIOR.
## COMMISSION TO THE FIVE CIVILIZED TRIBES.

IN RE APPLICATION FOR ENROLLMENT, as a citizen of the Choctaw Nation, of Martin A James, born on the 28 day of Feby, 1904

Name of Father: Allen W James         a citizen of the   Choctaw   Nation.
Name of Mother: Vicey James nee Fobb  a citizen of the   Choctaw   Nation.

Postoffice   Smithville, Ind. Ter.

### AFFIDAVIT OF MOTHER.

UNITED STATES OF AMERICA, Indian Territory, }
Central DISTRICT. }

I, Vicey James, on oath state that I am 21 years of age and a citizen by blood, of the Choctaw Nation; that I am the lawful wife of Allen W James, who is a citizen, by blood of the Choctaw Nation; that a male child was born to me on 28 day of Feby, 1904; that said child has been named Martin A James, and was living March 4, 1905.

Vicey James

Witnesses To Mark:
{ Harrison McGee
{ Elizen Gibson

Subscribed and sworn to before me this 4 day of August, 1905

C L Lester
Notary Public.

### AFFIDAVIT OF ATTENDING PHYSICIAN OR MID-WIFE.

UNITED STATES OF AMERICA, Indian Territory, }
Central DISTRICT. }

I, Sissy M$^c$Gee, a midwife, on oath state that I attended on Mrs. Vicey James, wife of Allen James on the 28 day of Feby, 1904; that there was born to her on said date a male child; that said child was living March 4, 1905, and is said to have been named Martin A James

Sissy McGee

# Applications for Enrollment of Choctaw Newborn
## Act of 1905   Volume XVIII

Witnesses To Mark:
{ Harrison McGee
{ Elizen Gibson

Subscribed and sworn to before me this 4 day of    August    , 1905

C L Lester
Notary Public.

---

7--NB--1327

Muskogee, Indian Territory, June 2, 1905.

Allen James,
Smithville, Indian Territory.

Dear Sir:

There is enclosed you herewith for execution application for the enrollment of your infant child, Martin A. James, Born[sic] February 28, 1904.

The affidavits heretofore filed in this office show the child was living on January 17, 1905. It is necessary, for the child to be enrolled, that she[sic] was living on March 4, 1905.

In having these affidavits executed care should be exercised to see that all names are written in full, as they appear in the body of the affidavit, and in the event that either of the persons signing the affidavit are unable to write, signatures by mark must be attested by two witnesses. Each affidavit must be executed before a Notary Public and the notarial seal and signature of the officer must be attached to each separate affidavit.

This matter should receive your immediate attention as no further action can be taken relative to the enrollment of said child until the Commission has been furnished these affidavits.

Respectfully,

[sic]

## Applications for Enrollment of Choctaw Newborn
## Act of 1905   Volume XVIII

7 NB 1327

Muskogee, Indian Territory, July 3, 1905.

Allen James,
Smithville, Indian Territory.

Dear Sir:

Receipt is hereby acknowledged of the affidavits of Vicy[sic] Tobb[sic] and Sisey McGee to the birth of Martin A. James, son of Allen James and Vicey Tobb, February 28, 1904, and the same have been filed with the records of this office in the matter of the enrollment of said child.

Respectfully,

Commissioner.

---

7-NB-1327

Muskogee, Indian Territory, July 28, 1905.

Allen W. James,
Smithville, Indian Territory.

Dear Sir:

There is inclosed you herewith for execution application for the enrollment of your infant child, Martin A. James, born February 28, 1904.

The affidavits executed June 26, 1905, heretofore filed in this office, show that your wife signed the mother's affidavit in her maiden name of Vicey Fobb, and that the mother's affidavit, and the affidavit of the midwife were executed before you as a Notary Public.

In having the inclosed application executed, see that your wife signs her married name, Vicey James, and that her affidavit and the affidavit of the midwife are executed before some other Notary that[sic] yourself. When the affidavits are properly executed return to this office.

This matter should receive your immediate attention as no further action can be taken relative to the enrollment of your said child until these affidavits in due form are filed in this office.

Respectfully,

Commissioner.

LM 1/28

## Applications for Enrollment of Choctaw Newborn
## Act of 1905 Volume XVIII

7-NB-1327

Muskogee, Indian Territory, August 1, 1905.

Allen James,
    Smithville, Indian Territory.

Dear Sir:

Receipt is hereby acknowledged of your letter of July 26, 1905, asking the status of the application for the enrollment of your baby Martin A. James.

In reply to your letter you are advised that on July 28, 1905, a letter was addressed to you from this office stating fully what further evidence was required in the matter of the application for the enrollment of your child, Martin A. James.

Respectfully,

Commissioner.

---

7-NB-1327

Muskogee, Indian Territory, August 9, 1905.

Allen W. James,
    Smithville, Indian Territory.

Dear Sir:

Receipt is hereby acknowledged of the affidavits of Vicey James and Sissy McGee to the birth of Martin A. James, son of Allen W. James and Vicey James nee Fobb, February 28, 1904, and the same have been filed with the records in the matter of the enrollment of said child.

Respectfully,

Acting Commissioner.

# Applications for Enrollment of Choctaw Newborn
## Act of 1905   Volume XVIII

7-NB-1327.

Muskogee, Indian Territory, September 27, 1905.

Allen W. James,
    Smithville, Indian Territory.

Dear Sir:

    Receipt is hereby acknowledged of your letter of September 16, 1905, requesting to be informed as to whether or not the enrollment of your minor son Martin A. James as a citizen by blood of the Choctaw Nation has been approved by the Secretary of the Interior.

    In reply to your letter you are advised that the enrollment of said child has not yet been approved by the Secretary of the Interior. As soon as the same is approved you will be duly notified.

                      Respectfully,

                                  Commissioner.

---

7-NB-1327

Muskogee, Indian Territory, December 26, 1905.

A. W. James,
    Smithville, Indian Territory.

Dear Sir:

    Receipt is hereby acknowledged of your letter of December 18, 1905, asking the status of your son, Martin A. James, and you ask if further action has been taken in this matter.

    In reply to your letter you are advised that the name of your son, Martin A. James has not yet been placed upon a schedule of citizens of the Choctaw Nation, prepared for forwarding to the Secretary of the Interior. In case further evidence is necessary to enable this office to determine the right to enrollment of your said child, you will be notified.

                      Respectfully,

                                  Commissioner.

# Applications for Enrollment of Choctaw Newborn
# Act of 1905   Volume XVIII

7-NB-1327

                              Muskogee, Indian Territory, February 26, 1906.

Allen W. James,
      Smithville, Indian Territory.

Dear Sir:

    Receipt is hereby acknowledged of your letter of February 19, 1906, stating that you have been advised that the enrollment of your child Martin A. James has been approved and you ask if this approval has reached this office.

    In reply to your letter you are advised that the name of your son Martin A. James has been placed upon a schedule of new born citizens of the Choctaw Nation which has been forwarded the Secretary of the Interior, but this office has not yet been advised of Departmental action thereon. You will be notified when the enrollment of this child is approved by the Department.

                    Respectfully,

                                  Acting Commissioner.

---

7-NB-1327

                              Muskogee, Indian Territory, April 13, 1906.

Ledbetter & Bledsoe,
      Attorneys at Law,
            Ardmore, Indian Territory.

Gentlemen:

    Receipt is hereby acknowledged of your letter of April 9, 1906, stating that you represent Allen W. James and asking to be advised if the records show that Martin A. James is the son of said Allen W. James and that he is now deceased; you also ask the relationship of Vicey Fobb to Martin A. James.

    In reply to your letter you are advised that it appears from the records of this office that Martin A. James is the son of Allen W. James and Vicey Fobb and that said Martin A. James died March 8, 1905.

    It further appears that the enrollment of Martin A. James as a new born citizen of the Choctaw Nation was approved by the Secretary of the Interior, March 14, 1906.

                    Respectfully,

                                  Acting Commissioner.

Applications for Enrollment of Choctaw Newborn
Act of 1905   Volume XVIII

Choc New Born 1328
    Rosie Ann Jones
    (Born Sep. 19, 1904)

# NEW BORN AFFIDAVIT

No ............

## CHOCTAW ENROLLING COMMISSION

IN THE MATTER OF THE APPLICATION FOR ENROLLMENT as a citizen of the Choctaw Nation, of   Rosanna[sic] Jones   born on the 19 day of September  190 4

Name of father   Willie Jones   a citizen of   Choctaw   Nation, final enrollment No. 9040
Name of mother   Ida Jones (nee Folsom)   a citizen of   ——   Nation, final enrollment No. 8001

Vireton I.T.   Postoffice.

### AFFIDAVIT OF MOTHER

UNITED STATES OF AMERICA  
    INDIAN TERRITORY  
DISTRICT    Central

I   Ida Jones (nee Folsom)   , on oath state that I am   23   years of age and a citizen by   blood   of the   Choctaw   Nation, and as such have been placed upon the final roll of the   Choctaw   Nation, by the Honorable Secretary of the Interior my final enrollment number being   8001   ; that I am the lawful wife of   Willie Jones   , who is a citizen of the   Choctaw   Nation, and as such has been placed upon the final roll of said Nation by the Honorable Secretary of the Interior, his final enrollment number being   9040   and that a   Female   child was born to me on the   19   day of   September   190 4; that said child has been named   Rosanna Jones   , and is now living.

Ida Jones

WITNESSETH:
    Must be two witnesses { Allen Perry
    who are citizens        { Nicholas J Nail

# Applications for Enrollment of Choctaw Newborn
## Act of 1905   Volume XVIII

Subscribed and sworn to before me this, the   17 day of   March   , 1905

James Bower
Notary Public.

My Commission Expires:
Sept 23, 1907

---

## *Affidavit of Attending Physician or Midwife*

UNITED STATES OF AMERICA,  
   INDIAN TERRITORY,  
 Central    DISTRICT

I,   Tennessee Kinkade   a   Midwife on oath state that I attended on Mrs. Ida Jones (nee Folsom)   wife of   Willie Jones on the   19   day of   Sept , 1904, that there was born to her on said date a   Female   child, that said child is now living, and is said to have been named   Rosanna Jones

            her  
Tennessee x Kinkade    M. D.  
           mark

Subscribed and sworn to before me this the   17   day of   March   1905

James Bower  
Notary Public.

**WITNESSETH:**

Must be two witnesses who are citizens and know the child.   {   Allen Perry  
           Nicholas J Nail

We hereby certify that we are well acquainted with   Tennessee Kinkade a   Midwife   and know   her   to be reputable and of good standing in the community.

Must be two citizen witnesses.   {   Allen Perry  
           Nicholas J Nail

# Applications for Enrollment of Choctaw Newborn
## Act of 1905 Volume XVIII

**BIRTH AFFIDAVIT.**

## DEPARTMENT OF THE INTERIOR.
## COMMISSION TO THE FIVE CIVILIZED TRIBES.

**IN RE APPLICATION FOR ENROLLMENT,** as a citizen of the   Choctaw   Nation, of Rosie Ann Jones  , born on the  19  day of  September  , 1904

Name of Father: Willie Jones        a citizen of the  Choc   Nation.
Name of Mother: Ida Jones nee Folsom    a citizen of the  Choc   Nation.

Postoffice   Vian I.T.

### AFFIDAVIT OF MOTHER.

UNITED STATES OF AMERICA, Indian Territory, }
   Central            DISTRICT.             }

I,  Ida Jones nee Folsom  , on oath state that I am  23  years of age and a citizen by  blood  , of the  Choc  Nation; that I am the lawful wife of  Willie Jones  , who is a citizen, by  blood  of the  Choc  Nation; that a female  child was born to me on  19  day of  September  , 1904; that said child has been named  Rosie Ann Jones  , and was living March 4, 1905.

                                    Ida Jones

Witnesses To Mark:
{

Subscribed and sworn to before me this  1st  day of  May  , 1905

                                    OL Johnson
                                        Notary Public.

### AFFIDAVIT OF ATTENDING PHYSICIAN OR MID-WIFE.

UNITED STATES OF AMERICA, Indian Territory, }
   Central            DISTRICT.             }

I,  Tennessee Kinkaid[sic]  , a midwife  , on oath state that I attended on Mrs.  Ida Jones  , wife of  Willie Jones  on the  19  day of  September  , 1904; that there was born to her on said date a  female  child; that said child was living March 4, 1905, and is said to have been named  Rosie Ann Jones

                                            her
                                 Tennessee x Kinkaid
                                            mark

# Applications for Enrollment of Choctaw Newborn
## Act of 1905   Volume XVIII

Witnesses To Mark:
{ Chas T Difendafer
{ OL Johnson

    Subscribed and sworn to before me this 1ˢᵗ day of   May  , 1905

                             OL Johnson
                             Notary Public.

---

Choc New Born 1329
    Levicy Harkins
    (Born July 24, 1904)

**NEW-BORN AFFIDAVIT.**

        Number..................

## ...Choctaw Enrolling Commission...

    IN THE MATTER OF THE APPLICATION FOR ENROLLMENT, as a citizen of the Choctaw   Nation, of   Levicy Harkins

born on the  24   day of   July     190 4

Name of father   Isaac Harkins         a citizen of   Choctaw
Nation final enrollment No.  1148
Name of mother   Alice Harkins         a citizen of   Choctaw
Nation final enrollment No.  559

                          Postoffice   Valliant IT

**AFFIDAVIT OF MOTHER.**

UNITED STATES OF AMERICA
INDIAN TERRITORY
   Central   DISTRICT

       I   Alice Harkins         , on oath state that I am   23   years of age and a citizen by   Intermarriage   of the   Choctaw Nation, and as such have been placed upon the final roll of the   Choctaw   Nation, by the Honorable Secretary of the Interior my final enrollment number being   559 ; that I am the lawful wife of  Isaac Harkins   , who is a citizen of the   Choctaw   Nation, and as

## Applications for Enrollment of Choctaw Newborn
## Act of 1905 Volume XVIII

such has been placed upon the final roll of said Nation by the Honorable Secretary of the Interior, his final enrollment number being   1148   and that a   female   child was born to me on the   24th   day of   July   190 4; that said child has been named   Levicy Harkins   , and is now living.

                         Allice[sic] Harkins

Witnesseth.

Must be two Witnesses who are Citizens.   William W Swink

H L Fowler

Subscribed and sworn to before me this   21   day of   Feb   190 5

                         W A Shoney
                                 Notary Public.

My commission expires:   Jan 10, 1909

---

### *Affidavit of Attending Physician or Midwife*

UNITED STATES OF AMERICA,
    INDIAN TERRITORY,
  Central     DISTRICT

I,   E. W. Hopson   a   Physician   on oath state that I attended on Mrs. Alice Harkins   wife of   Isaac Harkins   on the   24   day of   July   , 190 4, that there was born to her on said date a   female   child, that said child is now living, and is said to have been named   Levicy Harkins

                     Esa Hopson     M. D.

Subscribed and sworn to before me this the   3d   day of   February   1905

                     E.J. Gardner
                         Notary Public.

WITNESSETH:

Must be two witnesses who are citizens and know the child.   William W Swink

H L Fowler

We hereby certify that we are well acquainted with   E.W. Hopson   a   Physician   and know   him   to be reputable and of good standing in the community.

             Must be two citizen witnesses.   William W Swink
                                       H L Fowler

## Applications for Enrollment of Choctaw Newborn
## Act of 1905   Volume XVIII

BIRTH AFFIDAVIT.

### DEPARTMENT OF THE INTERIOR.
### COMMISSION TO THE FIVE CIVILIZED TRIBES.

IN RE APPLICATION FOR ENROLLMENT, as a citizen of the    Choctaw    Nation, of Levicy Harkins    , born on the 24$^{th}$    day of July  , 1904

Name of Father:  Isaac Harkins         a citizen of the   Choctaw    Nation.
Name of Mother:  Alice Harkins         a citizen of the   Choctaw    Nation.

Postoffice    Valliant Ind. Ter.

### AFFIDAVIT OF MOTHER.

UNITED STATES OF AMERICA, Indian Territory,
Central                            DISTRICT.

I,    Alice Harkins    , on oath state that I am  23   years of age and a citizen by blood  , of the   Choctaw    Nation; that I am the lawful wife of    Isaac Harkins   , who is a citizen, by blood   of the    Choctaw    Nation; that a   female    child was born to me on   24$^{th}$    day of   July    , 1904; that said child has been named   Levicy Harkins    , and was living March 4, 1905.

Alice Harkins

Witnesses To Mark:
  Phoebe Lucas
  Ida Austin

Subscribed and sworn to before me this 27$^{th}$   day of   June    , 1905

E.J. Gardner
Notary Public.

### AFFIDAVIT OF ATTENDING PHYSICIAN OR MID-WIFE.

UNITED STATES OF AMERICA, Indian Territory,
Central                            DISTRICT.

I,   E.W. Hopson      , a physician    , on oath state that I attended on Mrs.   Alice Harkins    , wife of   Isaac Harkins    on the 24$^{th}$   day of   July   , 1904; that there was born to her on said date a    female    child; that said child was living March 4, 1905, and is said to have been named  Levicy Harkins

E.W. Hopson

# Applications for Enrollment of Choctaw Newborn
## Act of 1905   Volume XVIII

Witnesses To Mark:

{

    Subscribed and sworn to before me this 27<sup>th</sup>　day of　June　, 1905

                                    E.J. Gardner
                                      Notary Public.

---

7--NB--1329

Muskogee, Indian Territory, June 2, 1905.

Isaac Harkins,
    Valliant, Indian Territory.

Dear Sir:

    There is enclosed you herewith for execution application for the enrollment of your infant child, Levicy Harkins, born July 24, 1904.

    The affidavits heretofore filed with the Commission show the child was living on February 21, 1905. It is necessary, for the child to be enrolled, that she was living on March 4, 1905.

    In having these affidavits executed care should be exercised to see that all names are written in full, as they appear in the body of the affidavit, and in the event that either of the persons signing the affidavit are unable to write, signatures by mark must be attested by two witnesses. Each affidavit must be executed before a Notary Public and the notarial seal and signature of the officer must be attached to each separate affidavit.

    This matter should receive your immediate attention as no further action can be taken relative to the enrollment of said child until the Commission has been furnished these affidavits.

                                        Respectfully,

Enc-FVK-5                                                                                                   [sic]

## Applications for Enrollment of Choctaw Newborn
## Act of 1905    Volume XVIII

7 NB 1329

Muskogee, Indian Territory, July 3, 1905.

Isaac Harkins,
    Valliant, Indian Territory.

Dear Sir:

    Receipt is hereby acknowledged of the affidavits of Alice Harkins and E. W. Hopson to the birth of Levicy Harkins, daughter of Isaac and Alice Harkins, July 24, 1904, and the same have been filed with the records of this office in the matter of the enrollment of said child.

Respectfully,

Commissioner.

---

Choc New Born 1330
    Lewie Curley
      (Born Apr. 6, 1904)

# NEW BORN AFFIDAVIT

No

## CHOCTAW ENROLLING COMMISSION

IN THE MATTER OF THE APPLICATION FOR ENROLLMENT as a citizen of the Choctaw Nation, of  Lee[sic] Curley  born on the 6 day of April 190 4

Name of father  James Curley    a citizen of  non  Nation, final enrollment No. ——
Name of mother  Roda Curley    a citizen of  Choctaw  Nation, final enrollment No.  6839

Summerfield I.T.    Postoffice.

# Applications for Enrollment of Choctaw Newborn
## Act of 1905   Volume XVIII

### AFFIDAVIT OF MOTHER

UNITED STATES OF AMERICA  
    INDIAN TERRITORY  
DISTRICT    Central

I   Roda Curley  , on oath state that I am   35   years of age and a citizen by   blood   of the   Choctaw   Nation, and as such have been placed upon the final roll of the   Choctaw   Nation, by the Honorable Secretary of the Interior my final enrollment number being   6839  ; that I am the lawful wife of   James Curley  , who is a citizen of the   non   Nation, and as such has been placed upon the final roll of said Nation by the Honorable Secretary of the Interior, his final enrollment number being   —   and that a   Male   child was born to me on the   6   day of   April   190 4; that said child has been named   Lee Curley  , and is now living.

                                                      her  
WITNESSETH:                                    Roda x Curley  
   Must be two witnesses {  Oscar Davis                     mark  
   who are citizens       Dave Colbert

Subscribed and sworn to before me this, the   17   day of   February  , 190 5

                                             James Bower  
                                                   Notary Public.

My Commission Expires:  
    Sept 23-1907

### *Affidavit of Attending Physician or Midwife*

UNITED STATES OF AMERICA,  
    INDIAN TERRITORY,  
Central      DISTRICT

I,   D^r A. R. Sisk    a    Practicing Physician on oath state that I attended on Mrs. Rhoda Curley   wife of   James Curley on the   6   day of   April  , 190 4, that there was born to her on said date a   male   child, that said child is now living, and is said to have been named   Lee Curley

                                       A.R. Sisk           M. D.

Subscribed and sworn to before me this the   18   day of   Jul     1905

                                      John W Dunlap  
                                            Notary Public.

WITNESSETH:  
   Must be two witnesses {  Oscar Davis  
   who are citizens and  
   know the child.       Dave Colbert

## Applications for Enrollment of Choctaw Newborn
## Act of 1905   Volume XVIII

We hereby certify that we are well acquainted with D$^r$. A.R. Sisk a Practicing Physician and know him to be reputable and of good standing in the community.

Must be two citizen witnesses. { Oscar Davis  
Dave Colbert

**BIRTH AFFIDAVIT.**

### DEPARTMENT OF THE INTERIOR.
### COMMISSION TO THE FIVE CIVILIZED TRIBES.

**IN RE APPLICATION FOR ENROLLMENT,** as a citizen of the   Choctaw   Nation, of Lewie Curley   , born on the  6  day of April  , 1904

Name of Father: James Curley         a citizen of the  U. States  Nation.  
Name of Mother: Rhoda Curley         a citizen of the  Choc  Nation.

Postoffice   Summerfield I.T.

**AFFIDAVIT OF MOTHER.**

UNITED STATES OF AMERICA, Indian Territory,  
   Central                DISTRICT.

I, Rhoda Curley  , on oath state that I am  35  years of age and a citizen by blood , of the  Choctaw  Nation; that I am the lawful wife of  James Curley  , who is a citizen, by ............of the  United States  Nation; that a  male  child was born to me on  6  day of April  , 1904; that said child has been named Lewie Curley  , and was living March 4, 1905.

                                  her  
                          Rhoda x Curley  
Witnesses To Mark:            mark  
 { Chas T Difendafer  
   OL Johnson

Subscribed and sworn to before me this  17  day of  April  , 1905

                          OL Johnson  
                              Notary Public.

# Applications for Enrollment of Choctaw Newborn
## Act of 1905   Volume XVIII

**AFFIDAVIT OF ATTENDING PHYSICIAN OR MID-WIFE.**

UNITED STATES OF AMERICA, Indian Territory, }
     Central                    DISTRICT. }

I, Louisa Smith, a ~~physician~~ *a woman*, on oath state that I attended on Mrs. Rhoda Curley, wife of James Curley on the 6th day of April, 1904; that there was born to her on said date a male child; that said child was living March 4, 1905, and is said to have been named Lewie Curley

                                    her
Witnesses To Mark:          Louisa x Smith
  { W.H. Smith                mark
  { W L Harris

Subscribed and sworn to before me this 29 day of April, 1905.

                        W.L. Harris
                             Notary Public.

---

                                      7--2362.

            Muskogee, Indian Territory, May 9, 1905.

James Curley,
    Summerfield, Indian Territory.

Dear Sir:

    Receipt is hereby acknowledged of the affidavits of Rhoda Curley and Louisa Smith to the birth of Lewie Curley, son of James and Rhoda Curley, April 6, 1904, and the same have been filed with our records as an application for the enrollment of said child.

                      Respectfully,

                                      Commissioner in Charge.

# Applications for Enrollment of Choctaw Newborn
## Act of 1905  Volume XVIII

7-NB-1330

Muskogee, Indian Territory, January 26, 1907.

Carr & Rogers,
    Pauls Valley, Indian Territory.

Gentlemen:

    Receipt is hereby acknowledged of your letter of January 16, 1907, stating that an ignorant Choctaw woman presented you a letter dated May 9, 1905, stating that the Commissioner to the Five Civilized Tribes was in possession of affidavits to the birth of Louie[sic] Curley, son of James and Roady[sic] Curley April 6, 1904; this woman states that she understands the child has been enrolled and that filing has been made upon its allotment of land but she has never received the certificate of the allotment, and she wishes to be advised in regard to this matter.

    In reply to your letter you are advised that on August 2, 1905, the Secretary of the Interior approved the enrollment of Lewie Curley, child of James and Rhoda Curley, as a new born citizen of the Choctaw Nation under the Act of Congress approved March 3, 1905.

    The matter of the allotments referred to in your letter will be made the subject of a separate communication.

                                Respectfully,

                                              Commissioner.

---

Choc New Born 1331
    Norris Cass
    (Born Dec. 29, 1902)

## Applications for Enrollment of Choctaw Newborn
## Act of 1905   Volume XVIII

**NEW-BORN AFFIDAVIT.**

Number................

## ...Choctaw Enrolling Commission...

IN THE MATTER OF THE APPLICATION FOR ENROLLMENT, as a citizen of the Choctaw Nation, of   Norris Cass

born on the   29$^{th}$   day of ___Dec___ 190 2

Name of father   Osborne Cass        a citizen of   Choctaw
Nation final enrollment No.  7194
Name of mother   Eliza Cass        a citizen of   Choctaw
Nation final enrollment No.  7195

Postoffice   Garland IT

**AFFIDAVIT OF MOTHER.**

UNITED STATES OF AMERICA
INDIAN TERRITORY
Central        DISTRICT

I   Eliza Cass   , on oath state that I am 28   years of age and a citizen by   blood   of the   Choctaw   Nation, and as such have been placed upon the final roll of the   Choctaw   Nation, by the Honorable Secretary of the Interior my final enrollment number being   7195 ; that I am the lawful wife of   Osborne Cass   , who is a citizen of the   Choctaw   Nation, and as such has been placed upon the final roll of said Nation by the Honorable Secretary of the Interior, his final enrollment number being   7194   and that a   Male   child was born to me on the 29   day of   December   190 2; that said child has been named   Norris Cass   , and is now living.

Eliza Cass

Witnesseth.
Must be two Witnesses who are Citizens.   } Ward Garland Jr
   Maurice N. Cass

Subscribed and sworn to before me this   6   day of   Jan   190 5

C.C. Jones
Notary Public.

My commission expires:   March 3$^{d}$ 1907

# Applications for Enrollment of Choctaw Newborn
## Act of 1905   Volume XVIII

## AFFIDAVIT OF ATTENDING PHYSICIAN OR MIDWIFE

UNITED STATES OF AMERICA
INDIAN TERRITORY
  Central   DISTRICT

I, Sallie Christy a midwife on oath state that I attended on Mrs. Eliza Cass wife of Osborne Cass on the 29th day of December, 190 2, that there was born to her on said date a male child, that said child is now living, and is said to have been named Norris Cass

                                                              her
                                                    Sallie x Christy
                                                              mark

Subscribed and sworn to before me this, the _____ day of Jan 3   190 5

WITNESSETH:                                James Bower    Notary Public.
Must be two witnesses { Wilson Christy
who are citizens
                        Mathew Henry

We hereby certify that we are well acquainted with Sallie Christy a midwife and know her to be reputable and of good standing in the community.

    Wilson Christy                          _____

    Mathew Henry                            _____

BIRTH AFFIDAVIT.

### DEPARTMENT OF THE INTERIOR.
### COMMISSION TO THE FIVE CIVILIZED TRIBES.

IN RE APPLICATION FOR ENROLLMENT, as a citizen of the Choctaw Nation, of Norris Cass, born on the 29 day of December, 1902

Name of Father: N. Osborne Cass         a citizen of the Choctaw Nation.
Name of Mother: Eliza Cass              a citizen of the Choctaw Nation.

                  Postoffice   Garland IT

# Applications for Enrollment of Choctaw Newborn
## Act of 1905   Volume XVIII

### AFFIDAVIT OF MOTHER.

UNITED STATES OF AMERICA, Indian Territory,
Central DISTRICT.

I, Eliza Cass, on oath state that I am _____ years of age and a citizen by Blood, of the Choctaw Nation; that I am the lawful wife of N. Osborne Cass, who is a citizen, by Blood of the Choctaw Nation; that a male child was born to me on 29$^{th}$ day of December, 1902; that said child has been named Norris Cass, and was living March 4, 1905.

Eliza Cass

Witnesses To Mark:

Subscribed and sworn to before me this 15$^{th}$ day of April, 1905.

C C Jones
Notary Public.

---

### AFFIDAVIT OF ATTENDING PHYSICIAN OR MID-WIFE.

UNITED STATES OF AMERICA, Indian Territory,
Central DISTRICT.

I, Sallie Christy, a midwife, on oath state that I attended on Mrs. Eliza Cass, wife of N. Osborne Cass on the 29$^{th}$ day of December, 1902; that there was born to her on said date a male child; that said child was living March 4, 1905, and is said to have been named Norris

this is
Sallie x Christy
mark

Witnesses To Mark:
  Wilson Christy
  Joshua Christy

Subscribed and sworn to before me this 15$^{th}$ day of April, 1905.

C C Jones
Notary Public.

Applications for Enrollment of Choctaw Newborn
Act of 1905   Volume XVIII

7--2460.

Muskogee, Indian Territory, May 10, 1905.

N. Osborne Cass,
    Garland, Indian Territory.

Dear Sir:

    Receipt is hereby acknowledged of the affidavits of Eliza Cass and Sallie Christy to the birth of Norris Cass, son of N. Osborne and Eliza Cass, December 29, 1902, and the same have been filed with our records as an application for the enrollment of said child.

                  Respectfully,

                                      Commissioner in Charge.

---

Choc New Born 1332
    Katie Barnhill
    (Born May 9, 1904)

# NEW BORN AFFIDAVIT

No _____

## CHOCTAW ENROLLING COMMISSION

IN THE MATTER OF THE APPLICATION FOR ENROLLMENT as a citizen of the Choctaw Nation, of Katie Barnhill born on the 9 day of May 190 4

    Name of father   Henry Barnhill      a citizen of    U. S. A.    Nation,
final enrollment No. ..................
    Name of mother   Mary J Barnhill      a citizen of    Choctaw    Nation,
final enrollment No.   4781

                          Arpelar I.T.               Postoffice.

# Applications for Enrollment of Choctaw Newborn
## Act of 1905 Volume XVIII

**AFFIDAVIT OF MOTHER**

UNITED STATES OF AMERICA }
INDIAN TERRITORY }
DISTRICT    Central }

I   Mary J. Barnhill   , on oath state that I am   20   years of age and a citizen by   Blood   of the   Choctaw   Nation, and as such have been placed upon the final roll of the   Choctaw   Nation, by the Honorable Secretary of the Interior my final enrollment number being   4781   ; that I am the lawful wife of   Henry Barnhill   , who is a citizen of the   U.S.A.   Nation, and as such has been placed upon the final roll of said Nation by the Honorable Secretary of the Interior, his final enrollment number being _____ and that a   Feamail[sic]   child was born to me on the   9   day of   May   190 4; that said child has been named   Katie Barnhill   , and is now living.

her mark<br>Mary J x Barnhill

WITNESSETH:
Must be two witheses { Levi Orphan
who are citizens { Rena Orphan

Subscribed and sworn to before me this, the   7   day of   April   , 190 5

Edward D. Sittel<br>Notary Public.

My Commission Expires:   March 20, 1909

---

## *Affidavit of Attending Physician or Midwife*

UNITED STATES OF AMERICA, }
INDIAN TERRITORY, }
Central   DISTRICT }

I,   Magie[sic] Long   a   Mid-wife   on oath state that I attended on Mrs.   Mary J Barnhill   wife of   Henry Barnhill   on the   9   day of   May   , 190 4, that there was born to her on said date a   Feamail   child, that said child is now living, and is said to have been named   Katie Barnhill

Mrs Maggie Long   M.D.

Subscribed and sworn to before me this the   1   day of   April   1905

Edward D Sittel<br>Notary Public.

WITNESSETH:
Must be two witnesses { Levi Orphan
who are citizens and
know the child. { Rena Orphan

# Applications for Enrollment of Choctaw Newborn
# Act of 1905   Volume XVIII

We hereby certify that we are well acquainted with   Henry Barnhill a   U.S.A.   and know   him   to be reputable and of good standing in the community.

Must be two citizen witnesses. { Levi Orphan
Rena Orphan

---

7-4781.

DEPARTMENT OF THE INTERIOR,
COMMISSION TO THE FIVE CIVILIZED TRIBES.
SOUTH MCALESTER, IND. TER. APRIL 24, 1905.

In the matter of the application for the enrollment of Katie Barnhill as a citizen by blood of the Choctaw Nation.

Henry F. Barnhill being first duly sworn testifies as follows:

EXAMINATION BY THE COMMISSION:

Q What is your name?  A Henry F. Barnhill.
Q What is your age?  A Thirty.
Q What is your post office address?  A Arpearler[sic].
Q For whom do you desire to make application today?  A For my child Katie Barnhill.
Q When was Katie Barnhill born?  A 9th day of May 1904.
Q Is she living at this time?  A Yes, sir.
Q What is the name of the mother of Katie Barnhill?  A Mary J. Baldwin.
Q That was her maiden name?  A Yes, sir.
Q Why is it your wife hasn't made application today for your child?  A My wife is dead.
Q When did she die?  A Died 3rd day last December 1904.

Witness excused.

Chas. T. Difendafer being first duly sworn states that the above and foregoing is a full, true and correct transcript of his stenographic notes taken in said cause on said date.

Chas T. Difendafer

Subscribed and sworn to before me this 24th day of April 1905.

OL Johnson
Notary Public.

# Applications for Enrollment of Choctaw Newborn
## Act of 1905   Volume XVIII

7-4781

BIRTH AFFIDAVIT.

### DEPARTMENT OF THE INTERIOR.
## COMMISSION TO THE FIVE CIVILIZED TRIBES.

IN RE APPLICATION FOR ENROLLMENT, as a citizen of the   Choctaw   Nation, of Katie Barnhill   , born on the   9 day of   May   , 1904

Name of Father: Henry F. Barnhill        a citizen of the   U. States   ~~Nation~~.
Name of Mother: Mary Barnhill nee Baldwin   a citizen of the   Choctaw   Nation.

Postoffice   Arpealer, I.T.

### AFFIDAVIT OF MOTHER.

UNITED STATES OF AMERICA, Indian Territory,
DISTRICT.

I, _____, on oath state that I am _____ years of age and a citizen by _____, of the _____ Nation; that I am the lawful wife of _____, who is a citizen, *See Testimony* of the _____ Nation; that a _____ child was born to me on ___ day of _____, 1___, that said child has been named _____, and was living March 4, 1905.

Witnesses To Mark:

Subscribed and sworn to before me this   28 day of   April   , 1905

Edward D Sittel
Notary Public.

### AFFIDAVIT OF ATTENDING PHYSICIAN OR MID-WIFE.

UNITED STATES OF AMERICA, Indian Territory,
Central   DISTRICT.

I,   Maggie Long   , a   midwife   , on oath state that I attended on Mrs.   Mary Barnhill   , wife of   Henry F. Barnhill   on the   9 day of May   , 1904; that there was born to her on said date a   female   child; that said child was living March 4, 1905, and is said to have been named   Katie Barnhill

Mrs Maggie Long

# Applications for Enrollment of Choctaw Newborn
## Act of 1905   Volume XVIII

Witnesses To Mark:
{

Subscribed and sworn to before me this  28  day of   April   , 1905

Edward D Sittel
Notary Public.

---

**BIRTH AFFIDAVIT.**

### DEPARTMENT OF THE INTERIOR.
### COMMISSION TO THE FIVE CIVILIZED TRIBES.

---

**IN RE APPLICATION FOR ENROLLMENT,** as a citizen of the   Choctaw   Nation, of Katie Barnhill  , born on the  9  day of   May   , 1904

Name of Father:  Henry  Barnhill          a citizen of the    U. S      ~~Nation~~.
Name of Mother: Mary Barnhill  nee Baldwin     a citizen of the   Choctaw   Nation.

Postoffice    Arpealer, I.T.

---

**AFFIDAVIT OF MOTHER.**

UNITED STATES OF AMERICA, Indian Territory,
                                DISTRICT.

I, _____ on oath state that I am _____ years of age and a citizen by _____, of the *See Testimony* Nation; that I am the lawful wife of _____, who is a citizen by _____ of the _____ Nation; that a child was born to me on ____ day of _____, 1____, that said child has been named _____, and was living March 4, 1905.

Witnesses To Mark:
{

Subscribed and sworn to before me this ____ day of _____, 1905.

Notary Public.

# Applications for Enrollment of Choctaw Newborn
## Act of 1905   Volume XVIII

### AFFIDAVIT OF ATTENDING PHYSICIAN OR MID-WIFE.

UNITED STATES OF AMERICA, Indian Territory,
Central                                    DISTRICT.

I,........................., a ——————, on oath state that I ~~attended on~~ *was personally acquainted with* Mrs. Mary Barnhill dec'd, wife of Henry F. Barnhill on the 9th day of May, 1904; that there was born to her on said date a female child; that said child was living March 4, 1905, and is said to have been named Katie Barnhill

Levi Orphan

Witnesses To Mark:
{

Subscribed and sworn to before me this 26 day of June, 1905

WG Weiner
Notary Public.

*Commission expires May 11, 1909*

---

**BIRTH AFFIDAVIT.**

### DEPARTMENT OF THE INTERIOR.
### COMMISSION TO THE FIVE CIVILIZED TRIBES.

IN RE APPLICATION FOR ENROLLMENT, as a citizen of the Choctaw Nation, of Katie Barnhill, born on the 9 day of May, 1904

Name of Father: Henry Barnhill      a citizen of the U. S ~~Nation~~.
Name of Mother: Mary Barnhill nee Baldwin    a citizen of the Choctaw Nation.

Postoffice   Arpealer, I.T.

---

### AFFIDAVIT OF MOTHER.

UNITED STATES OF AMERICA, Indian Territory,
......................... DISTRICT.

I,......................., on oath state that I am ............... years of age and a citizen by ............., of the ............... Nation; that I am the lawful wife of ..............., who is a citizen, by ............... of the ............... Nation; that a child was born to me on ....... day of ..........., I......, that said child has been named ..........................., and was living March 4, 1905.

*See Testimony*

30

## Applications for Enrollment of Choctaw Newborn
## Act of 1905 Volume XVIII

Witnesses To Mark:

Subscribed and sworn to before me this ____ day of ____, 1905.

Notary Public.

---

**AFFIDAVIT OF ATTENDING PHYSICIAN OR MID-WIFE.**

UNITED STATES OF AMERICA, Indian Territory,
Central DISTRICT.

*was personally acquainted with*
I, _____, a _____, on oath state that I ~~attended on~~ Mrs. Mary Barnhill, wife of Henry Barnhill on the 9 day of May, 1904; that there was born to her on said date a female child; that said child was living March 4, 1905, and is said to have been named Katie Barnhill

Ben Alberson

Witnesses To Mark:

Subscribed and sworn to before me this 26 day of June, 1905

WG Weiner

*Commission expires May 11, 1909*    Notary Public.

---

DEPARTMENT OF THE INTERIOR,
COMMISSION TO THE FIVE CIVILIZED TRIBES.
Muskogee, Indian Territory, June 27, 1905.

7-NB-1332.           --oOo--

In the matter of the application for the enrollment of Katie Barnhill, infant, as a citizen by blood of the Choctaw Nation.

Henry F. Barnhill, being first duly sworn, testifies as follows:

### EXAMINATION BY THE COMMISSION:

Q What is your name? A Henry F. Barnhill.
Q How old are you? A Thirty, last December.
Q What is your post office address? A Arpealar.
Q Do you make any claim to Choctaw citizenship? A No, sir.
Q Are you married? A I was married.

# Applications for Enrollment of Choctaw Newborn
## Act of 1905   Volume XVIII

Q  What was the name of your wife?  A  Mary Baldwin.
Q  What was the name of your wife's father?  A  George W. Baldwin.
Q  The name of her mother?  A  I don't know; I never saw her.
Q  Is your wife living?  A  No, sir.
Q  When did she die?  A  9th of last December.
Q  That would be December, 1904?  A  Yes, sir.
Q  You appeared before the Choctaw Enrolling Commission and made application for the enrollment of your infant child, Katie Barnhill, and at that time didn't you present an affidavit signed by your wife and subscribed to before Edward O. Sittel, dated April 7, 1905.  Now, you testified that your wife died in December last year, please explain about this affidavit you presented to the enrolling commission.  A  Well, Mr. Fulsom wrote me a private letter and said that as I was the father of the baby it would be alright for me to sign the affidavit in the presence of two witnesses of good standing; to sign her name to it.
Q  The affidavit you presented to the Choctaw Enrolling Commission was made out in accordance with the instructions you received from Mr. Fulsom?  A  Yes, sir.
Q  Who was he?  A  He was one of the Choctaw Enrolling Commission.
Q  When was Katie Barnhill born?  A  9th of May, 1904.
Q  Was she living on the 4th day of March, 1905?  A  Yes, sir.
Q  Who was she living with?  A  My uncle.
Q  Did a physician attend your wife in her last illness?  A  No, sir; yes, sir, when the baby was born we had a physician.
Q  What physician?  A  Dr. Troy at the Sisters Hospital at South McAlester.
Q  Can you get the testimony of two witnesses to the fact that your wife, the mother of Katie Barnhill, died on December 9, 1904?  A  Yes, sir; I think I can get them.
Q  The Commission requires the testimony or affidavits of two disinterested witnesses to the facts that your wife died in December, 1904, that she was the mother of Katie Barnhill, who was born on May 9, 1904; and that the child, Katie Barnhill, was living on March 4, 1905.  You will be allowed reasonable time to send these affidavits in, do you understand?  A  Yes, sir.

Witness excused.

----------------------------------

   Vester W. Rose, as stenographer to the Commission to the Five Civilized Tribes, on oath states that the above and foregoing is a full, true and correct transcript of his stenographic notes had in said case on said date.

Vester W Rose

Subscribed and sworn to before me this 28th day of June, 1905.

Frances R Long<br>Notary Public.

## Applications for Enrollment of Choctaw Newborn
## Act of 1905    Volume XVIII

7-NB-1332.

Muskogee, Indian Territory, June 14, 1905.

Henry Barnhill,
    Arpelar, Indian Territory.

Dear Sir:

    Referring to the application for the enrollment of your child, Katie Barnhill, born May 9, 1904, you state in your testimony taken on April 24, 1905, that Mary J. Baldwin, your wife and mother of the applicant, died on December 3, 1904, while it appears in an application filed with the Choctaw Enrolling Commission, that Mary J. Barnhill, your wife, executed an affidavit on April 7, 1905. Her signature to this affidavit was made by mark and witnesses by Levi Orphan and Rena Orphan.

    If your wife is still living you will please have the enclosed application executed and in addition thereto secure the affidavits of two disinterested parties to the fact that she is still living; but it she is dead, you will please secure the affidavit of the attending physician or midwife on the enclosed affidavit, and the affidavits of two persons who are disinterested and not related to the applicant, who have actual knowledge of the facts; that the child was born, the date of her birth, that she was living on March 4, 1905, and that Katie Barnhill, who is now dead, was her mother.

    This matter should receive your immediate attention, as no further action can be taken until these affidavits are furnished the Commission.

                    Respectfully,

                                          Chairman.

DeB--4/14

---

7 NB 1332

Muskogee, Indian Territory, June 30, 1905.

Henry Barnhill,
    South McAlester, Indian Territory.

Dear Sir:

    Receipt is hereby acknowledged of your letter of June 26, 1905, transmitting affidavits of Ben Alberson and Levi Orphan to the birth of Katie Bqrnhill[sic], daughter of Henry and Mary Barnhill, May 9, 1904, and the same have been filed with our records in the matter of the enrollment of said child.

# Applications for Enrollment of Choctaw Newborn
# Act of 1905   Volume XVIII

Respectfully,

Chairman.

7- NB 1332

Muskogee, Indian Territory, August 31, 1905.

Henry Barnhill,
    Arpelar, Indian Territory.

Dear Sir:-

    I am in receipt of your letter of August 27th in which you desire to be advised if the enrollment of your child, Katie Barnhill, has been approved.

    In reply to your letter you are advised that the enrollment of Katie Barnhill as a citizen by blood of the Choctaw Nation was approved by the Secretary of the Interior August 22, 1905, and the name of your child appears upon the roll of new-born citizens by blood of the Choctaw Nation, opposite number 1452.

Respectfully,

Commissioner.

---

Choc New Born 1333
    Benjamin Kemp
    (Born May 17, 1904)

## Applications for Enrollment of Choctaw Newborn
## Act of 1905   Volume XVIII

**NEW-BORN AFFIDAVIT.**

Number............

### ...Choctaw Enrolling Commission...

IN THE MATTER OF THE APPLICATION FOR ENROLLMENT, as a citizen of the Choctaw Nation, of Benjamin Kemp

born on the 17 day of May 190 4

Name of father   Martin Kemp         a citizen of   Choctaw
Nation final enrollment No.   12686
Name of mother   Rebecca Kemp         a citizen of   Choctaw
Nation final enrollment No.   13381

Postoffice   Vireton I.T.

**AFFIDAVIT OF MOTHER.**

UNITED STATES OF AMERICA
INDIAN TERRITORY
   Central        DISTRICT

I   Rebecca Kemp                       , on oath state that I am 35 years of age and a citizen by Blood of the Choctaw Nation, and as such have been placed upon the final roll of the Choctaw Nation, by the Honorable Secretary of the Interior my final enrollment number being 13381 ; that I am the lawful wife of Martin Kemp , who is a citizen of the Choctaw Nation, and as such has been placed upon the final roll of said Nation by the Honorable Secretary of the Interior, his final enrollment number being 12686 and that a Male child was born to me on the 17 day of May 190 4; that said child has been named Benjamin Kemp , and is now living.

Rebecca Kemp

Witnesseth.
   Must be two ⎫   Rufus Winlock
   Witnesses who ⎬
   are Citizens. ⎭   Jack Smith

Subscribed and sworn to before me this   18   day of   Feb   190 5

Allen C. Gregg
Notary Public.

My commission expires:
   Jan 9, 1907

35

# Applications for Enrollment of Choctaw Newborn
# Act of 1905 Volume XVIII

## AFFIDAVIT OF ATTENDING PHYSICIAN OR MIDWIFE

UNITED STATES OF AMERICA
INDIAN TERRITORY
Central DISTRICT

I, Mary Paisley a neighbor on oath state that I attended on Mrs. Rebecca Kemp wife of Martin Kemp on the 17 day of May, 1904, that there was born to her on said date a male child, that said child is now living, and is said to have been named Benjamin Kemp

 her
Mary x Paisley M.D.
 mark

WITNESSETH:
Must be two witnesses who are citizens and know the child.
{ Rufus Winlock
  Jack Smith

Subscribed and sworn to before me this, the 18 day of February 1905.

Allen C Gregg Notary Public.

We hereby certify that we are well acquainted with Mary Paisley a neighbor citizen and know her to be reputable and of good standing in the community.

{ Rufus Winlock
  Jack Smith

*I hereby certify that the name of the family should read Kemp and that I changed the writing from Cemp to Kemp in this new bon affidavit. Allen C Gregg Notary Public*

---

7-12636-13381.

DEPARTMENT OF THE INTERIOR,
COMMISSION TO THE FIVE CIVILIZED TRIBES.
SOUTH McALESTER, I.T.    APRIL 24th, 1905.

In the matter of the application for the enrollment of Benjamin Kemp as a citizen by blood of the Choctaw Nation.

Martin Kemp being first duly sworn testifies as follows:

EXAMINATION BY THE COMMISSION:

Q What is your name? A Martin Kemp.
Q What is your age? A About twenty or thirty I guess.

## Applications for Enrollment of Choctaw Newborn
## Act of 1905   Volume XVIII

Q  You have this day made application for the enrollment of your child Benjamin Kemp as a citizen of the Choctaw Nation; when was Benjamin born?  A  May 17, 1904.
Q  Who is the mother of this child?  A  Rebecca Kemp.
Q  Is this child living today?  A  Yes, sir.
Q  Who attended your wife when this child was born?  A  Mary Pusley.
Q  Where does she live?  A  She lives close by me at Vireton.

Witness excused.

Dave Mishamahtubbie being first duly sworn testified as follows:

EXAMINATION BY THE COMMISSION:

Q  What is your name?  A  Dave Mishamahtubbie.
Q  How old are you?  A  About forty-five.
Q  What is your post office address?  A  Vireton.
Q  Are you a citizen by blood of the Choctaw Nation?  A  Yes, sir.
Q  Are you acquainted with Martin Kemp and Rebecca who have this day made application for the enrollment of their child Benjamin Kemp as a citizen of the Choctaw Nation?  A  Yes sir.
Q  How far from Martin Kemp do you live?  A  About a mile.
Q  Do you know when Benjamin Kemp was born - what day?  A  Last May.
Q  May 1904?  A  Yes, sir.
Q  What day in May?  A  I don't remember the date.
Q  Is this child living today?  A  Yes, sir.

Witness excused.

Winie Mishamahtubbie being first duly sworn testifies as follows:

EXAMINATION BY THE COMMISSION:

Q  What is your name?  A  Winie Mishamahtabbie[sic].
Q  How old are you?  A  Thirty-five.
Q  What is your post office address?  A  Vireton.
Q  Are you a citizen by blood of the Choctaw Nation?  A  Yes, sir.
Q  Are you acquainted with Martin Kemp and Rebecca Kemp who have this day made application for the enrollment of their child Benjamin Kemp as a citizen of the Choctaw Nation?  A  Yes, sir.
Q  How far from Martin Kemp do you live?  A  Mile.
Q  When was Benjamin Kemp born?  A  Born May 17, 1904.
Q  Is Benjamin Kemp living today?  A  Yes, sir.

Witness excused.

## Applications for Enrollment of Choctaw Newborn
## Act of 1905   Volume XVIII

Chas. T. Difendafer being first duly sworn states that the above and foregoing is a full, true and correct transcript of his stenographic notes taken in said cause on said date.

Chas. T. Difendafer

Subscribed and sworn to before me this 24th day of April 1905.

OL Johnson
Notary Public.

7-12636 - 7-13381

BIRTH AFFIDAVIT.

DEPARTMENT OF THE INTERIOR.
**COMMISSION TO THE FIVE CIVILIZED TRIBES.**

IN RE APPLICATION FOR ENROLLMENT, as a citizen of the   Choc   Nation, of Benjamin Kemp   , born on the 17 day of May , 1904

Name of Father: Martin Kemp          a citizen of the  Choc   Nation.
Name of Mother: Rebecca Kemp nee Jones   a citizen of the  Choc   Nation.

Postoffice   Vireton I.T.

AFFIDAVIT OF MOTHER.

UNITED STATES OF AMERICA, Indian Territory,
Central        DISTRICT.

I, Rebecca Kemp  , on oath state that I am  28  years of age and a citizen by blood , of the Choctaw Nation; that I am the lawful wife of Martin Kemp , who is a citizen, by blood of the Choctaw Nation; that a male child was born to me on  17  day of  May , 1904; that said child has been named  Benjamin Kemp  , and was living March 4, 1905.

her
Rebecca x Kemp
mark

Witnesses To Mark:
{ Chas. T. Difendafer
{ OL Johnson

Subscribed and sworn to before me this  24  day of  April    , 1905

OL Johnson
Notary Public.

# Applications for Enrollment of Choctaw Newborn
## Act of 1905   Volume XVIII

Choc New Born 1334
   Thomas Scruggs Collier
   (Born Oct. 28, 1903)

**NEW-BORN AFFIDAVIT.**

Number..........

## ...Choctaw Enrolling Commission...

IN THE MATTER OF THE APPLICATION FOR ENROLLMENT, as a citizen of the Choctaw Nation, of Thomas Scruggs Collier

born on the 28$^{th}$ day of ___October___ 190 3

Name of father   Oliver Collier           a citizen of   white
Nation final enrollment No. ..........
Name of mother   Martha Collier           a citizen of   Choctaw
Nation final enrollment No.   12372

                              Postoffice   Enterprise I.T.

### AFFIDAVIT OF MOTHER.

UNITED STATES OF AMERICA
INDIAN TERRITORY
   Western       DISTRICT

I   Martha Collier   , on oath state that I am 23 years of age and a citizen by blood of the Choctaw Nation, and as such have been placed upon the final roll of the Choctaw Nation, by the Honorable Secretary of the Interior my final enrollment number being   12372 ; that I am the lawful wife of   Oliver Collier   , who is a citizen of the   white   Nation, and as such has been placed upon the final roll of said Nation by the Honorable Secretary of the Interior, his final enrollment number being ——  and that a   male   child was born to me on the   28   day of   October   190 3; that said child has been named   Thomas Scruggs Collier   , and is now living.

                              Martha Collier

Witnesseth.
   Must be two  ⎫   James Fizer
   Witnesses who ⎬
   are Citizens. ⎭   Jess Walls

# Applications for Enrollment of Choctaw Newborn
## Act of 1905   Volume XVIII

Subscribed and sworn to before me this   15   day of   Jan     190 5

                                      John M Lentz
                                                   Notary Public.

My commission expires:   Nov 29 1907

## AFFIDAVIT OF ATTENDING PHYSICIAN OR MIDWIFE

UNITED STATES OF AMERICA
INDIAN TERRITORY
  Western    DISTRICT

    I,   D.S. Billington   a   practicing physician on oath state that I attended on Mrs.   Martha Collier   wife of   Oliver Collier on the   $28^{th}$   day of   October   , 190 3 , that there was born to her on said date a   male child, that said child is now living, and is said to have been named   Thomas Scruggs Collier

                                      D.S. Billington     *M.D.*

    Subscribed and sworn to before me this, the   5   day of   January   190 5

                                    John M Lentz     Notary Public.

WITNESSETH:
Must be two witnesses who are citizens { James Fizer
                      Jess Walls

    We hereby certify that we are well acquainted with   D S Billington   a   practicing physician   and know   him   to be reputable and of good standing in the community.

    James Fizer

    Jess Walls

BIRTH AFFIDAVIT.
### DEPARTMENT OF THE INTERIOR.
### COMMISSION TO THE FIVE CIVILIZED TRIBES.

    IN RE APPLICATION FOR ENROLLMENT, as a citizen of the   Choctaw   Nation, of   Thomas Scruggs Collier   , born on the   28   day of   October   , 1903

Name of Father: Oliver Collier        a citizen of the   Choctaw   Nation.
Name of Mother: Martha Collier       a citizen of the   Choctaw   Nation.

                          Postoffice   Enterprise Ind Ter

# Applications for Enrollment of Choctaw Newborn
# Act of 1905   Volume XVIII

### AFFIDAVIT OF MOTHER.

UNITED STATES OF AMERICA, Indian Territory,
Western    DISTRICT.

I, Martha Collier, on oath state that I am 23 years of age and a citizen by Blood, of the Choctaw Nation; that I am the lawful wife of Oliver Collier, who is a citizen, by Marriage of the Choctaw Nation; that a Male child was born to me on 28 day of October, 1903; that said child has been named Thomas Scruggs Collier, and was living March 4, 1905.

Martha Collier

Witnesses To Mark:
 C C Cornelius
 T.F. Pearson

Subscribed and sworn to before me this 15 day of April, 1905

My commission
Expires Nov 29 1907

John M Lentz
Notary Public.

### AFFIDAVIT OF ATTENDING PHYSICIAN OR MID-WIFE.

UNITED STATES OF AMERICA, Indian Territory,
Western    DISTRICT.

I, D.S. Billington, a Physician, on oath state that I attended on Mrs. Martha Collier, wife of Oliver Collies on the 28 day of October, 1903; that there was born to her on said date a male child; that said child was living March 4, 1905, and is said to have been named Thomas Scruggs Collier

Dr. D.S. Billington

Witnesses To Mark:
 C C Cornelius
 T.F. Pearson

Subscribed and sworn to before me this 15 day of April, 1905

My commission
Expires Nov 29 1907

John M Lentz
Notary Public.

# Applications for Enrollment of Choctaw Newborn
## Act of 1905   Volume XVIII

Muskogee, Indian Territory, April 20, 1905.

Oliver Collier,
    Enterprise, Indian Territory.

Dear Sir:

    Receipt is hereby acknowledged of the affidavits of Martha Collier and Dr. D. S. Billington to the birth of Thomas Scruggs Collier, son of Oliver and Martha Collier, October 28, 1903.

    It is stated in the affidavit of the mother that she is a citizen by blood of the Choctaw Nation. If this is correct you are requested to state the name under which she was enrolled, the names of her parents, and if she has selected an allotment of the lands of the Choctaw or Chickasaw Nation please give her roll number as it appears upon her allotment certificate.

                            Respectfully,

                                              Chairman.

---

<u>Choc New Born 1335</u>
    Harold J. Bays
    (Born Nov. 1, 1904)

**NEW-BORN AFFIDAVIT.**

                    Number..................

## ...Choctaw Enrolling Commission...

    IN THE MATTER OF THE APPLICATION FOR ENROLLMENT, as a citizen of the Choctaw      Nation, of      Harold J. Bays

born on the  1$^{st}$  day of __November__ 190 4

Name of father  John Bays                a citizen of     ———
Nation final enrollment No. ———
Name of mother  Emma Bays          a citizen of    Choctaw
Nation final enrollment No.  11363

                                        Postoffice    Coalgate IT

Applications for Enrollment of Choctaw Newborn
Act of 1905   Volume XVIII

**AFFIDAVIT OF MOTHER.**

UNITED STATES OF AMERICA
INDIAN TERRITORY
Central   DISTRICT

I   Emma Bays   , on oath state that I am 27 years of age and a citizen by blood of the Choctaw Nation, and as such have been placed upon the final roll of the Choctaw Nation, by the Honorable Secretary of the Interior my final enrollment number being 11363 ; that I am the lawful wife of John Bays , who is a citizen of the ——— Nation, and as such has been placed upon the final roll of said Nation by the Honorable Secretary of the Interior, his final enrollment number being —— and that a Male child was born to me on the $1^{st}$ day of November 190 4; that said child has been named Harold J. Bays , and is now living.

Emma Bays

Witnesseth.

Must be two Witnesses who are Citizens.   } J.M. Harrison

   *(Name Illegible)*

Subscribed and sworn to before me this   $2^d$   day of   March   190 5

A.E. Folsom
Notary Public.

My commission expires:
Jan 9-1909

## AFFIDAVIT OF ATTENDING PHYSICIAN OR MIDWIFE

UNITED STATES OF AMERICA
INDIAN TERRITORY
Central   DISTRICT

I,   T.J. Allen   a   Practicing Physician on oath state that I attended on Mrs.   Emma Bays   wife of   John Bays on the   $1^{st}$   day of   November , 190 4, that there was born to her on said date a   male child, that said child is now living, and is said to have been named   Harold J. Bays

T.J. Allen   M.D.

WITNESSETH:

Must be two witnesses who are citizens and know the child.   { J.M. Harrison
   LC LeFlore

Subscribed and sworn to before me this, the   3rd   day of   March   190 5

JR Wood   Notary Public.

43

## Applications for Enrollment of Choctaw Newborn
## Act of 1905  Volume XVIII

We hereby certify that we are well acquainted with    D$^r$ T.J. Allen a    Practician[sic]    and know    him    to be reputable and of good standing in the community.

> SW Lance
> J M$^c$C Heflin

**BIRTH AFFIDAVIT.**

## DEPARTMENT OF THE INTERIOR.
## COMMISSION TO THE FIVE CIVILIZED TRIBES.

**IN RE APPLICATION FOR ENROLLMENT**, as a citizen of the    Choctaw    Nation, of Harold J. Bays    , born on the  1$^{st}$    day of   November   , 1904

Name of Father: John Bays          a citizen of the    ——    Nation.
Name of Mother: Emma Bays         a citizen of the   Choctaw   Nation.

Postoffice    Coalgate, Ind. Ter.

**AFFIDAVIT OF MOTHER.**

**UNITED STATES OF AMERICA, Indian Territory,**
Central                **DISTRICT.**

I,   Emma Bays   , on oath state that I am  27   years of age and a citizen by blood   , of the   Choctaw   Nation; that I am the lawful wife of   John Bays   , who is a citizen, by   ——   of the   ——   Nation; that a   male   child was born to me on  1$^{st}$   day of   November   , 1904; that said child has been named   Harold J Bays   , and was living March 4, 1905.

Emma Bays

Witnesses To Mark:

Subscribed and sworn to before me this  5th   day of   June    , 1905

*(Name Illegible)*
Notary Public.

# Applications for Enrollment of Choctaw Newborn
# Act of 1905   Volume XVIII

**AFFIDAVIT OF ATTENDING PHYSICIAN OR MID-WIFE.**

UNITED STATES OF AMERICA, Indian Territory,
Central                DISTRICT.

I, T.J. Allen, a physician, on oath state that I attended on Mrs. Emma Bays, wife of John Bays on the 1$^{st}$ day of November, 1904; that there was born to her on said date a male child; that said child was living March 4, 1905, and is said to have been named Harold J Bays

T.J. Allen, M.D.

Witnesses To Mark:
{

Subscribed and sworn to before me this 5th day of June, 1905.

*(Name Illegible)*
Notary Public.

7--NB--1338

Muskogee, Indian Territory, June 2, 1905.

James[sic] Bays,
   Coalgate, Indian Territory.

Dear Sir:

There is enclosed you herewith for execution application for the enrollment of your infant child, Harold J. Bays, born November 1, 1904.

The affidavits heretofore filed with the Commission show the child was living on March 2, 1905. It is necessary, for the child to be enrolled, that he was living on March 4, 1905.

In having these affidavits executed care should be exercised to see that all names are written in full, as they appear in the body of the affidavit, and in the event that either of the persons signing the affidavit are unable to write, signatures by mark must be attested by two witnesses. Each affidavit must be executed before a Notary Public and the notarial seal and signature of the officer must be attached to each separate affidavit.

This matter should receive your immediate attention as no further action can be taken relative to the enrollment of said child until the Commission has been furnished these affidavits.

Respectfully,

[sic]

## Applications for Enrollment of Choctaw Newborn
## Act of 1905   Volume XVIII

7-NB-1335

Muskogee, Indian Territory, June 10, 1905.

John Bays,
    Coalgate, Indian Territory.

Dear Sir:

    Receipt is hereby acknowledged of the affidavits of Emma Bays and T. J. Allen to the birth of Harold J. Bays, son of John and Emma Bays, November 1, 1904, and the same have been filed with our records in the matter of the enrollment of said child.

Respectfully,

Chairman.

---

Choc. New Born 1336
    Leroy Pierce
    (Born Aug. 24, 1903)

**NEW-BORN AFFIDAVIT.**

Number................

...Choctaw Enrolling Commission...

IN THE MATTER OF THE APPLICATION FOR ENROLLMENT, as a citizen of the Choctaw Nation, of Leroy Pierce

born on the 24 day of __August__ 190 3

Name of father   Robert L Pierce      a citizen of   Choctaw
Nation final enrollment No.   13792
Name of mother   Maude M Pierce      a citizen of   Choctaw
Nation final enrollment No.   850

    Postoffice   Antlers I T

## Applications for Enrollment of Choctaw Newborn
## Act of 1905  Volume XVIII

### AFFIDAVIT OF MOTHER.

UNITED STATES OF AMERICA
INDIAN TERRITORY
Central   DISTRICT

I  Maude M Pierce  , on oath state that I am 24 years of age and a citizen by marriage of the Choctaw Nation, and as such have been placed upon the final roll of the Choctaw Nation, by the Honorable Secretary of the Interior my final enrollment number being Eight hundred fifty *(850)* ; that I am the lawful wife of Robert L. Pierce , who is a citizen of the Choctaw Nation, and as such has been placed upon the final roll of said Nation by the Honorable Secretary of the Interior, his final enrollment number being 13792 and that a Male child was born to me on the 24th day of August 190 3; that said child has been named Leroy Pierce , and is now living.

Maude M Pierce

Witnesseth.
Must be two Witnesses who are Citizens.   Paul C Harris
James Frazier

Subscribed and sworn to before me this 25 day of Feb 190 5

John Cocke
Notary Public.

My commission expires:
Dec 6, 1908

---

## AFFIDAVIT OF ATTENDING PHYSICIAN OR MIDWIFE

UNITED STATES OF AMERICA
INDIAN TERRITORY
Central   DISTRICT

I, Mrs Sarah J Haynes a midwife on oath state that I attended on Mrs. Mrs Maude M Pierce wife of Robert L Pierce on the 24th day of August , 190 3 , that there was born to her on said date a male child, that said child is now living, and is said to have been named Leroy Pierce

her
Sarah J x Haynes   *midwife*
mark

Subscribed and sworn to before me this, the 20" day of February 190 5

WITNESSETH:
Must be two witnesses who are citizens   Paul C Harris
James Frazier

John Cocke  Notary Public.

# Applications for Enrollment of Choctaw Newborn
## Act of 1905   Volume XVIII

We hereby certify that we are well acquainted with   Sarah J Haynes   a   midwife   and know   her   to be reputable and of good standing in the community.

Paul C Harris

James Frazier

---

**BIRTH AFFIDAVIT.**

### DEPARTMENT OF THE INTERIOR.
### COMMISSION TO THE FIVE CIVILIZED TRIBES.

---

IN RE APPLICATION FOR ENROLLMENT, as a citizen of the   Choctaw   Nation, of Leroy Pierce   , born on the 24th   day of   August   , 1903

Name of Father: Robert L Pierce           a citizen of the   Choctaw   Nation.
Name of Mother: Maudie[sic] May Pierce    a citizen of the   Choctaw   Nation.

Postoffice   Antlers, Ind. Ter.

---

### AFFIDAVIT OF MOTHER.

UNITED STATES OF AMERICA, Indian Territory,
Central                  DISTRICT.

I,   Maudie May Pierce   , on oath state that I am   24   years of age and a citizen by   marriage   , of the   Choctaw   Nation; that I am the lawful wife of Robert L. Pierce   , who is a citizen, by blood   of the   Choctaw   Nation; that a   male   child was born to me on   24th   day of   August   , 1903; that said child has been named   Leroy Pierce   , and was living March 4, 1905.

Maude May Pierce

Witnesses To Mark:

Subscribed and sworn to before me this 26th   day of   April   , 1905

Wirt Franklin
Notary Public.

## Applications for Enrollment of Choctaw Newborn
## Act of 1905   Volume XVIII

### AFFIDAVIT OF ATTENDING PHYSICIAN OR MID-WIFE.

UNITED STATES OF AMERICA, Indian Territory,
Central                                DISTRICT.

I, Sarah Haynes, a mid-wife, on oath state that I attended on Mrs. Maudie May Pierce, wife of Robert L. Pierce on the 24th day of August, 1903; that there was born to her on said date a male child; that said child was living March 4, 1905, and is said to have been named Leroy Pierce

                                                      her
                                        Sarah x Haynes

Witnesses To Mark:                mark
   { Robert Anderson
     Vester Rose

Subscribed and sworn to before me this 26th day of April, 1905

                                      Wirt Franklin
                                              Notary Public.

*Maudie May Pierce*
*I.W. No 850*

*Robert L Pierce*
*Roll No 13792*

---

Choc. New Born 1337
    Emma Thomas
    (Born July 14, 1903)

BIRTH AFFIDAVIT.

### DEPARTMENT OF THE INTERIOR.
### COMMISSION TO THE FIVE CIVILIZED TRIBES.

**IN RE APPLICATION FOR ENROLLMENT,** as a citizen of the Chocktaw[sic] Nation, of Emma Thomas, born on the 14 day of July, 1903

Name of Father: Josiah Thomas        a citizen of the Chocktaw Nation.
Name of Mother: Melvina[sic]           a citizen of the Chocktaw Nation.

# Applications for Enrollment of Choctaw Newborn
# Act of 1905   Volume XVIII

Postoffice   Corinne

### AFFIDAVIT OF MOTHER.

UNITED STATES OF AMERICA, Indian Territory, }
Central   DISTRICT. }

I,   Melvina Thomas   , on oath state that I am   30   years of age and a citizen by   Blood   , of the   Chocktaw   Nation; that I am the lawful wife of   Josiah Thomas   , who is a citizen, by Blood   of the   Chocktaw   Nation; that a Female   child was born to me on   14   day of   July   , 1903; that said child has been named   Emma Thomas   , and was living March 4, 1905.

                          her
               Melvina x Thomas
Witnesses To Mark:         mark
  { Paul Homer
    Tobias Anderson

Subscribed and sworn to before me this   21   day of   April   , 1905

My Com expires   Jno. E. Talbert
Dec 12, 1908   Notary Public.

### AFFIDAVIT OF ATTENDING PHYSICIAN OR MID-WIFE.

UNITED STATES OF AMERICA, Indian Territory, }
Central   DISTRICT. }

I,   Josiah Thomas (Acting)   , a   Midwife   , on oath state that I attended on Mrs.   Josiah Thomas   , wife of   Josiah Thomas   on the   14   day of July   , 1903; that there was born to her on said date a   female   child; that said child was living March 4, 1905, and is said to have been named   Emma Thomas

                         Josiah Thomas

Witnesses To Mark:
  { Paul Homer
    Tobias Anderson

Subscribed and sworn to before me this   21   day of   April   , 1905

My Com expires   Jno. E. Talbert
Dec 12, 1908   Notary Public.

# Applications for Enrollment of Choctaw Newborn
## Act of 1905   Volume XVIII

DEPARTMENT OF THE INTERIOR,
COMMISSIONER TO THE FIVE CIVILIZED TRIBES.

Valliant, Indian Territory, April 16, 1906.

-------00------

In the matter of the enrollment of Emma Thomas, Choctaw New Born, *Card* Number 1337.

Testimony taken two miles northeast of Corinne, Indian Territory, April 12, 1906.

ELBINA THOMAS, being first duly sworn, testified as follows:

Through Interpreter, Jacob Homer.

BY THE COMMISSIONER:

Q What is your name? A Elbina Thomas.
Q What is your age? A About 31.
Q What is your post office address? A Corinne, I.T.
Q Are you a citizen by blood of the Choctaw Nation? A Yes, sir.

Witness is here identified as a Choctaw by blood, Roll Number 3197.

Q What is your husband's name? A Josiah Thomas.
Q Are you the mother of Emma Thomas? A Yes, sir.
Q When was Emma Thomas born?
A July 14, 1903.
Q Is the child now living?
A Yes, sir, here is the child right here ( indicating a small child, apparently a full-blood, of age corresponding to that of applicant).
Q Were you attended by a physician or mid-wife at the birth of this child?
A No.
Q Did you appear before John E. Tolbert on the 21st of April, 1905, as Melvina Thomas, and make affidavit to the birth of this child as occuring[sic] on the 14th of July, 1903?
A Yes, sir.
Q Your name appears on this affidavit as "Melvina" Thomas: should it have been "Elbina" Thomas? A Yes.
Q Affidavit is here exhibited witness: who witnessed the mark to your signature?
A It was Tobias Anderson and Paul Homer, but Paul Homer is dead now.

Witness Excused.
----------------------------------

Testimony taken two and one-half miles east of Corinne, Indian Territory, April 12, 1906.

# Applications for Enrollment of Choctaw Newborn
## Act of 1905 Volume XVIII

SALLIE TOM, being first duly sworn, testified as follows:

Through Interpreter, Jacob Homer.

BY THE COMMISSIONER:

Q What is your name? A Sallie Tom?[sic]
Q How old are you? A About 50.
Q What is your post office address? A Corinne, I T.
Q Are you a citizen by blood of the Choctaw Nation? A Yes.
Q Do you know a little Choctaw girl named Emma Thomas?
A Yes.
Q Who are the parents of this child?
A Josiah Thomas and Elbina Thomas.
Q Were you living near Josiah and Elbina Thomas at the time of the birth of this child?
A Yes, sir, I was living in less than a mile of them.
Q Are the parents of this Child--Josiah and Elbina Thomas--citizens by blood of the Choctaw Nation?
A Yes, sir.
Q When was Emma Thomas born?
A It was in July over two years ago.
Q Will the child be three years of age next July?
A Yes, sir.
Q Is this child, Emma Thomas, now living?
A Yes, sir.
Q Are you interested directly or indirectly in any allotment to which Emma Thomas may be entitled of the lands of the Choctaw-Chickasaw Tribes of Indians by reason of her enrollment as a citizen by blood of the Choctaw Nation? A No.

Witness Excused.

-----------------------------------------

Two and one-half miles southeast of Corinne, I. T. April 12, 1905.

JESSE TOM, being first duly sworn, testified, through interpreter Jacob Homer, as follows:

BY THE COMMISSIONER:

Q What is your name? A Jesse Tom.
Q How old are you? A 24/[sic]
Q What is your post office address? A Corinne, I. T.
Q Are you a citizen by blood of the Choctaw Nation? A Yes, sir.
Q Do you know a little Choctaw girl named Emma Thomas?
Q Yes, sir.
Q Who are the father and mother of this child?
A Josiah and Elbina Thomas.

# Applications for Enrollment of Choctaw Newborn
# Act of 1905   Volume XVIII

Q  Are they citizens by blood of the Choctaw Nation?
A  Yes, sir, both full-blood Choctaw.
Q  When was Emma Thomas born?
A  This coming July will be three years.
Q  The child was born in July 1903, then, was it?
A  Yes.
Q  Is Emma Thomas now living?   A  Yes, sir.
Q  How near do you live to Josiah and Elbina Thomas?
A  About a mile.
Q  Have you any interest in any allotment to which Emma Thomas may be entitled by reason of her enrollment as a citizen by blood of the Choctaw Nation?   A  No, sir.

Witness Excused.

W. P. Covington, being first duly sworn, states that the above and foregoing is a full, true and correct transcript of his stenographic notes taken in said case on said date.

W.P. Covington

Subscribed and sworn to before me, this   16<sup>th</sup>   day of April, 1906.

Lacey P Bobo<br>Notary Public.

---

$W^m O.B.$

COMMISSIONERS:
TAMS BIXBY,
THOMAS B. NEEDLES,
C.R. BRECKINBRIDGE.

WM. O. BEALL
Secretary

**DEPARTMENT OF THE INTERIOR,**
**COMMISSIONER TO THE FIVE CIVILIZED TRIBES.**

REFER IN REPLY TO THE FOLLOWING:

7-1175

ADDRESS ONLY THE
COMMISSION TO THE FIVE CIVILIZED TRIBES.

Muskogee, Indian Territory, May 3, 1905.

Josiah Thomas,
    Corrinne[sic], Indian Territory.

Dear Sir:

Receipt is hereby acknowledged of the affidavits of Melvina Thomas and Josiah Thomas to the birth of Emma Thomas, daughter of Josiah and Melvina Thomas, July 14, 1903, and the same have been filed with our records as an application for the enrollment of said child.

For the further identification of the mother of this child you are requested to state the names of her parents, and if she has selected an allotment of the lands of the Choctaw

## Applications for Enrollment of Choctaw Newborn
## Act of 1905   Volume XVIII

and Chickasaw Nations, give her roll number as it appears upon her certificate of allotment.

>Respectfully,
>Tams Bixby
>Chairman.

---

*(The letter below typed as given.)*

>Corinne, Ind. Ter May 19, 1905.

Sirs:

In answer to your inquiry will say That my wifes fathers name is Tom Nollet. Don't know what her mother's name was. My wife Elbina Thomas has allotted her land Certificate No. 1175 Roll No. 3197.

Hoping this will be satisfactory I remain

>Josiah Thomas.

---

>Choctaw N B 1337

>Muskogee, Indian Territory, June 9, 1905.

Josiah Thomas,
   Corinne, Indian Territory.

Dear Sir:

Receipt is hereby acknowledged of your letter of May 19, giving information relative to your wife's enrollment, and she has been identified as an enrolled citizen by blood of the Choctaw Nation, under the name of Elbina Thomas, and the information has been made a part of the record in the matter of the enrollment of your child, Emma Thomas.

>Respectfully,
>Chairman.

## Applications for Enrollment of Choctaw Newborn
## Act of 1905   Volume XVIII

7-NB-1337.

Muskogee, Indian Territory, June 14, 1905.

Josiah Thomas,
    Corinne, Indian Territory.

Dear Sir:

    Referring to the application for the enrollment of your infant child, Emma Thomas, born July 14, 1903, it is noted in the affidavits heretofore filed in this office that you attended upon your wife at the time of the birth of the applicant.

    If there was no physician or midwife besides yourself in attendance you will please secure his or her affidavit, but if you were the only one in attendance, it will be necessary for you to file in this office the affidavits of two persons who are disinterested and not related to the applicant, who have actual knowledge of the facts; that the child was born, the date of her birth, that she was living on March 4, 1905, and that Elbina Thomas is her mother.

                  Respectfully,

                                      Chairman.

---

7-NB-1337

Muskogee, Indian Territory, July 25, 1905.

Josiah Thomas,
    Corinne, Indian Territory.

Dear Sir:

    Your attention is called to a communication addressed to you by the Commission to the Five Civilized Tribes under date of June 14, 1905, requesting additional evidence in the matter of the enrollment of your infant child, Emma Thomas, born July 14, 1903.

    In said letter you were informed if you had attended upon your wife at the time of the birth of the applicant it was necessary for the child to be enrolled, that you furnish the affidavit of the physician or midwife, if any in attendance, or the affidavits of two persons who are disinterested and not related to the applicant, who have actual knowledge of the facts, that the child was born, date of her birth, that she was living March 4, 1905, and that Elbina Thomas is her mother. No reply to this letter has been received.

# Applications for Enrollment of Choctaw Newborn
## Act of 1905 Volume XVIII

You are requested to give this matter your immediate attention as no further action can be taken relative to the enrollment of said child until the evidence requested has been supplied.

        Respectfully,

                Commissioner.

---

7-NB-1337

        Muskogee, Indian Territory, August 19, 1905.

Josiah Thomas,
  Corinne, Indian Territory.

Dear Sir:

  Receipt is hereby acknowledged of your letter of August 14, 1905, asking that a blank be forwarded you for the purpose of making such additional proof as is necessary in the matter of the application for the enrollment of your infant child, Emma Thomas, born July 14, 1903. In compliance with your request, There is inclosed you herewith for execution application for the enrollment of your infant child, partially executed, an affidavit, which you should have filled out by two disinterested witnesses who know of the birth of your child, Emma Thomas, that your wife, Elbina Thomas is her mother, and whether or not she was living March 4, 1905.

  The affidavit of the mother should also be executed, and you should be careful to see that her name is signed to said affidavit as Elbina Thomas, as it appears in the body of the affidavit. If any of the persons signing the affidavit are unable to write, signature by mark must be attested by two witnesses who can sign their own names.

  Please give this matter your immediate attention.

        Respectfully,

              Acting Commissioner.

LM 3/19

# Applications for Enrollment of Choctaw Newborn
# Act of 1905   Volume XVIII

Choc. New Born 1338
    Abbin Underwood
    (Born Apr. 26[sic], 1903)

BIRTH AFFIDAVIT.

## DEPARTMENT OF THE INTERIOR.
## COMMISSION TO THE FIVE CIVILIZED TRIBES.

**IN RE APPLICATION FOR ENROLLMENT,** as a citizen of the Choctaw Nation, of Abbin Underwood, born on the 27th day of April, 1903

Name of Father: Alexander Underwood    a citizen of the Choctaw Nation.
Name of Mother: Patsy Underwood    a citizen of the Choctaw Nation.

    Postoffice    Antlers, Ind. Ter.

### AFFIDAVIT OF MOTHER.

UNITED STATES OF AMERICA, Indian Territory,
    Central    DISTRICT.

    I, Patsy Underwood, on oath state that I am 23 years of age and a citizen by blood, of the Choctaw Nation; that I am the lawful wife of Alexander Underwood, who is a citizen, by blood of the Choctaw Nation; that a male child was born to me on 27th day of April, 1903; that said child has been named Abbin Underwood, and was living March 4, 1905.

                      her
              Patsy x Underwood
Witnesses To Mark:        mark
  { Vester Rose
    Robert Anderson

    Subscribed and sworn to before me this 25th day of April, 1905

                      Wirt Franklin
                          Notary Public.

# Applications for Enrollment of Choctaw Newborn
## Act of 1905   Volume XVIII

### AFFIDAVIT OF ATTENDING PHYSICIAN OR MID-WIFE.

UNITED STATES OF AMERICA, Indian Territory,
    Central      DISTRICT.

I, Molsey Nelson, a mid-wife, on oath state that I attended on Mrs. Patsy Underwood, wife of Alexander Underwood on the 27th day of April, 1903; that there was born to her on said date a male child; that said child was living March 4, 1905, and is said to have been named Abbin Underwood

                          her
                     Molsey x Nelson
Witnesses To Mark:       mark
   { Robert Anderson
     Vester Rose

Subscribed and sworn to before me this 26th day of April, 1905

                     Wirt Franklin
                       Notary Public.

---

Choc. New Born 1339
    John Thomas Daniels
    (Born Aug. 12, 1904)

### NEW-BORN AFFIDAVIT.

      Number..............

## Choctaw Enrolling Commission.

IN THE MATTER OF THE APPLICATION FOR ENROLLMENT, as a citizen of the Choctaw Nation, of     John Thomas Daniels

born on the 12th day of August     190 4

Name of father    William Daniels        a citizen of    white
Nation final enrollment No ...............    (now *Daniels*)
Name of mother    Lina Coston        a citizen of    Choctaw
Nation final enrollment No    4123

                Postoffice     Antlers IT

## Applications for Enrollment of Choctaw Newborn
## Act of 1905   Volume XVIII

### AFFIDAVIT OF MOTHER.

UNITED STATES OF AMERICA, }
   INDIAN TERRITORY,
  Central    DISTRICT

    I  Lina Coston now Daniels  on oath state that I am 16 years of age and a citizen by blood of the Choctaw Nation, and as such have been placed upon the final roll of the Choctaw Nation, by the Honorable Secretary of the Interior my final enrollment number being 4123 ; that I am the lawful wife of William Daniels , who is a citizen of the ~~Cho~~ white Nation, and as such has been placed upon the final roll of said Nation by the Honorable Secretary of the Interior, his final enrollment number being —— and that a male child was born to me on the 12$^{th}$ day of August 190 4; that said child has been named John Thomas Daniels , and is now living.

                                                    *Daniels*
                                    Lina Coston *now*

WITNESSETH:

Must be two Witnesses who are Citizens. }  Martin B Crowder
                      Eliza Harris

    Subscribed and sworn to before me this  17  day of  Jan  190 5

                                W A Shoney
                                      Notary Public.

My commission expires  Jan 10, 1909

---

### *Affidavit of Attending Physician or Midwife*

UNITED STATES OF AMERICA, }
   INDIAN TERRITORY,
  Central    DISTRICT

    I,  Dr W. M. Wallace  a  Physician on oath state that I attended on Mrs. Lina Coston now M$^c$Daniels[sic] wife of William Daniels on the 12$^{th}$ day of August , 190 4, that there was born to her on said date a male child, that said child is now living, and is said to have been named John Thomas Daniels

                                W.M. Wallace    M. D.

    Subscribed and sworn to before me this the  21  day of  Jan  1905

      *My commission expires*
        *July 9$^{th}$, 1908.*            W.E. Larecy
                                      Notary Public.

WITNESSETH:

Must be two witnesses who are citizens and know the child. }  T.J. Oakes
                          Joe Nail

# Applications for Enrollment of Choctaw Newborn
## Act of 1905 Volume XVIII

We hereby certify that we are well acquainted with Dr W.M. Wallace a Physician and know him to be reputable and of good standing in the community.

Must be two citizen witnesses. { TJ Oakes
Joe Nail

**BIRTH AFFIDAVIT.**

## DEPARTMENT OF THE INTERIOR.
## COMMISSION TO THE FIVE CIVILIZED TRIBES.

IN RE APPLICATION FOR ENROLLMENT, as a citizen of the Choctaw Nation, of John Thomas Daniels , born on the 12th day of August , 1904

Name of Father: William Daniels a citizen of the United States Nation.
Name of Mother: Lina Daniels a citizen of the Choctaw Nation.

Postoffice Antlers, Ind. Ter.

**AFFIDAVIT OF MOTHER.**

UNITED STATES OF AMERICA, Indian Territory, Central DISTRICT.

I, Lina Daniels , on oath state that I am 17 years of age and a citizen by blood , of the Choctaw Nation; that I am the lawful wife of William Daniels , who is a citizen, by ................ of the United States ~~Nation~~; that a male child was born to me on 12th day of August , 1904; that said child has been named John Thomas Daniels , and was living March 4, 1905.

Lina Daniels

Witnesses To Mark:
{

Subscribed and sworn to before me this 25th day of April , 1905

Wirt Franklin
Notary Public.

## Applications for Enrollment of Choctaw Newborn
## Act of 1905 Volume XVIII

#### AFFIDAVIT OF ATTENDING PHYSICIAN OR MID-WIFE.

UNITED STATES OF AMERICA, Indian Territory,
Central DISTRICT.

I, W.M. Wallace , a physician , on oath state that I attended on Mrs. Lina Daniels , wife of William Daniels on the 12th day of August , 1904; that there was born to her on said date a male child; that said child was living March 4, 1905, and is said to have been named John Thomas Daniels

W.M. Wallace

Witnesses To Mark:
{

Subscribed and sworn to before me this 25th day of April , 1905

*My commission expires*
*July 9th, 1908.*

W.E. Larecy
Notary Public.

7-NB-1339

Muskogee, Indian Territory, July 10, 1905.

W. N. Daniels,
Antlers, Indian Territory.

Dear Sir:

Receipt is hereby acknowledged of your letter of July 3, 1905, asking if the name of your son John Thomas Daniels has been approved.

In reply to your letter you are advised that the name of your son John Thomas Daniels has been placed upon a schedule of citizens by blood of the Choctaw Nation which has been forwarded the Secretary of the Interior, but this office has not yet been advised of Departmental action thereon.

Respectfully,

Commissioner.

## Applications for Enrollment of Choctaw Newborn
## Act of 1905   Volume XVIII

Choc. New Born 1340
    Richard Harkins
    (Born Feb. 20, 1903)

**BIRTH AFFIDAVIT.**

### DEPARTMENT OF THE INTERIOR.
### COMMISSION TO THE FIVE CIVILIZED TRIBES.

IN RE APPLICATION FOR ENROLLMENT, as a citizen of the  Choctaw  Nation, of  Richard Harkins  , born on the 20$^{th}$  day of  Feb  , 1903

Name of Father: James Harkins      a citizen of the  Choctaw  Nation.
Name of Mother: Viney Harkins      a citizen of the  Choctaw  Nation.

        Postoffice    Swink Ind Ter

**AFFIDAVIT OF MOTHER.**

UNITED STATES OF AMERICA, Indian Territory, }
    Central        DISTRICT. }

    I, Viney Harkins  , on oath state that I am ............ years of age and a citizen by inter marred[sic]  , of the  Choctaw  Nation; that I am the lawful wife of  James Harkins  , who is a citizen, by Blood  of the  Choctaw  Nation; that a male  child was born to me on  20 day of  Feb  , 1903; that said child has been named  Richard Harkins  , and was living March 4, 1905.

                                Viney Harkins

Witnesses To Mark:
{

    Subscribed and sworn to before me this  22  day of  April  , 1905

                                Thomas Fennell
                                Notary Public.

**AFFIDAVIT OF ATTENDING PHYSICIAN OR MID-WIFE.**

UNITED STATES OF AMERICA, Indian Territory, }
    Central        DISTRICT. }

    I, ................................... , a  Midwife  , on oath state that I attended on Mrs.  Viney Harkins  , wife of  James Harkins  on the 20  day of  Feb  ,

# Applications for Enrollment of Choctaw Newborn
## Act of 1905  Volume XVIII

1903; that there was born to her on said date a   male   child; that said child was living March 4, 1905, and is said to have been named  Richard Harkins

Nellie B. Browning

Witnesses To Mark:

{ Subscribed and sworn to before me this  22   day of    April       , 1905

Thomas Fennell<br>Notary Public.

---

7-1497.

Muskogee, Indian Territory, May 3, 1905.

James Harkins,
    Swink, Indian Territory.

Dear Sir:

    Receipt is hereby acknowledged of your letter of April 22, enclosing the affidavits of Viney Harkins and Nellie B. Browning to the birth of Richard Harkins, son of James and Viney Harkins, February 20, 1903, and the same have been filed with our records as an application for the enrollment of said child.

Respectfully,

Chairman.

---

Choc. New Born 1341
    Freddierica Jones
    (Born March 7, 1904)
    Cleo Jones
    (Born March 4, 1905)

**Applications for Enrollment of Choctaw Newborn**
**Act of 1905   Volume XVIII**

*(Below typed as given.)*

# NEW BORN
## CHOCTAW
### ENROLLMENT

FREDDIERICA JONES
(BORN MARCH 7, 1904)

CLEO JONES
(BORN MARCH 4, 1905)

CLEO JONES transferred to N. B. (April 26 1906)
#757
No. 2 born March 4, 1905)

(2) decision rendered as to No. (2 Jun. 30, 1905

As Citizen of the
CHOCTAW NATION
Act of Congress
Approved March 3, 1905

Decline to receive or consider June 30, 1905
copy of decision forwarded attorneys; Jun 30 1905
for Choctaw and Chickasaw nations. June 30, 1905

COPY OF DECISION FORWARDED APPLICANT'S
FATHER    JUNE 30, 1905

Action approved by Secretary of interior.
Dec. 8, 1905
Notice of departmental action forwarded
attorneys for Choctaw and Chickasaw nations
Dec. 20, 1905
Notice of departmental action mailed applicant's
father.    Dec. 20, 1905.

RECORD FORWARDED DEPARTMENT    JUNE 30, 1905

## Applications for Enrollment of Choctaw Newborn
### Act of 1905   Volume XVIII

*Affidavit of Attending Physician or Midwife*

UNITED STATES OF AMERICA,
INDIAN TERRITORY,
Central    DISTRICT

I, H.E. Rappoole a Practicing Physician on oath state that I attended on Mrs. Lucetta Boydstun now Jones wife of Charles W. Jones on the 7$^{th}$ day of March, 1904, that there was born to her on said date a Female child, that said child is now living, and is said to have been named Freddierica Jones

H E Rappolee    M. D.

Subscribed and sworn to before me this the 16$^{th}$ day of February 1905

A.E. Folsom
Notary Public.

WITNESSETH:
Must be two witnesses who are citizens and know the child.
{ Alfred E Boydstun
  George A Boydstun

We hereby certify that we are well acquainted with D$^r$ Rappolee a Physician and know him to be reputable and of good standing in the community.

*Jan 9.1909*

Must be two citizen witnesses.
{ Alfred E Boydstun
  George A Boydstun

# NEW BORN AFFIDAVIT

No ............

## CHOCTAW ENROLLING COMMISSION

IN THE MATTER OF THE APPLICATION FOR ENROLLMENT as a citizen of the Choctaw Nation, of Freddierica Jones born on the 7$^{th}$ day of March 1904

Name of father Charles W Jones   a citizen of Choctaw Nation, final enrollment No. 598   *now Jones*

Name of mother Lucetta Boydstun   a citizen of Choctaw Nation, final enrollment No. 13557

Caddo I.T.   Postoffice.

# Applications for Enrollment of Choctaw Newborn
## Act of 1905   Volume XVIII

### AFFIDAVIT OF MOTHER

UNITED STATES OF AMERICA  
INDIAN TERRITORY  
DISTRICT   Central

I   Lucetta Boydstun  *now* Jones  , on oath state that I am   21   years of age and a citizen by   blood   of the   Choctaw   Nation, and as such have been placed upon the final roll of the   Choctaw   Nation, by the Honorable Secretary of the Interior my final enrollment number being   13557   ; that I am the lawful wife of   Charles W Jones  , who is a citizen of the   Choctaw   Nation, and as such has been placed upon the final roll of said Nation by the Honorable Secretary of the Interior, his final enrollment number being   598   and that a   Female   child was born to me on the   7$^{th}$   day of   March   190 4; that said child has been named   Freddierica Jones  , and is now living.

Lucetta Boydstun *now* Jones

WITNESSETH:  
Must be two witnesses who are citizens { Alfred E Boydstun  
George A Boydstun

Subscribed and sworn to before me this, the   13$^{th}$   day of   February  , 190 5

A.E. Folsom  
Notary Public.

My Commission Expires:  
Jan - 9 - 1909

---

BIRTH AFFIDAVIT.

### DEPARTMENT OF THE INTERIOR.
## COMMISSION TO THE FIVE CIVILIZED TRIBES.

IN RE APPLICATION FOR ENROLLMENT, as a citizen of the   Choctaw   Nation, of   Fred R. Jones  , born on the 7th   day of   March  , 1904

Name of Father:  Charles W. Jones       a citizen of the   Choctaw   Nation.  
Name of Mother:  Lucetta Jones       a citizen of the   Choctaw   Nation.

Postoffice   Caddo Indian Territory

# Applications for Enrollment of Choctaw Newborn
## Act of 1905   Volume XVIII

### AFFIDAVIT OF MOTHER.

UNITED STATES OF AMERICA, Indian Territory, }
    Central                          DISTRICT.

    I, Lucetta Jones, on oath state that I am 21 years of age and a citizen by blood, of the Choctaw Nation; that I am the lawful wife of Charles W. Jones, who is a citizen, by marriage of the Choctaw Nation; that a female child was born to me on 7th day of March, 1904; that said child has been named Rred[sic] R. Jones, and was living March 4, 1905.

                                                Lucetta Jones

Witnesses To Mark:
{

    Subscribed and sworn to before me this 26th day of May, 1905

                                                  JL Rappolee
                                                         Notary Public.

---

### AFFIDAVIT OF ATTENDING PHYSICIAN OR MID-WIFE.

UNITED STATES OF AMERICA, Indian Territory, }
    Central                          DISTRICT.

    I, H. E. Rappolee, a Physician, on oath state that I attended on Mrs. Lucetta Jones, wife of Charles W. Jones on the 7th day of March, 1904; that there was born to her on said date a female child; that said child was living March 4, 1905, and is said to have been named Fred R. Jones

                                                 H.E. Rappolee

Witnesses To Mark:
{

    Subscribed and sworn to before me this 26th day of May, 1905

                                                  JL Rappolee
                                                         Notary Public.

## Applications for Enrollment of Choctaw Newborn
### Act of 1905  Volume XVIII

BIRTH AFFIDAVIT.

### DEPARTMENT OF THE INTERIOR.
### COMMISSION TO THE FIVE CIVILIZED TRIBES.

IN RE APPLICATION FOR ENROLLMENT, as a citizen of the Choctaw Nation, of Freddierica Jones, born on the 7th day of March, 1904

Name of Father: Charles W. Jones  Roll 7 W 598  a citizen of the Choctaw Nation.
Name of Mother: Lucetta Jones  " 13559  a citizen of the Choctaw Nation.

Postoffice  Caddo I.T.

### AFFIDAVIT OF MOTHER.

UNITED STATES OF AMERICA, Indian Territory, }
Central  DISTRICT. }

I, Lucetta Jones, on oath state that I am 21 years of age and a citizen by blood, of the Choctaw Nation; that I am the lawful wife of Charles W. Jones, who is a citizen, by marriage of the Choctaw Nation; that a female child was born to me on 7th day of March, 1904; that said child has been named Freddierica Jones, and was living March 4, 1905.

Lucetta Jones

Witnesses To Mark:
{

Subscribed and sworn to before me this 12 day of June, 1905

JL Rappolee
Notary Public.

### AFFIDAVIT OF ATTENDING PHYSICIAN OR MID-WIFE.

UNITED STATES OF AMERICA, Indian Territory, }
Central  DISTRICT. }

I, H. E. Rappolee, a Physician, on oath state that I attended on Mrs. Lucetta Jones, wife of Charles W. Jones on the 7th day of March, 1904; that there was born to her on said date a female child; that said child was living March 4, 1905, and is said to have been named Freddierica Jones

H.E. Rappolee

Witnesses To Mark:
{

## Applications for Enrollment of Choctaw Newborn
## Act of 1905 Volume XVIII

Subscribed and sworn to before me this 12$^{th}$ day of June , 1905

JL Rappolee
Notary Public.

---

7-5351.

Muskogee, Indian Territory, May 3, 1905.

Charles W. Jones,
    Caddo, Indian Territory.

Dear Sir:

    Receipt is hereby acknowledged of the affidavits of Lucetta Jones and H. E. Rappolee to the birth of Fred R. Jones, child of Charles w. and Lucetta Jones, March 7, 1904, and the same have been filed with our records as an application for the enrollment of said child.

    There have been received at this office from the Principal Chief of the Choctaw Nation affidavits to the birth of Freddierica Jones, and the information contained therein has enabled the Commission to identify Lucetta Jones upon our records as an enrolled citizen by blood of the Choctaw Nation, and it will not, therefore, be necessary for you to forward the information requested in our letter of May 1, 1905.

    Receipt is also acknowledged of the affidavits of Lucetta Jones and H. E. Rappolee to the birth of Cleo Jones, daughter of Charles W. and Lucetta Jones, March 4, 1905.

    You are advised that the Commission is authorized by the Act of Congress approved March 3, 1905, for a period of sixty days from that date, to receive applications for the enrollment of children born to enrolled citizens by blood of the Choctaw and Chickasaw Nations between September 25, 1902 and March 4, 1905, and living on the latter date.

Respectfully,

Chairman.

# Applications for Enrollment of Choctaw Newborn
## Act of 1905   Volume XVIII

7-NB-1341.

Muskogee, Indian Territory, June 3, 1905.

Charles W. Jones,
    Caddo, Indian Territory.

Dear Sir:

    There is enclosed you herewith for execution application for the enrollment of your infant child, born March 7, 1904.

    In the affidavit of February 13, 1905, heretofore filed in this office, the name of the applicant is given as Freddierica Jones, while in those of April 26, 1905, her name is given as Fred R. Jones. In the enclosed application the name of the child is left blank. Please insert the correct name and when the affidavits are properly executed return them to this office.

    In having these affidavits executed care should be exercised to see that all names are written in full, as they appear in the body of the affidavit, and in the event that either of the persons signing the affidavit are unable to write, signatures by mark must be attested by two witnesses. Each affidavit must be executed before a Notary Public and the notarial seal and signature of the officer must be attached to each separate affidavit.

                        Respectfully,

VR 3-4.                                                                                           [sic]

---

7 NB 1341

Muskogee, Indian Territory, June 21, 1905.

Charles W. Jones,
    Caddo, Indian Territory.

Dear Sir:

    Receipt is hereby acknowledged of the affidavits of Lucetta Jones and H. E. Rappolee to the birth of Freddierica Jones, daughter of Charles W. and Lucetta Jones, March 7, 1904, and the same have been filed with our records in the matter of the enrollment of said child.

                        Respectfully,

                                                     Chairman.

## Applications for Enrollment of Choctaw Newborn
## Act of 1905   Volume XVIII

Choc. New Born 1342
    Pearl Anderson
    (Born Nov. 1, 1904)

**BIRTH AFFIDAVIT.**

### DEPARTMENT OF THE INTERIOR.
### COMMISSION TO THE FIVE CIVILIZED TRIBES.

    **IN RE APPLICATION FOR ENROLLMENT,** as a citizen of the   Choctaw   Nation, of   Pearl Anderson   , born on the   1st   day of   November   , 1904

Name of Father: Charley Anderson      a citizen of the   Choctaw   Nation.
Name of Mother: Lue Anderson      a citizen of the   Choctaw   Nation.

    Postoffice    Farris, Ind. Ter.

**AFFIDAVIT OF MOTHER.**

UNITED STATES OF AMERICA, Indian Territory, }
    Central             DISTRICT.  }

    I,   Lue Anderson   , on oath state that I am   34   years of age and a citizen by   marriage   , of the   Choctaw   Nation; that I am the lawful wife of   Charley Anderson   , who is a citizen, by blood   of the   Choctaw   Nation; that a   female   child was born to me on   1st   day of   November   , 1904; that said child has been named   Pearl Anderson   , and was living March 4, 1905.

                              Lue Anderson

Witnesses To Mark:
  {

    Subscribed and sworn to before me this   26th   day of   April   , 1905

                              Wirt Franklin
                                  Notary Public.

**AFFIDAVIT OF ATTENDING PHYSICIAN OR MID-WIFE.**

UNITED STATES OF AMERICA, Indian Territory, }
    Central             DISTRICT.  }

    I,   W.H. Hamlet   , a physician   , on oath state that I attended on   Mrs.   Lue Anderson   , wife of   Charley Anderson   on the   1st   day of

## Applications for Enrollment of Choctaw Newborn
## Act of 1905   Volume XVIII

November    , 1904; that there was born to her on said date a    female    child; that said child was living March 4, 1905, and is said to have been named  Pearl Anderson

W.H. Hamlet

Witnesses To Mark:
{

   Subscribed and sworn to before me this   26th   day of    April     , 1905

Wirt Franklin<br>Notary Public.

---

DEPARTMENT OF THE INTERIOR,

COMMISSION TO THE FIVE CIVILIZED TRIBES,

CHOCTAW LAND OFFICE,

ATOKA, INDIAN TERRITORY, SEPTEMBER 7, 1906.

---

IN THE MATTER of the application of Lue Anderson, Choctaw by intermarriage, approved roll No. 898, field card No. 1901, to make selection in allotment for her child Pearl Anderson, Choctaw new born (Act of Congress approved March 3, 1905), roll No. 1184, field card No. 1342.

---

LUE ANDERSON, being duly sworn testified as follows:

EXAMINATION

BY THE COMMISSIONER:

Q  What is your name?  A  Lue Anderson.
Q  How old are you?  A  Thirty-five.
Q  What is your postoffice address?  A  Farris, I. T.
Q  Are you a duly enrolled citizen by intermarriage of the Choctaw Nation?  A  Yes sir.
Q  What is the name of your father?  A  J. B. Saddlefield.
Q  Is his given name Joe?  A  Yes sir.
Q  What is the name of your mother?  A  Eliza Jane.
Q  What was the name of your former husband?  A  Charley Anderson.
Q  Are you the mother of Eva and Lillie Anderson?  A  Yes sir.

## Applications for Enrollment of Choctaw Newborn
## Act of 1905   Volume XVIII

THE COMMISSIONER:   The name of Lue Anderson appears as No. 898 upon the approved Choctaw roll by intermarriage, field card No. 1901.

Q Have you another child? A Yes sir.
Q What is the name of that child? A Pearl Anderson.
Q Do you appear at the land office today to select an allotment for Pearl Anderson? A Yes sir.
Q Is Pearl Anderson living? A Yes sir.
Q When was Pearl Anderson born? A First of November, 1904.
Q She was born on the first day of November, 1904? A Yes sir.
Q Is she now living with you? A Yes sir.
Q What is the name of Pearl Anderson's father? A Charley Anderson.
Q Is he a citizen by blood of the Choctaw Nation? A Yes sir.
Q Do you know the name of his father? A Yes sir.
Q What is his name? A Rodgers Anderson.
Q Do you know the name of his mother? A Lucinda, - Square I believe was the last man she married; she married a man by the name of Square.
Q Is your husband Charley Anderson living? A Yes sir.
Q Are you and he living together now as husband and wife? A No sir.
Q Have you been separated? A Yes sir.
Q Have you been divorced? A No sir, never been divorced.
Q When were you separated at first? A Well, you know he went to the penitentiary; is that what you want to know? He went to the penitentiary in 1896.
Q How long was he confined in the penitentiary? A Five years.
Q When was he released? A I think, - I don't know, - in 1900, as well as I remember.
Q After he returned from the penitentiary, did you and he go back and live together as husband and wife? A Yes sir.
Q Immediately upon his return? A No sir.
Q When did you commence living together after he returned from the penitentiary? A In February, 1904. I quit getting letters from him; I wrote and never got no answer from him until he come in. I had heard of him coming in, but I never knew if he was living or not.
Q When did you say you next lived together after he returned from the penitentiary, first of February of what year? A 1904; that time I lived at Coalgate.
Q Were you living at Coalgate then? A Yes sir.
Q Where had Charles Anderson been living before that time, after he was released from the penitentiary? A First one place and then another; he was hunting me, but didn't know where I was at.
Q Did you at one time make affidavit to an official of the Commission to the Five Civilized Tribes to the effect that Charles Anderson was dead? A Yes sir.
Q Was that while he was in the penitentiary? A No sir, he was out then.
Q What did you make that affidavit for? A Because, there was two persons told me he died after he come out.
Q Had you ever seen Charles Anderson from the time he was released from the penitentiary until in February, 1904? A No sir.
Q How did you happen to see him then? A He come to where I was at.

# Applications for Enrollment of Choctaw Newborn
## Act of 1905   Volume XVIII

Q Where?  A Coalgate.
Q What day of the month?  A I can't tell you the exact date.
Q With whom were you living at Coalgate?  A I was living by myself in a house there at Coalgate on some land I had filed on for the children.
Q How long did Charles Anderson live with you?  A He lived with me until in June.
Q Did he live with you continuously from the time he came there in February, 1904, until June of the same year?  A I don't know as he did. He went to see his folks several times; to his Uncle's in the Chickasaw; would be gone two or three days may be.
Q Did you and Charles Anderson assume the relations of husband and wife after he came to you at Coalgate in February 1904?  A Yes sir.
Q You never was divorced from Charles Anderson?  A Never was.
Q Did you ever apply for a divorce?  A No sir.
Q Did he ever apply for a divorce?  A No sir.
Q With whom are you living now?  A George Hammer.
Q Is he a citizen of the Choctaw Nation?  A No sir.
Q Is he a white man?  A Yes sir.
Q Have you been married to him?  A Yes sir.
Q When were you married to George Hammer?  A On the 24th of December.
Q Of what year?  A 1904, I guess.
Q Were you married to him before or after Pearl Anderson was born?  A After.
Q You never had been divorced from Charles Anderson, had you?  A No I hadn't, and aint[sic] yet.
Q How did you come to marry another man?  A I just married, I reckon.
Q Where did you get your marriage license?  A Atoka.
Q From the clerk of the United States Court?  A Yes sir.
Q Who married you?  A Man at Coalgate.
Q What is his name?  A I don't know, I have forgot.
Q Some minister of the Gospel?  A Yes sir.
Q You procured a marriage license from the Clerk of the United States Court at Atoka when you married George Hammer?  A Yes sir.
Q You are sure about that?  A Yes sir.
Q Who got the marriage license?  A George Hammer.
Q Were you living at Coalgate at that time?  A Yes sir.
Q Where were you married there?  A In the preacher's room, in the presence of him and his wife; I knowed[sic] his name, but I have forgot it now.
Q Have you been living with George Hammer ever since as husband and wife?
A Yes sir.
Q Where is Charles Anderson now?  A Chickasaw Nation
Q What is his postoffice address?  A I don't know. He was in the Chickasaw Nation last year at some little station there, I have forgot.
Q When was Pearl Anderson born?  A In November, first of November.
Q Of what year?  A 1904.
Q Mrs. Anderson, will you state on oath that your former husband Charles Anderson is the father of Pearl Anderson?  A Yes sir.
Q How long did you live with this man Hammer before you married him?  A I didn't live with him.

# Applications for Enrollment of Choctaw Newborn
## Act of 1905  Volume XVIII

Q Never lived with him at all until you married him? A Never did.
Q Did you ever live with any other man before you married this man Hammer after you and Charles Anderson separated? A No sir.
Q When did Charles Anderson go to the penitentiary? A In 1898.
Q What was he charged with? A Horse stealing
Q Do you state on oath that you and Charles Anderson resumed the marriage relations and lived together as husband and wife from February, 1904, until along in June of that same year, and that he is the father of your child Pearl Anderson? A Yes sir.
Q Is he the father of your other two children, Lillie and Eva? A Yes sir.
Q Are these three children all the children you have? A Yes; no, I have got a boy mighty near grown.
Q Is he living? A Yes sir, he is living.
Q What is his name? A Lee Samuels.
Q What is the name of his father? A John Samuels.
Q Were you ever married to John Samuels? A Yes sir.
Q Was he dead when you married Charles Anderson? A Yes sir.
Q Were you ever married after Charles Anderson was sent to the penitentiary?
A No sir
Q That is, until you married this man Hammer? A No sir.
Q You never did live with any other man while Charles Anderson was in the penitentiary, or after he returned from the penitentiary until you married this man Hammer? A No.
Q You will swear that, will you? A Yes sir.
Q This office received a letter from Charles Anderson, dated August 18, 1905, in which he state that he never did live with you after he returned from the penitentiary, what about that? A Well, he did; if he states it, - what is he at?
Q You say that you lived with him after he came back? A Yes/
Q What do you suppose he states he didn't for? A I presume because we parted.
Q How did you ever come to live together; you didn't get along after he came back, did you? A We didn't get along before, either.
Q How did you commence to live together after he came back? A He didn't know where I was at.
Q Didn't he try to find you? A Why, he did.
Q Why do you suppose he would make that statement that he had never lived with you since he returned from the penitentiary? A I can't tell you why he would make it, but then I can face him; you can get us both together if you want to.
Q Have you any witnesses that you can prove the fact that you did live with Charles Anderson during that period of time you state, as husband and wife? A Several lived there, of course, but then they have moved away. They are all gone.
Q Who are they? A Moons.
Q What Moons? A I don't know what his name was; Mr. Moons and his family.
A Any body else? A Yes.
Q Who? A Mr. Williams.
Q What is his name? A John Williams.
Q Where does he live? A I don't know where he lives at.
Q Where did he live? A There on my place.

## Applications for Enrollment of Choctaw Newborn
## Act of 1905   Volume XVIII

Q At the time you were living there? A Yes sir.
Q What month? A Why, he had been there several years.
Q Where did Charles Anderson come from when he came to you at Coalgate that time? A Hartshorne.
Q Did he go back to Hartshorne? A No sir.
Q Where did he go? A Down to Kiamichi, I think.
Q Who were you living with before he came there? A Living with just me and the children.
Q Just you and the children? A Yes sir, just me and the children there on that place I had filed on.
Q Who had you lived with since Charles Anderson went to the penitentiary until that time?   A Well I was with a family most of the time, or close to a family, generally lived though, by myself.
Q Did you ever live with any man? A No sir.
Q None at all? A No sir.
Q Did you live with any man after that time until you married this man Hammer? A No sir.
Q Did you live with Hammer before you married him? A No sir.
Q You don't know the name of the preacher that married you and Hammer? A No sir. You can find out by the marriage license.
Q You have the marriage license at home? A Yes sir, they are at home.
Q How many times have you been married? A I have been married three times?[sic]
Q What was your first husband's name? A John Williams.
Q What was your second husband's name? A Charley Anderson.
Q What is the name of your third husband? A George Hammer.
Q You married him before you were divorced from Charles Anderson? A Yes sir.
Q You have never been divorced from him? A No sir.
Q You and this man Hammer are now living together as husband and wife? A Yes sir.
Q Do you know what the penalty is for swearing falsely about a matter of this kind? A I reckon so, I don't know.
Q What do you think it is? A I haven't swore false.
Q You are willing to state under oath that Charles Anderson is the father of this child? A Certainly.
Q And that you and he lived together as husband and wife from February, 1904, until June, 1904? A Yes sir.

(Witness dismissed).

---

W. M. DAVIS, being duly sworn, testified as follows:

### EXAMINATION
BY THE COMMISSIONER:

Q What is your name? A W. M. Davis.
Q What is your postoffice? A Farris.
Q How old are you? A Fifty-two.

## Applications for Enrollment of Choctaw Newborn
## Act of 1905   Volume XVIII

Q  Are you a citizen of either the Choctaw or Chickasaw Nation? A  No sir.
Q  How long have you lived at Farris? A  I have lived there, about, I think it will be six years this Fall.
Q  Do you know Lue Anderson? A  Yes sir.
Q  Do you know her former husband Charles Anderson? A  Yes sir.
Q  How long have you known him? A  In the neighborhood of thirteen years.
Q  How long has Lue Anderson lived close to Farris? A  Why, I think may be she has lived there some where near one year.
Q  Where did she live prior to that time? A  Before she married, she staid[sic] at Coalgate.
Q  When did she come to Farris? A  She come there, let me see, if I can study out the time; last year we raised a crop and this year is a crop; they come there sometime in the winter I think, this here is two years, they have just made two crops. I don't remember the time of year that they moved in there and filed on a piece of land.
Q  Who lived with her down there? A  Man by the name of George Hammer.
Q  Where did she live before that, close to Coalgate? A  About seven miles north of Coalgate.
Q  Did you live close to her then? A  No sir, I lived at Farris.
Q  Did you see her any time while she was living near Coalgate? A  Yes, I went up to her place.
Q  When? A  Some where, I can't recollect, some where in February, some time in '94.
Q  1904? A  Yes sir, 1904, in February I think along about the first of the month.
Q  How long did you stay up there? A  Why I went up there one day and come away the same day.
Q  What was the occasion of your visit? A  To see about getting the place she owned.
Q  Did you stay all night at her place? A  No sir.
Q  With whom was she living near Coalgate then? A  I don't know. When I went up there Charley Anderson went with me from this place. I met him here in Atoka.
Q  You met Charles Anderson here in Atoka and went with him? A  Yes sir.
Q  Before that time, had Lue Anderson and Charles Anderson been living together since he was sent to the penitentiary? A  I don't know; I knowed[sic] him before he was ever sent to the penitentiary.
Q  You don't know whether he and Lue had lived together after he was released up until the time you went up there? A  No sit.
Q  When you went up there did Charles Anderson stay? A  Yes, I left him there.
Q  With whom did you leave him there? A  At Mrs. Anderson's, on her place.
Q  With her? A  Yes, at her house.
Q  Do you know how long he remained there? A  No sir, I don't know, I went on back here.
Q  Do you know whether he stayed with her that night you stayed in that section?
A  No sir.
Q  You were at her house? A  Yes sir.
Q  Charles Anderson was with her the same time you were there? A  Yes, he went there with me.
Q  Did he stay there? A  Yes sir.
Q  Was that in the day time? A  Yes sir.
Q  You doN't[sic] know whether he remained that night or not? A  No sir.

## Applications for Enrollment of Choctaw Newborn
## Act of 1905   Volume XVIII

Q  You don't know how long he stayed with her, or whether they lived together as husband and wife after that?  A  No sir, I don't; I never saw him for a long time, and aint[sic] seen him since.
Q  All you know about them living together is that Charles Anderson went from Atoka up to her place and you left him at her house one day?  A  Yes sir.
Q  You don't know whether he staid[sic] there any longer that time or not?  A  No sir.
Q  You don't know whether they lived together as husband and wife or not?  A  No sir.
Q  That was about the first of February, 1904?  A  Some time along about that time of year, I think it was about the first of February; It was in the spring I know.
Q  Did Charles Anderson make any statement to you relative to living with his wife Lue Anderson?  A  No sir, never said anything about it.
Q  How did he happen to go with you that time?  A  I met him right here on the other side of the railroad track, and talked to him and told him where I was going to; he said he was going up there, too.
Q  Did he say anything about whether he intended to go back and live with her as husband and wife or not?  A  No sir, I never asked him about his affairs.
Q  Do you know anything about who the father of Lue Anderson's child, Pearl Anderson, is?  A  No sir.
Q  With whom does she live now?  A  George Hammer.
Q  Have they been married?  A  I don't know, I have heard they are.
Q  Do you know how long they have been living together?  A  No sir. They was living together when they move down there.
Q  That was two years ago this coming winter?  A  Yes, the second crop they have made on the place.
Q  Do you know whether this child Pearl Anderson was born after they moved down there or before?  A  I don't know where it was born; I think it was born before they moved down there. I know it is a pretty good sized chap.
Q  Do you know Charles Anderson's present postoffice address?  A  No sir.

(Witness dismissed).

KATIE MAXEY, being duly sworn testified as follows:

### EXAMINATION
BY THE COMMISSIONER:

Q  What is your postoffice address?  A  Farris.
Q  How old are you?  A  Twenty-five.
Q  Are you a citizen of either the Choctaw or Chickasaw Nation?  A  I am not.
Q  How long have you lived at Farris?  A  I got in Farris the 4th day of last April a year ago.
Q  The 4th day of April, 1905?  A  Yes sir.
Q  Where had you lived before that time?  A  I lived in Texas.
Q  Did you come from Texas to Farris?  A  Yes sir.
Q  Do you know Lue Anderson?  A  I do.
Q  Do you know her husband Charles Anderson?  A  Yes sir.

## Applications for Enrollment of Choctaw Newborn
## Act of 1905   Volume XVIII

Q Where did you know them? A I knew Charles Anderson and her when they lived at Quinton Spur near Tuskahoma on Kiamichi.
Q When was that? A Ten or twelve years ago.
Q Before Charles Anderson was sent to the penitentiary? A Yes sir.
Q How long was it before you moved to Farris a year ago, that you had seen Lue Anderson? A I saw Lue Anderson when she lived at Coalgate in 1904. I went up there to her house on a visit. It was in the first week of January, - to see her, - she lived at Coalgate.
Q First week in January, 1904, you visited Lue Anderson near Coalgate? A Yes sir.
Q What she living alone at that time? A Her and her children.
Q There was no mane living with her? A Charley Anderson, - I was there when Charley Anderson was there.
Q When did Charley Anderson come there? A I come there the day he come there.
Q Was he there when you arrived at her place? A Yes sir.
Q You found him there? A Yes sir.
Q What time did you say that was? A In 1904, it was in the first week of January, if I disremember the very date, - of February, I mean.
Q If was February, then instead of January? A Yes sir.
Q You are sure of that? A I am sure that is when I was there. That is what I said at first, but I got mixed up.
Q Charles Anderson was there? A Yes sir.
Q Do you know how long he had been there? A Come that day.
Q How do you know? A She said he did.
Q How long did you stay with Lue Anderson then? A Two weeks.
Q Then where did you go? A Back home to Texas and my father.
Q How long did Charles Anderson stay with Lue Anderson? A There when I left.
Q Did he remain there all the time? A No, not all the time, no sir.
Q How long would he be gone at a time? A He was there three times at the place while I was there. He staid[sic] a couple of nights while I was there.
Q Well, now did he stay a couple of nights all the time you were there, or a couple of nights each time? A He staid[sic] two nights the first time I was there, and then he would come in and out. I don't know where he went to when he would be gone.
Q Did he stay at Lue Anderson's house? A Yes sir.
Q Did she and he stay together in the same room at night? A I don't know, they was always settin' up and talking when me and the children went to bed.
Q Have you ever seen Charles Anderson since you left there? A No sir.
Q Do you know who he come there with that time? A This gentleman (W. M. Davis).
Q Was this gentleman (W. M. Davis) there when you got there? A Yes sir.
Q Do you know Charles Anderson and Lue Anderson lived together after that? A No sir, I do not.
Q Do you know where Charles Anderson is now? A No, I do not.
Q Did you ever hear Charles Anderson or Lue Anderson say anything about them going to live together as husband and wife? A No sir, I didn't; I think they was, but I don't know whether they did or not.
Q Do you know Lue Anderson's child, Pearl Anderson? A Yes sir.

# Applications for Enrollment of Choctaw Newborn
# Act of 1905   Volume XVIII

Q  Do you know when this child was born? A Born while she lived at Coalgate, Indian Territory I think; I wasn't there when she was born.
Q  With whom did Lue Anderson live during the time Charles Anderson was in the penitentiary and after his release from the penitentiary until you saw her at Coalgate that time? A Lue Anderson lived alone, her and her children while they lived in the neighborhood where I did; I don't know who she has lived with since then.
Q  Do you know whether she has ever lived with any body else since she and Charles separated the first time? A No sir.
Q  Did you ever hear she did? A No sir.
Q  With whom does she live now? A George Hammer.
Q  Are they married? A I suppose; I never seen them married but they claim they are married.
Q  Do you know how long George Hammer has been living with her? A No sir, they have been living together ever since I come to Farris, Indian Territory there where they lived. That is as far as I know, when I come there 4th of April.
Q  Do you know whether they lived together when Lue Anderson lived near Coalgate? A They wasn't when I was there.
Q  Do you know Hammer? A Yes sir.
Q  Where did you get acquainted with him? A I got acquainted with him on Kiamichi, near Tuskahoma.
Q  Did any one go with you up to Lue Anderson's this time when you went up there? A No sir.
Q  Was any one else there at the same time you were? A Mr. Davis here and Charley Anderson.
Q  You staid[sic] there about two weeks? A Yes sir.
Q  Then you went back to Texas? A Yes sir.
Q  You didn't see Lue Anderson any more until you moved up to Farris about a year ago? A No sir.
Q  You don't know anything about who is the father of her child Pearl Anderson? A No sir.
Q  Did you ever hear Lue Anderson and Charley Anderson has been divorced? A No sir.
Q  You don't know how long he staid[sic] with her up near Coalgate after you left there? A No sir, I do not.

(Witness dismissed).

---

I, S. T. Wright, stenographer to the Commissioner to the Five Civilized Tribes, on oath state that I recorded the testimony and proceedings had in the above entitled cause on September 7, 1906, and that the above and foregoing is a true and correct transcript of my stenographic notes thereof.

S.T. Wright

# Applications for Enrollment of Choctaw Newborn
## Act of 1905   Volume XVIII

Subscribed and sworn to before me this October 31, 1906.

Walter W. Chappell<br>NOTARY PUBLIC.

---

(COPY)

7-NB-1342

Atoka, Indian Territory, August 16, 1905.

Charles Anderson,
    Ti, Indian Territory.

Dear Sir:

    You are requested to advise this office at once if you and your former wife, Lou Anderson, have lived together as husband and wife since your first separation; if so, please give the date when you commenced to live together again, and the date you again separated, stating particularly whether you and she were living together during the winter and Spring of last year, 1904.

    Also please state if you are the father of her child, Pearl Anderson, born November 1, 1904.

    This matter is important and you are requested to give same immediate attention.

Respectfully,<br>Tams Bixby,<br>Commissioner.

---

*(The letter below typed as given.)*

Aug 18, 1905.

Department of the
    Interior Commissioner to
        the Five Civilized Sir

    Here is an answer I give I and my wife Lou Anderson Separated the Year of 1895, Jan. and I have never Seen her Senc, and when we Separated we had two child and here is the name Ever Anderson, Liley Anderson and Ever was Born in the year of 1893 Jan 22, and Liliy Anderson was Born in the Year of 1895 Nov 12, there two girls is only the two I claim By this woman Lou Anderson So this is all I will say for this time although if you want found anything I any thing more by me write again.

## Applications for Enrollment of Choctaw Newborn
## Act of 1905 Volume XVIII

Charles Anderson,
Tie[sic], I. T.

7-1901
7-NB-1342.

W. M. H.
W. H. A.

Atoka, Indian Territory, September 2, 1905.

Commissioner to the Five Civilized Tribes,
    Muskogee, Indian Territory.

Dear Sir:

    Referring to the enrollment of Pearl Anderson, Choctaw New Born Card No. 1342, Approved Roll No. 1184, father's name appearing as Charles Anderson, Choctaw by blood, Roll No. 5434, and the mother's name as Lue Anderson, Choctaw by Intermarriage, Roll No. 898, you are advised that on August 16, 1905, Lue Anderson appeared at this office for the purpose of selecting an allotment for Pearl Anderson above mentioned.

    This office was in possession of unofficial information to the effect that Charles Anderson and his wife, Lue Anderson, separated a number of years ago and had not lived together since. Therefore, it being thought questionable whether Charles Anderson was the father of the child, Pearl Anderson, we refused to permit Lue Anderson to make selection in allotment for said child pending investigation in the matter.

    This office accordingly on August 16, 1905, addressed a letter to Charles Anderson, at his postoffice, Ti, Indian Territory, relative to the matter, a copy of which letter is enclosed herewith, together with a letter received from Charles Anderson in reply thereto dated August 18, 1905, which is self explanatory.

    This matter is referred to the General Office for proper action, and pending further instructions no selection in allotment will be permitted by this office in behalf of said Pearl Anderson.

                                           Respectfully,
                                          (Signed) W. H. Angell
                                                    Chief Clerk.

EncL[sic]. CB 207

# Applications for Enrollment of Choctaw Newborn
## Act of 1905   Volume XVIII

7-NB-1342.

Muskogee, Indian Territory, September 8, 1905.

Chief Clerk,
    Choctaw-Chickasaw Allotment Division,
        General Office.

Dear Sir:

A question having arisen as to the right to enrollment as a citizen by blood of the Choctaw Nation of Pearl Anderson, whose name appears on Choctaw New Born Card No. 1342, approved roll No. 1184; you are directed to take no action relative to an allotment to said Pearl Anderson, pending an investigation.

Respectfully,

Acting Commissioner.

---

X-1184.

Muskogee, Indian Territory, September 9, 1905.

Chief Clerk,
    Choctaw Land Office,
        Atoka, Indian Territory.

Dear Sir:

Receipt is hereby acknowledged of your letter of the 2nd instant in which you state that Lue Anderson, Choctaw by intermarriage, Roll No. 898, appeared before you on August 16, 1905, and made application for selection of lands in allotment for her minor child, Pearl Anderson, Choctaw new born, Roll No. 1184; that said child is enrolled as a daughter of Charles Anderson, Choctaw by blood, Roll No. 5434. You further state that, at the time of the appearance of Lue Anderson for the purpose of making such selections, you were in possession of unofficial information to the affect that Charles Anderson and his wife, Lue Anderson, separated a number of years ago and had not lived together since; that it being questionable whether Charles Anderson was the father of the child, Pearl Anderson, you refused to permit Lue Anderson to make selection in allotment for said child pending an investigation; that on August 16, 1905, you addressed a letter to Charles Anderson at Ti, Indian Territory, relative to *(illegible...)*ter and inclose his reply in which he states that he *(illegible)* from his wife in January, 1895, and has not lived wit*(illegible...)* that time.

In reply, you are informed that your action in refusing to permit Lue Anderson to make selection of allotment for her infant child, Pearl Anderson, is confirmed, and that an

# Applications for Enrollment of Choctaw Newborn
# Act of 1905   Volume XVIII

investigation of the matter will be made and pending such investigation your office is directed to take no further action relative to an allotment to said Pearl Anderson.

Respectfully,

Acting Commissioner.

---

REFER IN REPLY TO THE FOLLOWING:

X-1184.

DEPARTMENT OF THE INTERIOR,
**COMMISSIONER TO THE FIVE CIVILIZED TRIBES.**

Muskogee, Indian Territory, September 9, 1905.

United States District Attorney,
Antlers, Indian Territory.

*5/6/06 Write Commissioner Bixby to know when affidavit made Etc.*

Dear Sir:

There is inclosed herewith the record in the matter of the enrollment, as a citizen by blood of the Choctaw Nation, of Pearl Anderson, whose enrollment as such was approved by the Secretary of the Interior August 2, 1905, her name appearing upon the final rolls of new born citizens of the Choctaw Nation as No. 1184.  Said record shows that on April 26, 1905, Lue Anderson, a citizen by intermarriage of the Choctaw Nation, Roll No. 898, appeared before a representative of the Commission to the Five Civilized Tribes at Antlers, Indian Territory, and made application for the enrollment of her infant child, Pearl Anderson, as a citizen by blood of the Choctaw Nation, under the Act of Congress approved March 3, 1905 (Public 212), at which time she made affidavit before Wirt Franklin, a Notary Public and an employee of the Commission to the Five Civilized Tribes, to the affect that she was thirty-four years of age and a citizen by blood of the Choctaw Nation intermarriage of the Choctaw Nation; the lawful wife of Charley Anderson, a citizen by blood of the Choctaw Nation; that a female child was born to her on the 1st day of November, 1904; that said child has been named Pearl Anderson, and was living March 4, 1905.

At the same time and date W. H. Hamlet made affidavit that he was a physician and attended Mrs. Lue Anderson, wife of Charley Anderson, on the 1st day of November, 1904; that a female child was born to her; that said child was living March 4, 1905, and is said to have been named Pearl Anderson.

It appears from the record that on August 16, 1905, Lue Anderson appeared before the Choctaw Land Office at Atoka, Indian Territory, and made application for the selection of land in allotment for her said child, Pearl Anderson; that at the time of her appearance the Chief Clerk of the Choctaw Land Office was in possession of information that raised a doubt as to whether the child, Pearl Anderson, was a decendant[sic] of a

## Applications for Enrollment of Choctaw Newborn
## Act of 1905   Volume XVIII

citizen by blood of the Choctaw Nation and refused to permit selection of allotment to be made for said child.

On August 16, 1905, the Chief Clerk of the Choctaw Land Office addressed a letter to Charles Anderson, the reputed father of said child, at his post office address at Ti, Indian Territory, in which he requested information as to whether he and his wife, Lue Anderson, had lived together since their separation. The reply of Charley Anderson, in which he states that he has not lived with his wife since January, 1895, is a part of the record inclosed herewith.

It is clear that an undoubted fraud is attempted and the papers in this case are respectfully submitted for such action as you deem proper.

It is believed that the last paragraph of Section 21 of the Act of Congress approved June 28, 1898 (30 Stats., L. 495), is applicable to this case.

Said paragraph is, as follows:

> "The members of said Commission shall, in performing all duties required of them by law, have authority to administer oaths, examine witnesses, and send for persons and papers; and any person who shall willfully and knowingly make any false affidavit or oath to any material fact or matter before any member of said Commission, or before any other officer authorized to administer oaths, to any affidavit or other paper to be filed or oath taken before said Commission, shall be deemed guilty of perjury, and on conviction thereof shall be punished[sic] as for such offense."

The original papers are sent you and you are requested to return them to this office as soon as they have answred[sic] your purpose.

Respectfully,
W$^m$. O. Beall
Acting Commissioner.

Registered.
VR. 9-4.

# Applications for Enrollment of Choctaw Newborn
# Act of 1905   Volume XVIII

Department of Justice.

OFFICE of UNITED SATES[sic] ATTORNEY
Central District of Indian Territory.

Antlers, Indian Territory, September 13, 1905.

Commission to the Five Civilized Tribes,
   Muskogee, Indian Territory.

Sirs:

     Yours of the 9th, instant, enclosing affidavit of Mrs. Lou[sic] Anderson and Dr. W. H. Hamlet in behalf of the formers child for an enrollment as an Indian by blood, submitted for my consideration, received, late this afternoon. Our grand Jury which convened here Monday closed its work and was dismissed before I had time to open my mail, and upon a careful examination of the affidavits I find that if it be true that Charles Anderson, although the lawful husband of Lou Anderson, had not seen his wife since 1895, it is not certain that the woman has committed perjury, since her affidavit on this line only state that she is the lawful wife of Charles Anderson; that she is 34 years of age; that Charles Anderson is a citizen by blood of the Choctaw Nation, and that said child has been named Pearl Anderson, and was living March 4, 1905. You will observe that she no where swears that Charles Anderson is the father of her child, and therefore in this affidavit she has not committed perjury. I cannot determine just now whether she and the Dr. have committed any other offence or not, but will examine carefully within a few days, as soon as our criminal trials here are over, and determine the matter, after which the papers will be returned to you as requested.

     Very respectfully,
     (Signed) J. H. Wilkins
     U. S. Attorney.

---

7-1901

Muskogee, Indian Territory, May 15, 1906.

T. B. Latham,
   United States Attorney,
     South McAlester, Indian Territory.

Dear Sir:

     Receipt is hereby acknowledged of your letter of May 7, 1906, inclosing papers in the matter of the application for the enrollment of Pearl Anderson as a new born citizen of the Choctaw Nation as you state you were informed by your predecessor the matter had been closed before you came into office.

# Applications for Enrollment of Choctaw Newborn
## Act of 1905   Volume XVIII

Respectfully,

Acting Commissioner.

---

7-NB-1342

Muskogee, Indian Territory, December 18, 1906.

Lue Anderson,
    Farris, Indian Territory.

Dear Madam:

You are hereby advised that you will be permitted to make selection of allotment for your child Pearl Anderson upon your personal appearance at the Land Office for the nation in which the land you desire to select for said child is located.

Respectfully,

Commissioner.

---

7-NB-1342

Muskogee, Indian Territory, December 18, 1906.

Chief Clerk,
    Choctaw Land Office,
        Atoka, Indian Territory.

Dear Sir:

September 9, 1905, your office was directed to withhold the issuance of citizenship certificate and the making of allotment to Pearl Anderson whose name appears at No. 1184 upon the approved roll of citizens by blood of the Choctaw Nation of the Choctaw Nation under the Act of March 3, 1905.

Additional testimony was taken in this case at the Choctaw Land Office September 7, 1906 and you are now directed to allow Lue Anderson, the mother of this child, to make application for an allotment for said child upon her personal appearance at your office.

Respectfully,

Commissioner.

## Applications for Enrollment of Choctaw Newborn
## Act of 1905   Volume XVIII

Choc. New Born 1343
    Dicy Guess
    (Born Nov. 26, 1904)

**BIRTH AFFIDAVIT.**

### DEPARTMENT OF THE INTERIOR.
### COMMISSION TO THE FIVE CIVILIZED TRIBES.

**IN RE APPLICATION FOR ENROLLMENT,** as a citizen of the Choctaw Nation, of Dicy Guess, born on the 26th day of November, 1904 *Choctaw*

Name of Father: Billy Guess    a citizen of the Freedman Nation.
Name of Mother: Sophia Guess    a citizen of the Choctaw Nation.

Postoffice    Hamden, Ind. Ter.

### AFFIDAVIT OF MOTHER.

UNITED STATES OF AMERICA, Indian Territory, } 
   Central     DISTRICT.

I, Sophia Guess, on oath state that I am about 23 years of age and a citizen by blood, of the Choctaw Nation; that I am the lawful wife of Billy Guess, who is a ~~citizen, by~~ Choctaw ~~of the~~ Freedman ~~Nation~~; that a female child was born to me on 26th day of November, 1904; that said child has been named Dicy Guess, and was living March 4, 1905.

                            her
                    Sophia x Guess
Witnesses To Mark:      mark
  { Vester W Rose
    W.P. Clark

Subscribed and sworn to before me this 27th day of April, 1905

                    Wirt Franklin
                        Notary Public.

# Applications for Enrollment of Choctaw Newborn
## Act of 1905   Volume XVIII

### AFFIDAVIT OF ATTENDING PHYSICIAN OR MID-WIFE.

UNITED STATES OF AMERICA, Indian Territory, }
   Central               DISTRICT.

      I,   Dicy Hunter  , a  mid-wife  , on oath state that I attended on Mrs.  Sophia Guess  , wife of  Billy Guess  on the 26th day of November, 1904; that there was born to her on said date a  female  child; that said child was living March 4, 1905, and is said to have been named  Dicy Guess

                                            her
                                  Dicy x Hunter
Witnesses To Mark:              mark
  { Vester W Rose
    W.P. Clark

      Subscribed and sworn to before me this  27th day of  April  , 1905

                                  Wirt Franklin
                                    Notary Public.

---

Choc. New Born 1344
      Vannie Elizabeth Fennel
      (Born Nov. 30[sic], 1904)

**BIRTH AFFIDAVIT.**
### DEPARTMENT OF THE INTERIOR.
### COMMISSION TO THE FIVE CIVILIZED TRIBES.

      IN RE APPLICATION FOR ENROLLMENT, as a citizen of the    Choctaw    Nation, of Vannie Elizabeth Fennel    , born on the  20th  day of  November  , 1904

Name of Father: Jack Fennel          a citizen of the  Choctaw    Nation.
Name of Mother: Louisa Fennel       a citizen of the  Choctaw    Nation.

                        Postoffice    Hugo Ind. Ter.

# Applications for Enrollment of Choctaw Newborn
## Act of 1905   Volume XVIII

### AFFIDAVIT OF MOTHER.

UNITED STATES OF AMERICA, Indian Territory,  
Central   DISTRICT.

I, Louisa Fennel, on oath state that I am 22 years of age and a citizen by blood, of the Choctaw Nation; that I am the lawful wife of Jack Fennel, who is a citizen, by Interm of the Choctaw Nation; that a female child was born to me on 20 day of November, 1904; that said child has been named Vannie Elizabeth Fennel, and was living March 4, 1905.

Louisa Fennel

Witnesses To Mark:

Subscribed and sworn to before me this 25th day of April, 1905

Arthur Adams  
Notary Public.

---

### AFFIDAVIT OF ATTENDING PHYSICIAN OR MID-WIFE.

UNITED STATES OF AMERICA, Indian Territory,  
Central   DISTRICT.

I, J.S. Miller, a physician, on oath state that I attended on Mrs. Louisa Fennel, wife of Jack Fennel on the 20th day of November, 1904; that there was born to her on said date a female child; that said child was living March 4, 1905, and is said to have been named Vannie Elizabeth Fennel

J.S. Miller M.D.

Witnesses To Mark:

Subscribed and sworn to before me this 25th day of April, 1905

Arthur Adams  
Notary Public.

## Applications for Enrollment of Choctaw Newborn
## Act of 1905   Volume XVIII

7-2901.

Muskogee, Indian Territory, May 3, 1905.

Arthur Adams,
    Hugo, Indian Territory.

Dear Sir:

    Receipt is hereby acknowledged of your letter of April 27, enclosing the affidavits of Louisia[sic] Fennel and J. S. Miller to the birth of Vannie Elizabeth Fennel, daughter of Jack and Louisa Fennel, November 20, 1904, and the same have been filed with our records as an application for the enrollment of said child.

                Respectfully,

                          Chairman.

---

<u>Choc. New Born 1345</u>
    Thomas Walter McMurtrey
    (Born July 17, 1903)

7-6341

**BIRTH AFFIDAVIT.**

**DEPARTMENT OF THE INTERIOR.**
**COMMISSION TO THE FIVE CIVILIZED TRIBES.**

    **IN RE APPLICATION FOR ENROLLMENT**, as a citizen of the    Choctaw    Nation, of Thomas Walter M$^c$Murtrey    , born on the  17  day of  July  , 1903

Name of Father: Joseph B. M$^c$Murtrey    a citizen of the  Choctaw  Nation.
Name of Mother: Minnie L. M$^c$Murtrey    a citizen of the  U.S.  Nation.

                Postoffice    Hartshorne, I.T.

# Applications for Enrollment of Choctaw Newborn
# Act of 1905  Volume XVIII

### AFFIDAVIT OF MOTHER.

UNITED STATES OF AMERICA, Indian Territory, }
Central    DISTRICT.

    I, Minnie L. M<sup>c</sup>Murtrey, on oath state that I am 18 years of age and a citizen by Marriage, of the Choctaw Nation; that I am the lawful wife of Joseph B. M<sup>c</sup>Murtrey, who is a citizen, by Blood of the Choctaw Nation; that a Male child was born to me on 17 day of July, 1903; that said child has been named Thomas Walter M<sup>c</sup>Murtrey, and was living March 4, 1905.

                                      Minnie L M<sup>c</sup>Murtrey

Witnesses To Mark:
{

    Subscribed and sworn to before me this 27 day of April, 1905

                                      David A. Bailey
                                      Notary Public.

---

### AFFIDAVIT OF ATTENDING PHYSICIAN OR MID-WIFE.

UNITED STATES OF AMERICA, Indian Territory, }
Central    DISTRICT.

    I, J. Bruton, a Mid Wife, on oath state that I attended on Mrs. Minnie L. M<sup>c</sup>Murtrey, wife of Joseph B. M<sup>c</sup>Murtrey on the 17 day of July, 1903; that there was born to her on said date a Male child; that said child was living March 4, 1905, and is said to have been named Thomas Walter M<sup>c</sup>Murtrey

                                      J. Bruton

Witnesses To Mark:
{

    Subscribed and sworn to before me this 27 day of April, 1905

                                      David A. Bailey
                                      Notary Public.

My Commission Expires
Jan 11-1909.

## Applications for Enrollment of Choctaw Newborn
## Act of 1905   Volume XVIII

*(The marriage certificate below typed as given.)*

Certificate of Marriage.

This is to Certify that

J.B. McMurtry and Miss.M.L.Barnes

of Hartshorne,IT.                of Hartshorne,I.T.

have been by me joined together in the

Holy Bonds of Matrimony.

this 14th day of September,1902.

(Signed)  Frank Battles.

Witness John Barnes.              County Judge Gains

County, C.N.

Filed in the Clerk's

Office

Dec.20, 1902.

Page 66

Eastmon Nelson.

Clerk of Gaines County,C.N.


AFFIDAVIT.

I, J. B. McMurtry do solemnly swear that the above Certificate of Marriage is a true copy of the one which I hold and is signed by Frank Battles, County Judge of Gaines County,C.M., and filed in the Clerk's Office by Eastmon Nelson.

J B McMurtrey

Sworn and subscribed to before me this the 29th day of April, 1905.

Samuel A Maysey   Notary Public.

My C0mmission Expires
MAY 20 1908

# Applications for Enrollment of Choctaw Newborn
## Act of 1905   Volume XVIII

7 N.B. 1345.

Muskogee, Indian Territory, May 9, 1906.

Joseph B. McMurtry,
    Hartshorne, Indian Territory.

Dear Sir:

    Receipt is hereby acknowledged of certified copy of marriage certificate between J. D. McMurtry and Miss M. L. Barnes, which is offered in support of the application for the enrollment of your child, Thomas Walter McMurtry, and the same has been filed with the records in this case.

                  Respectfully,

                  Commissioner in Charge.

---

Choc. New Born 1346
    Vester M. Dana
    (Born Sep. 12, 1904)

**BIRTH AFFIDAVIT.**

### DEPARTMENT OF THE INTERIOR.
### COMMISSION TO THE FIVE CIVILIZED TRIBES.

**IN RE APPLICATION FOR ENROLLMENT,** as a citizen of the   Choctaw   Nation, of  Vester M Dana   , born on the  12  day of  September  , 1904

Name of Father: Charles A Dana        a citizen of the   Choctaw   Nation.
Name of Mother: Eliza Dana        a citizen of the   Choctaw   Nation.

              Postoffice     Boggy Depot I T

### AFFIDAVIT OF MOTHER.

UNITED STATES OF AMERICA, Indian Territory, }
    Central             DISTRICT.

    I,   Eliza Dana   , on oath state that I am  27  years of age and a citizen by blood , of the   Choctaw   Nation; that I am the lawful wife of  Charles A Dana  , who is a citizen, by Blood   of the   Choctaw   Nation; that a   male   child

## Applications for Enrollment of Choctaw Newborn
## Act of 1905  Volume XVIII

was born to me on the 12th day of September , 1904; that said child has been named Vester M Dana , and was living March 4, 1905.

             her
            Eliza x Dana
Witnesses To Mark:        mark
 { C. S. Cotton
  J. A. Lewis

  Subscribed and sworn to before me this 27 day of April , 1905

          SC Hieronymus
           Notary Public.

---

**AFFIDAVIT OF ATTENDING PHYSICIAN OR MID-WIFE.**

UNITED STATES OF AMERICA, Indian Territory, }
  Central    DISTRICT.

  I, Sallie Louis , a Mid Wife , on oath state that I attended on Mrs. Eliza Dana , wife of Charles Dana on the 12 day of September , 1904; that there was born to her on said date a male child; that said child was living March 4, 1905, and is said to have been named Vester M Dana

          Sallie Louis

Witnesses To Mark:
 {

  Subscribed and sworn to before me this 27 day of April , 1905

          SC Hieronymus
           Notary Public.

---

7-NB-1346

       Muskogee, Indian Territory, August 7, 1905.

Charles A. Dana,
  Caney, Indian Territory.

Dear Sir:

  Receipt is hereby acknowledged of your letter of July 31, 1905, asking if your child Vester M. Dana has been enrolled.

## Applications for Enrollment of Choctaw Newborn
## Act of 1905 Volume XVIII

In reply to your letter you are advised that the name of your son Vester M. Dana has been placed upon a schedule of citizens by blood of the Choctaw Nation which has been forwarded the Secretary of the Interior and you will be advised when his enrollment is approved by the Department.

Respectfully,

Commissioner.

---

Choc. New Born 1347
    Emma Moore
    (Born Dec. 3, 1904)

# NEW BORN AFFIDAVIT

No ............

### CHOCTAW ENROLLING COMMISSION

IN THE MATTER OF THE APPLICATION FOR ENROLLMENT as a citizen of the Choctaw Nation, of Emma Moore born on the 3$^{rd}$ day of December 1904

Name of father Willie Moore    a citizen of Choctaw Nation, final enrollment No. 10562

Name of mother Fannie Moore    a citizen of Choctaw Nation, final enrollment No. 11794

Calloway I. T.    Postoffice.

**AFFIDAVIT OF MOTHER**

UNITED STATES OF AMERICA
    INDIAN TERRITORY
DISTRICT    Central

I Fannie Moore , on oath state that I am 22 years of age and a citizen by blood of the Choctaw Nation, and as such have been placed upon the final roll of the Choctaw Nation, by the Honorable Secretary of the Interior my final enrollment number being 11794 ; that I am the lawful wife of Willie

## Applications for Enrollment of Choctaw Newborn
## Act of 1905  Volume XVIII

Moore         , who is a citizen of the    Choctaw           Nation, and as such has been placed upon the final roll of said Nation by the Honorable Secretary of the Interior, his final enrollment number being   10562     and that a   female   child was born to me on the   3<sup>rd</sup> day of    December  190 4; that said child has been named   Emma    , and is now living.

                                              her
                                    Fannie  x  Moore

WITNESSETH:                      mark
  Must be two witnesses { Austin Jacob
  who are citizens         (Name Illegible)

Subscribed and sworn to before me this,  22<sup>=</sup>   day of   February   , 190 5

                                      A.E. Folsom
                                              Notary Public.

My Commission Expires:
Jan 9 - 1909

---

### *Affidavit of Attending Physician or Midwife*

UNITED STATES OF AMERICA,
   INDIAN TERRITORY,
Central           DISTRICT

   I,   Sylphie Homer       a       Midwife      on oath state that I attended on Mrs. Fannie Moore        wife of  Willie Moore  on the   3<sup>rd</sup>   day of  December   , 190 4, that there was born to her on said date a    female child, that said child is now living, and is said to have been named   Emma Moore

                                       her                  *mid wife*
                                Sylphie x Homer         ~~M. D.~~
                                       mark
Subscribed and sworn to before me this the   22<sup>d</sup>   day of   February     1905

                                     A.E. Folsom
                                            Notary Public.

WITNESSETH:
  Must be two witnesses { Austin Jacob
  who are citizens and
  know the child.         (Name Illegible)

   We hereby certify that we are well acquainted with       Sylphie Homer         a   Midwife          and know   her         to be reputable and of good standing in the community.

                              Must be two citizen { Austin Jacob
                              witnesses.             (Name Illegible)

## Applications for Enrollment of Choctaw Newborn
## Act of 1905  Volume XVIII

BIRTH AFFIDAVIT.

### DEPARTMENT OF THE INTERIOR.
### COMMISSION TO THE FIVE CIVILIZED TRIBES.

IN RE APPLICATION FOR ENROLLMENT, as a citizen of the Choctaw Nation, of Emma Moore, born on the 3$^{rd}$ day of December, 1904

Name of Father: Willis[sic] Moore     a citizen of the Choctaw Nation.
Name of Mother: Fannie Moore     a citizen of the Choctaw Nation.

Postoffice    Calloway, I.T.

### AFFIDAVIT OF MOTHER.

UNITED STATES OF AMERICA, Indian Territory, }
     Central            DISTRICT.

I, Fannie Moore, on oath state that I am 22 years of age and a citizen by blood, of the Choctaw Nation; that I am the lawful wife of Willis Moore, who is a citizen, by blood of the Choctaw Nation; that a female child was born to me on 3$^{rd}$ day of December, 1904; that said child has been named Emma Moore, and was living March 4, 1905.

                                   her
                          Fannie x Moore
Witnesses To Mark:          mark
   { James Culberson
   { *(Name Illegible)*

Subscribed and sworn to before me this 28$^{th}$ day of April, 1905

                         W.H. Angell
                              Notary Public.

### AFFIDAVIT OF ATTENDING PHYSICIAN OR MID-WIFE.

UNITED STATES OF AMERICA, Indian Territory, }
     Central            DISTRICT.

I, Adeline Homer, a midwife, on oath state that I attended on Mrs. Fannie Moore, wife of Willis Moore on the 3$^{rd}$ day of December, 1904; that there was born to her on said date a female child; that said child was living March 4, 1905, and is said to have been named Emma Moore

                                   her
                          Adeline x Homer
                               mark

## Applications for Enrollment of Choctaw Newborn
## Act of 1905   Volume XVIII

Witnesses To Mark:
{ James Culberson
{ *(Name Illegible)*

Subscribed and sworn to before me this  28$^{th}$  day of   April   , 1905

W.H. Angell
Notary Public.

---

7-NB-1347.

Muskogee, Indian Territory, June 1, 1905.

Commissioner in Charge,
    Choctaw Land Office,
        Atoka, Indian Territory.

Dear Sir:

    There is enclosed herewith application for the enrollment of Emma Moore, born December 3, 1904, which appears to have been executed in your office, in which the Notary Public failed to attach his signature to the affidavits, and the signature by mark must be attested by two witnesses. were attested by only one witness.

    You will please have the Notary, before whom the affidavits were executed, to attach his signature and also to secure an additional witness to the signatures of Fannie Moore and Adeline Homer.

Respectfully,

Chairman.

VR 1-6.

---

Choc. New Born 1348
    Sampson Bond
    (Born Feb. 24, 1904)

Applications for Enrollment of Choctaw Newborn
Act of 1905 Volume XVIII

**NEW-BORN AFFIDAVIT.**

Number............

...Choctaw Enrolling Commission...

---

IN THE MATTER OF THE APPLICATION FOR ENROLLMENT, as a citizen of the Choctaw Nation, of Sampson Bond

born on the 24$^{th}$ day of Feby 190 4

Name of father  Simeon Bond                a citizen of  Choctaw
Nation final enrollment No.  11814
Name of mother  Silway Bond                a citizen of  Choctaw Nation
Nation final enrollment No.  11815

Postoffice  Stringtown, I.T.

**AFFIDAVIT OF MOTHER.**

UNITED STATES OF AMERICA
INDIAN TERRITORY
Central     DISTRICT

I  Silway Bond                      , on oath state that I am 33 years of age and a citizen by  blood  of the  Choctaw  Nation, and as such have been placed upon the final roll of the  Choctaw  Nation, by the Honorable Secretary of the Interior my final enrollment number being  11815 ; that I am the lawful wife of  Simeon Bond  , who is a citizen of the  Choctaw  Nation, and as such has been placed upon the final roll of said Nation by the Honorable Secretary of the Interior, his final enrollment number being  11814  and that a  Male  child was born to me on the  24  day of  February  190 4; that said child has been named  Sampson Bond  , and is now living.

                                                         her
                                              Silway x Bond
Witnesseth.                                       mark

Must be two ⎫ J B Spring
Witnesses who ⎬
are Citizens. ⎭ Henry J Bond

Subscribed and sworn to before me this  10$^{th}$  day of  Feby  190 5

D S Kennedy
Notary Public.

My commission expires:  Nov 1$^{st}$ 1905

# Applications for Enrollment of Choctaw Newborn
## Act of 1905 Volume XVIII

## AFFIDAVIT OF ATTENDING PHYSICIAN OR MIDWIFE

UNITED STATES OF AMERICA
INDIAN TERRITORY
Central Judicial DISTRICT

I, Simeon Bond _____
on oath state that I attended on Mrs. Silway Bond wife of Simeon Bond on the 24th day of Feby, 1904, that there was born to her on said date a Male child, that said child is now living, and is said to have been named Sampson Bond

Witness
Thos M Bell
M Reid

WITNESSETH:
Must be two witnesses who are citizens and know the child.
{ Henry J Bond
  Justin McIntosh

his
Simeon x Bond      M.D.
mark

Subscribed and sworn to before me this, the 10th day of Feby 1905

D S Kennedy    Notary Public.

We hereby certify that we are well acquainted with Simeon Bond a attendant and know him to be reputable and of good standing in the community.

{ Henry J Bond
  Silas Byington

BIRTH AFFIDAVIT.

## DEPARTMENT OF THE INTERIOR.
### COMMISSION TO THE FIVE CIVILIZED TRIBES.

IN RE APPLICATION FOR ENROLLMENT, as a citizen of the Choctaw Nation, of Sampson Bond, born on the 24th day of February, 1904

Name of Father: Simeon Bond      a citizen of the Choctaw Nation.
Name of Mother: Silway Bond      a citizen of the Choctaw Nation.

Postoffice    Stringtown, I.T.

# Applications for Enrollment of Choctaw Newborn
# Act of 1905 Volume XVIII

### AFFIDAVIT OF MOTHER.

UNITED STATES OF AMERICA, Indian Territory,
Central DISTRICT.

I, Christopher D. Moore, on oath state that I am 38 years of age and a citizen by blood, of the Choctaw Nation; that I am ~~the lawful wife of~~ *am personally acquainted with Silway Bond, wife of Simeon Bond*, who is a citizen, by blood of the Choctaw Nation; that a male child was born to ~~me~~ *her* on 24th day of February, 1904; that said child has been named Sampson Bond, and was living March 4, 1905.

Christopher D. Moore

Witnesses To Mark:

Subscribed and sworn to before me this 28th day of April, 1905.

W.H. Angell
Notary Public.

---

### AFFIDAVIT OF ATTENDING PHYSICIAN OR MID-WIFE.

UNITED STATES OF AMERICA, Indian Territory,
Central DISTRICT.

I, Anna Noah, ~~a~~, *am personally acquainted with* on oath state that I ~~attended on~~ Mrs. Silway Bond, wife of Simeon Bond *that* on the 24th day of February, 1904; that there was born to her on said date a male child; that said child was living March 4, 1905, and is said to have been named Sampson Bond

her
Anna x Noah
mark

Witnesses To Mark:
William H Cunningham
Arthur O. Archer

Subscribed and sworn to before me this 28th day of April, 1905.

W.H. Angell
Notary Public.

## Applications for Enrollment of Choctaw Newborn
## Act of 1905 Volume XVIII

**BIRTH AFFIDAVIT.**

### DEPARTMENT OF THE INTERIOR.
### COMMISSION TO THE FIVE CIVILIZED TRIBES.

IN RE APPLICATION FOR ENROLLMENT, as a citizen of the Choctaw Nation, of Sampson Bond, born on the 24th day of February, 1904

Name of Father: Simeon Bond     a citizen of the Choctaw Nation.
Name of Mother: Silway Bond     a citizen of the Choctaw Nation.

Postoffice    Stringtown, I.T.

**AFFIDAVIT OF MOTHER.**

UNITED STATES OF AMERICA, Indian Territory, } 
Central     DISTRICT.

I, Silway Bond, on oath state that I am 34 years of age and a citizen by blood, of the Choctaw Nation; that I am the lawful wife of Simeon Bond, who is a citizen, by blood of the Choctaw Nation; that a male child was born to me on 24th day of February, 1904; that said child has been named Sampson Bond, and was living March 4, 1905.

                 her
          Silway x Bond
Witnesses To Mark:       mark
   { William H Cunningham
     Arthur O. Archer

Subscribed and sworn to before me this 28th day of April, 1905

          W.H. Angell
            Notary Public.

**AFFIDAVIT OF ATTENDING PHYSICIAN OR MID-WIFE.**

UNITED STATES OF AMERICA, Indian Territory, }
Central     DISTRICT.

I, Simeon Bond, a citizen by blood of the Choctaw Nation, on oath state that I attended on Mrs. Silway Bond, my, wife of ———— on the 24th day of February, 1905[sic]; that there was born to her on said date a male child; that said child was living March 4, 1905, and is said to have been named Sampson Bond; and that no one was present on the date of the birth of said Sampson Bond except myself and said wife.

# Applications for Enrollment of Choctaw Newborn
## Act of 1905   Volume XVIII

            his
          Sampson x Bond
Witnesses To Mark:      mark
 { William H Cunningham
  Arthur O. Archer

Subscribed and sworn to before me this 28th day of April, 1905

          W.H. Angell
            Notary Public.

---

BIRTH AFFIDAVIT.

DEPARTMENT OF THE INTERIOR.
## COMMISSION TO THE FIVE CIVILIZED TRIBES.

IN RE APPLICATION FOR ENROLLMENT, as a citizen of the Choctaw Nation, of Sampson Bond, born on the 24 day of Feb, 1904

Name of Father: Simeon Bond  a citizen of the Choctaw Nation.
Name of Mother: Silway Bond  a citizen of the Choctaw Nation.

       Postoffice  Stringtown

---

### AFFIDAVIT OF MOTHER.

UNITED STATES OF AMERICA, Indian Territory, }
 Central Judicial  DISTRICT.

  I, Silway Bond, on oath state that I am 33 years of age and a citizen by blood, of the Choctaw Nation; that I am the lawful wife of Simeon Bond, who is a citizen, by blood of the Choctaw Nation; that a male child was born to me on 24 day of February, 1904; that said child has been named Sampson Bond, and was living March 4, 1905.

          her
         Silway x Bond
Witnesses To Mark:    mark
 { CD Moore
  Thos M Bell

Subscribed and sworn to before me this 4th day of July, 1905

         D S Kennedy
          Notary Public.

# Applications for Enrollment of Choctaw Newborn
## Act of 1905  Volume XVIII

#### AFFIDAVIT OF ATTENDING PHYSICIAN OR MID-WIFE.

UNITED STATES OF AMERICA, Indian Territory,  
Central Judicial  DISTRICT.

I, *Simeon Bond, a citizen by blood of the Choctaw Nation*, on oath state that I attended on Mrs. Silway Bond, *my*, wife of ———— on the 24 day of February, 1904; that there was born to her on said date a Male child; that said child was living March 4, 1905, and is said to have been named Sampson Bond; *and that no one was present on the date of the birth of said Sampson Bond except myself and said wife.*

                                        his  
   Witnesses To Mark:         Sampson x Bond  
    { CD Moore                  mark  
     Thos M Bell

Subscribed and sworn to before me this 4$^{th}$ day of July, 1905.

                                      D S Kennedy  
                                      Notary Public.

---

                                                              7-NB-1348.

                           Muskogee, Indian Territory, June 21, 1905.

Simeon Bond,  
      Stringtown, Indian Territory.

Dear Sir:

    Referring to the application for the enrollment of your infant child, Sampson Bond, the affidavits of Silway Bond, Christopher D. Moore and Anna Noah give the date of the applicant's birth as February 24, 1904, while your affidavit gives it as February 24, 1905.

    You are requested to insert the correct date in the enclosed affidavit and when it is properly executed return it to this office.

                                Respectfully,

                                                         Chairman.

DeB--5/21

## Applications for Enrollment of Choctaw Newborn
## Act of 1905   Volume XVIII

7-NB-1348

Muskogee, Indian Territory, July 10, 1905.

Simeon Bond,
    Stringtown, Indian Territory.

Dear Sir:

    Receipt is hereby acknowledged of the affidavits of Silway Bond and Simeon Bond, to the birth of Sampson Bond February 24, 1904, and the same have been filed with the records of this office in the matter of the enrollment of said child.

        Respectfully,

        Commissioner.

---

Choc. New Born 1349
    Joseph David Roff
    (Born Sep. 22, 1903)

# NEW BORN AFFIDAVIT

No ............

## CHOCTAW ENROLLING COMMISSION

IN THE MATTER OF THE APPLICATION FOR ENROLLMENT as a citizen of the Choctaw Nation, of Joseph David Roff born on the $22^{nd}$ day of Sept 190 3

Name of father Andrew V. Roff    a citizen of Choctaw Nation, final enrollment No. 70

Name of mother Pearl Roff    a citizen of Choctaw Nation, final enrollment No. ———

Lula Ind. Ter.      Postoffice.

## Applications for Enrollment of Choctaw Newborn
## Act of 1905   Volume XVIII

**AFFIDAVIT OF MOTHER**

UNITED STATES OF AMERICA  
   INDIAN TERRITORY  
DISTRICT     Central

I     Pearl Roff                , on oath state that I am   23   years of age and a citizen by  ———  of the  ———  Nation, and as such have been placed upon the final roll of the  ———  Nation, by the Honorable Secretary of the Interior my final enrollment number being .................. that I am the lawful wife of   Andrew V Roff   , who is a citizen of the   Choctaw   Nation, and as such has been placed upon the final roll of said Nation by the Honorable Secretary of the Interior, his final enrollment number being   70   and that a   Male   child was born to me on the   22$^{nd}$   day of   Sept   190 3; that said child has been named   Joseph David Roff   , and is now living.

WITNESSETH:                              Pearl Roff

  Must be two witnesses { John Wallace  
  who are citizens              WE Jones

Subscribed and sworn to before me this, the   4   day of   march   , 190 5

                       John H Cross  
                             Notary Public.

My Commission Expires:   Sept 24-1908

---

### *Affidavit of Attending Physician or Midwife*

UNITED STATES OF AMERICA,  
   INDIAN TERRITORY,  
  Central       DISTRICT

I,   Pennie Moore   a   Midwife   on oath state that I attended on Mrs.   Pearl Roff   wife of   Andrew V Roff   on the   22$^{nd}$   day of   Sept   , 190 3, that there was born to her on said date a   Male   child, that said child is now living, and is said to have been named   Joseph David Roff

                        her                *midwife*  
                  Pennie x Moore       ~~M.D~~.  
                      mark

Subscribed and sworn to before me this the   4   day of   March   1905

                       John H Cross  
                            Notary Public.

WITNESSETH:  
  Must be two witnesses { John Wallace  
  who are citizens and  
  know the child.              WE Jones

# Applications for Enrollment of Choctaw Newborn
## Act of 1905   Volume XVIII

We hereby certify that we are well acquainted with     Pennie Moore     a     Midwife     and know     her     to be reputable and of good standing in the community.

Must be two citizen witnesses. { MG Mullens
John Wallace

**BIRTH AFFIDAVIT.**

## DEPARTMENT OF THE INTERIOR.
## COMMISSION TO THE FIVE CIVILIZED TRIBES.

IN RE APPLICATION FOR ENROLLMENT, as a citizen of the     Choctaw     Nation, of     Joseph David Roff     , born on the   22   day of   September   , 1905[sic]

Name of Father: Andrew V. Roff         a citizen of the   Choctaw   Nation.
Name of Mother: Pearl Roff              a citizen of the   Choctaw   Nation.

Postoffice     Lula, Choc. Nat. Ind. Ter.

### AFFIDAVIT OF MOTHER.

UNITED STATES OF AMERICA, Indian Territory, }
Central                       DISTRICT.

I,   Pearl Roff   , on oath state that I am   23   years of age and a citizen by marriage   , of the   Choctaw   Nation; that I am the lawful wife of   Andrew V Roff   , who is a citizen, by   blood   of the   Choctaw   Nation; that a   male   child was born to me on   22   day of   September   , 1903; that said child has been named   Joseph David Roff   , and was living March 4, 1905.

Pearl Roff

Witnesses To Mark:
{

Subscribed and sworn to before me this   22   day of   April   , 1905

(Seal)                                        D. Allen
                                    Notary Public. *for*
                                    *Central District*

108

## Applications for Enrollment of Choctaw Newborn
## Act of 1905   Volume XVIII

### AFFIDAVIT OF ATTENDING PHYSICIAN OR MID-WIFE.

UNITED STATES OF AMERICA, Indian Territory,
Central   DISTRICT.

I, Pennie Moore, a midwife, on oath state that I attended on Mrs. Pearl Roff, wife of Andrew V Roff on the 22 day of Sept, 1903; that there was born to her on said date a male child; that said child was living March 4, 1905, and is said to have been named Joseph David Roff

                          her
                    Pennie x Moore

Witnesses To Mark:           mark
   M L Allen
   Jessie Allen

Subscribed and sworn to before me this 22 day of April, 1905

                  D. Allen
(Seal)                      Notary Public.
                      for Central District

---

BIRTH AFFIDAVIT.

### DEPARTMENT OF THE INTERIOR.
### COMMISSION TO THE FIVE CIVILIZED TRIBES.

IN RE APPLICATION FOR ENROLLMENT, as a citizen of the Chocktaw[sic] Nation, of Joseph David Roff, born on the 22 day of September, 1903

Name of Father: Andrew V. Roff     a citizen of the Chocktaw Nation.
Name of Mother: Pearl Roff        a citizen of the   "   Nation.

               Postoffice    Lula I.T.

---

### AFFIDAVIT OF MOTHER.

UNITED STATES OF AMERICA, Indian Territory,
Southern   DISTRICT.

I, Pearl Roff, on oath state that I am 23 years of age and a citizen by intermarriage, of the Chocktaw Nation; that I am the lawful wife of Andrew V Roff, who is a citizen, by blood of the Chocktaw Nation; that a male child was born to me on 22 day of September, 1903; that said child has been named Joseph David Roff, and was living March 4, 1905.

                    Pearl Roff

# Applications for Enrollment of Choctaw Newborn
## Act of 1905   Volume XVIII

Witnesses To Mark:
{

    Subscribed and sworn to before me this   1   day of    May    , 1905

                             J.E. Williams
                                  Notary Public.

**AFFIDAVIT OF ATTENDING PHYSICIAN OR MID-WIFE.**

UNITED STATES OF AMERICA, Indian Territory, }
   Southern                DISTRICT.

    I, Mrs. Pennie Moore    , a   midwife   , on oath state that I attended on Mrs.   Pearl Roff   , wife of   Andrew V Roff    on the  22 day of  September  , 1903; that there was born to her on said date a    male    child; that said child was living March 4, 1905, and is said to have been named Joseph David Roff

                            Pennie Moore

Witnesses To Mark:
{

    Subscribed and sworn to before me this   1   day of    May    , 1905

                             J.E. Williams
                                  Notary Public.

---

Choc. New Born 1350
      Ollie May Coplen
      (Born Sep. 24, 1904)

BIRTH AFFIDAVIT.
                         DEPARTMENT OF THE INTERIOR.
                  **COMMISSION TO THE FIVE CIVILIZED TRIBES.**

    IN RE APPLICATION FOR ENROLLMENT, as a citizen of the    Choctaw    Nation, of   Ollie May Coplen      , born on the  24$^{th}$    day of  September  , 1904
                                    *white*
Name of Father: Lemm Joseph Coplen     a ^citizen of the United States Nation.
Name of Mother: Myrtle Palmer-Coplen    a citizen of the   Choctaw    Nation.
*Roll No 13813-Choctaw by blood*
                          Postoffice    Kinta, formerly Stigler, I.T.

# Applications for Enrollment of Choctaw Newborn
## Act of 1905   Volume XVIII

### AFFIDAVIT OF MOTHER.

UNITED STATES OF AMERICA, Indian Territory,  
Central         DISTRICT.

I, Myrtle Palmer-Coplen, on oath state that I am nineteen years of age and a citizen by blood, of the Choctaw Nation; *enrolled as No. 13813 under the name of Myrtle Palmer* that I am the lawful wife of Lemm Joseph Coplen, who is a *white* citizen, by .................. of the United States Nation; that a female child was born to me on 24$^{th}$ day of September, 1904; that said child has been named Ollie May Coplen, and was living March 4, 1905.

*My father's name was Frank Palmer*
*My mother's name was Adeline Palmer*                    Myrtle Palmer Coplen

Witnesses To Mark:

{

Subscribed and sworn to before me this 28$^{th}$ day of April, 1905

W$^m$ O. Carr
Notary Public.

### AFFIDAVIT OF ATTENDING PHYSICIAN OR MID-WIFE.

UNITED STATES OF AMERICA, Indian Territory,  
Central         DISTRICT.

I, L.K. Stephens, a Physician, on oath state that I attended on Mrs. Myrtle Palmer-Coplen, wife of Lem Joseph Coplen on the 24$^{th}$ day of September, 1904; that there was born to her on said date a female child; that said child was living March 4, 1905, and is said to have been named Ollie May Coplen

L. K. Stephens MD

Witnesses To Mark:

{

Subscribed and sworn to before me this 28$^{th}$ day of April, 1905

W$^m$ O. Carr
Notary Public.

## Applications for Enrollment of Choctaw Newborn
## Act of 1905   Volume XVIII

7-5442.

Muskogee, Indian Territory, May 3, 1905.

Lemm Joseph Coplen,
    Kinta, Indian Territory.

Dear Sir:

    Receipt is hereby acknowledged of the affidavits of Myrtle Palmer Coplen and L. K. Stephens to the birth of Ollie May Coplen, daughter of Lemm Joseph and Myrtle Palmer Coplen, September 24, 1904, and the same have been filed with our records as an application for the enrollment of said child.

Respectfully,

Chairman.

---

Choc. New Born 1351
    Catherine Reed
    (Born June 4, 1903)

**NEW-BORN AFFIDAVIT.**

Number..................

## Choctaw Enrolling Commission.

IN THE MATTER OF THE APPLICATION FOR ENROLLMENT, as a citizen of the Choctaw    Nation, of    Catherine Reed

born on the   4   day of   June        190 3

Name of father    M. F. Reed                a citizen of    ———
Nation final enrollment No   ——
Name of mother    Arlee Reed              a citizen of     Choctaw
Nation final enrollment No    9815

Postoffice    Durant I.T.

## Applications for Enrollment of Choctaw Newborn
## Act of 1905   Volume XVIII

### AFFIDAVIT OF MOTHER.

UNITED STATES OF AMERICA,
INDIAN TERRITORY,
Central   DISTRICT

I   Arlee Reed   on oath state that I am 22 years of age and a citizen by blood of the Choctaw Nation, and as such have been placed upon the final roll of the Choctaw Nation, by the Honorable Secretary of the Interior my final enrollment number being 9815 ; that I am the lawful wife of M.F. Reed, who is a citizen of the ——— Nation, and as such has been placed upon the final roll of said Nation by the Honorable Secretary of the Interior, his final enrollment number being ——— and that a female child was born to me on the 4 day of June 190 3 ; that said child has been named Catherine, and is now living.

Arlee Reed

WITNESSETH:
Must be two Witnesses who are Citizens.
C.D. Robinson
William M. Harkins

Subscribed and sworn to before me this 16 day of January 190 5

James Bower
Notary Public.

My commission expires Sept 23-1907

### AFFIDAVIT OF ATTENDING PHYSICIAN OR MIDWIFE

UNITED STATES OF AMERICA
INDIAN TERRITORY
Central   DISTRICT

I, M. A. Damron a midwife on oath state that I attended on Mrs. Arlee Reed wife of M. F. Reed on the 4 day of June , 190 3 , that there was born to her on said date a Female child, that said child is now living, and is said to have been named Catherine Reed

M.A. Damron   M.D.

Subscribed and sworn to before me this, the 13 day of Feb 190 5

T.C. Keller
Notary Public.

WITNESSETH:
Must be two witnesses who are citizens and know the child.
C.D. Robinson
William M Harkins

## Applications for Enrollment of Choctaw Newborn
## Act of 1905   Volume XVIII

We hereby certify that we are well acquainted with   M.A. Damron a Midwife   and know   her   to be reputable and of good standing in the community.

   C.D. Robinson

   William M Harkins

BIRTH AFFIDAVIT.

### DEPARTMENT OF THE INTERIOR.
### COMMISSION TO THE FIVE CIVILIZED TRIBES.

IN RE APPLICATION FOR ENROLLMENT, as a citizen of the   Choctaw   Nation, of Catherine Reed   , born on the   4th   day of   June   , 1903

Name of Father: M.F. Reed   *a noncitizen*   ~~a citizen of the~~   ~~Nation~~.
Name of Mother: Arlee Reed   a citizen of the   Choctaw   Nation.

Postoffice   Durant, Ind. Ter.

### AFFIDAVIT OF MOTHER.

UNITED STATES OF AMERICA, Indian Territory,
   Central   DISTRICT.

I,   Arlee Reed   , on oath state that I am   22   years of age and a citizen by blood   , of the   Choctaw   Nation; that I am the lawful wife of   M. F. Reed, *who is a noncitizen*   , ~~who is a citizen, by~~   of the   Choctaw   Nation; that a female   child was born to me on   the 4th   day of   June   , 1903; that said child has been named   Catherine   , and was living March 4, 1905.

   Arlee Reed

Witnesses To Mark:
   Green Thompson

Subscribed and sworn to before me this  26th   day of   April   , 1905

   J. V. Connell
   Notary Public.

My term of office expires *Nov* the *13-* 190*7*

## Applications for Enrollment of Choctaw Newborn
## Act of 1905 Volume XVIII

### AFFIDAVIT OF ATTENDING PHYSICIAN OR MID-WIFE.

UNITED STATES OF AMERICA, Indian Territory,　}
　Central　　　　　　　　DISTRICT.

I, Catherine[sic] O'Riley[sic] , a Mid-wife , on oath state that I attended on Mrs. Arlee Reed , wife of M. F. Reed on the 4th day of June , 1903; that there was born to her on said date a female child; that said child was living March 4, 1905, and is said to have been named Catherine

　　　　　　　　　　　　　　　Catharine O Riley

Witnesses To Mark:
　{　　　　　Green Thompson

Subscribed and sworn to before me this 26th day of April , 1905

　　　　　　　　　　　J. V. Connell
　　　　　　　　　　　　　Notary Public.

My term of office expires Nov the 13- 1907

---

　　　　　　　　　　　　　　　　　　7-3449.

　　　　　　Muskogee, Indian Territory, May 3, 1905.

M. F. Reed,
　　Durant, Indian Territory.

Dear Sir:

Receipt is hereby acknowledged of the affidavits of Arlee Reed and Catharine O. Riley to the birth of Catherine Reed, daughter of M. F. and Arlee Reed, June 4, 1903, and the same have been filed with our records as an application for the enrollment of said child.

　　　　　　　　　Respectfully,

　　　　　　　　　　　　　　　　Chairman.

# Applications for Enrollment of Choctaw Newborn
# Act of 1905   Volume XVIII

Choc. New Born 1352
    Joel Nail
    (Born Feb. 9, 1903)

---

In re. application for enrollment, as a citizen of the Choctaw Nation of Joel Nail born on the 9 day of February 1903.

Name of father, Richard Nail a citizen of the Choctaw Nation.
Name of mother, Salina Nail a citizen of the Choctaw Nation.

                        Post Office, Ryan Ind. Ter.

                        Affidavit of Mother.

UNITES STATES OF AMERICA.

Indian Territory
                SS.
Southern District.

    I, Salina Nail on oath state that I am about 30 years of age and a citizen by blood of the Choctaw Nation; That I am the lawful wife of Richard Nail who is a citizen, by blood of the Choctaw Nation, That a male child was born to me on the 9$^{th}$ day of February 190 3. That said child has been named Joel Nail and is now living. *Witness to mark*                       her
        *CA McBrian*                   signed Salina x Nail
        *(Name Illegible)*                       mark

Subscribed and sworn to before me this 20$^{th}$ day of March 190 5

                              Cham Jones
                              Notary Public.

        AFFIDAVIT OF ATTENDING PHYSICIAN OR MIDWIFE.

United States of America,

    Indian Territory, Southern District, SS.

    I, Mary Ann Ramsey acting midwife on oath state that I attended Mrs. Salina Nail wife of Richard Nail on the 9" day of Feby , 190 3 that there was born to her on said date a male child; That said child is now living and is said to have been named Joel Nail                       her
        *Witness to mark*             Mary Ann x Ramsey
        *Mores Johnson*                    mark
        *P.C. Crowder*

## Applications for Enrollment of Choctaw Newborn
## Act of 1905 Volume XVIII

Subscribed and sworn to before me this 22 day of April 1905

                        T M Sullivan
                        Notary Public.

7-4851.

Muskogee, Indian Territory, May 3, 1905.

Dick Nail,
    Ryan, Indian Territory.

Dear Sir:

    Receipt is hereby acknowledged of the affidavits of Salina Nail and Mary Ann Ramsey to the birth of Joel Nail, son of Richard and Saline Nail, February 9, 1903, and the same have been filed with our records as an application for the enrollment of said child.

                Respectfully,

                              Chairman.

---

Choc. New Born 1353
    Cornelius Bascomb
    (Born July 5, 1903)

**NEW-BORN AFFIDAVIT.**

        Number

...Choctaw Enrolling Commission...

    IN THE MATTER OF THE APPLICATION FOR ENROLLMENT, as a citizen of the Choctaw Nation, of Cornelius Bascomb

born on the 5 day of July 190 3

Name of father Charles Bascomb      a citizen of Choctaw Nation final enrollment No. 10554

## Applications for Enrollment of Choctaw Newborn
## Act of 1905   Volume XVIII

Name of mother   Jincy Bascomb            a citizen of   Choctaw
Nation final enrollment No.  13873

                                                 Postoffice    Quinton, I. T.

### AFFIDAVIT OF MOTHER.

UNITED STATES OF AMERICA
INDIAN TERRITORY
  Western    DISTRICT

I   Jincy Bascomb   , on oath state that I am   29   years of age and a citizen by   blood   of the   Choctaw   Nation, and as such have been placed upon the final roll of the   Choctaw   Nation, by the Honorable Secretary of the Interior my final enrollment number being   13873 ; that I am the lawful wife of   Charles Bascomb   , who is a citizen of the   Choctaw   Nation, and as such has been placed upon the final roll of said Nation by the Honorable Secretary of the Interior, his final enrollment number being   10554   and that a   Male   child was born to me on the   5th   day of   July   190 3; that said child has been named   Cornelius Bascomb   , and is now living.

                                                                Jincy Bascomb

Witnesseth.
   Must be two  }   Noel Pope
   Witnesses who
   are Citizens.    Stanley Hoklotubbe

Subscribed and sworn to before me this   6th   day of   Jan   190 5

                                            Guy A. Curry
                                                     Notary Public.

My commission expires:
  Apr 27-1907

---

## AFFIDAVIT OF ATTENDING PHYSICIAN OR MIDWIFE

UNITED STATES OF AMERICA
INDIAN TERRITORY
  Western    DISTRICT

    I,   Milly Carney   a   woman on oath state that I attended on Mrs.   Jincy Bascomb   wife of   Charles Bascomb   on the   5th   day of   July  , 190 3 , that there was born to her on said date a   Male   child, that said child is now living, and is said to have been named   Cornelius Bascomb

                                                her
                                     Milly  x  Carney
                                        mark    midwife

## Applications for Enrollment of Choctaw Newborn
## Act of 1905 Volume XVIII

    Subscribed and sworn to before me this, the   6th      day of
    January    190 5

                 Guy A Curry    Notary Public.

WITNESSETH:
Must be two witnesses { Noel Pope
who are citizens
         Stanley Hoklotubbe

  We hereby certify that we are well acquainted with    Milly Carney
a    woman    and know    her    to be reputable and of good standing in the community.

  Noel Pope             _____

  Stanley Hoklotubbe         _____

                 *Choctaw by Blood*
**BIRTH AFFIDAVIT.**           *Roll No. of mother 13873*

### DEPARTMENT OF THE INTERIOR.
### COMMISSION TO THE FIVE CIVILIZED TRIBES.

  **IN RE APPLICATION FOR ENROLLMENT**, as a citizen of the    Choctaw    Nation, of Cornelius Bascomb    , born on the   5th   day of   July   , 1903

Name of Father: Charles Bascomb     a citizen of the   Choctaw   Nation.
Name of Mother: Jincy Bascomb      a citizen of the   Choctaw   Nation.

          Postoffice    Quinton, Indian Territory

**AFFIDAVIT OF MOTHER.**

UNITED STATES OF AMERICA, Indian Territory, }
   Western      DISTRICT.

  I,   Jincy Bascomb   , on oath state that I am   30   years of age and a citizen by   blood   , of the   Choctaw   Nation; that I am the lawful wife of   Charles Bascomb   , who is a citizen, by blood   of the   Choctaw   Nation; that a Male   child was born to me on   5th   day of   July   , 1903; that said child has been named   Cornelius Bascomb   , and was living March 4, 1905.

             Jincy Bascomb

Witnesses To Mark:
{

# Applications for Enrollment of Choctaw Newborn
## Act of 1905   Volume XVIII

Subscribed and sworn to before me this   27th  day of    April   , 1905

                                   Guy A. Curry
                                   Notary Public.

---

### AFFIDAVIT OF ATTENDING PHYSICIAN OR MID-WIFE.

UNITED STATES OF AMERICA, Indian Territory, ⎫
    Western                  DISTRICT. ⎭

       I,   Milly Carney   , a  mid-wife   , on oath state that I attended on Mrs.   Jincy Bascomb   , wife of   Charles Bascomb   on the  5th day of   July , 1903; that there was born to her on said date a   Male    child; that said child was living March 4, 1905, and is said to have been named   Cornelius Bascomb

                                       her
                               Milly x  Carney
Witnesses To Mark:           mark
   ⎰ A C Bullard
   ⎱ *(Name Illegible)*

Subscribed and sworn to before me this   27th day of    April   , 1905

                                   Guy A. Curry
                                   Notary Public.

---

                                                   7-5465.

                     Muskogee, Indian Territory, May 3, 1905.

Charles Bascomb,
     Quinton, Indian Territory.

Dear Sir:

       Receipt is hereby acknowledged of the affidavits of Jincy Bascomb and Millie Carney to the birth of Cornelius Bascomb, son of Charles and Jincy Bascomb, July 5, 1903, and the same have been filed with our records as an application for the enrollment of said child.

                         Respectfully,

                                            Chairman.

## Applications for Enrollment of Choctaw Newborn
## Act of 1905 Volume XVIII

Choc. New Born 1354
    James Lillian Theresa Moore
    (Born Apr. 6, 1904)

BIRTH AFFIDAVIT.

### DEPARTMENT OF THE INTERIOR.
### COMMISSION TO THE FIVE CIVILIZED TRIBES.

IN RE APPLICATION FOR ENROLLMENT, as a citizen of the Choctaw Nation, of James Lillian Theresa Moore , born on the 6$^{th}$ day of April , 1904

Name of Father: James E. Moore      a citizen of the Choctaw Nation.
Name of Mother: Elizabeth Moore      a citizen of the Choctaw Nation.

        Postoffice    Alex, Ind. Ter.

### AFFIDAVIT OF MOTHER.

UNITED STATES OF AMERICA, Indian Territory,
    Southern          DISTRICT.

    I, Elizabeth Moore , on oath state that I am 21 years of age and a citizen by Intermarriage , of the Choctaw Nation; that I am the lawful wife of James E. Moore , who is a citizen, by Blood of the Choctaw Nation; that a Female child was born to me on 6$^{th}$ day of April , 1904; that said child has been named James Lillian Theresa Moore , and was living March 4, 1905.

                      Elizabeth Moore
Witnesses To Mark:

    Subscribed and sworn to before me this 27 day of April , 1905

                      J.A. Bohart
                          Notary Public.

### AFFIDAVIT OF ATTENDING PHYSICIAN OR MID-WIFE.

UNITED STATES OF AMERICA, Indian Territory,
    Southern          DISTRICT.

    I, Nanie Campbell , a midwife , on oath state that I attended on Mrs. Elizabeth Moore , wife of James E. Moore on the 6$^{th}$ day of April ,

# Applications for Enrollment of Choctaw Newborn
## Act of 1905 Volume XVIII

1904; that there was born to her on said date a Female child; that said child was living March 4, 1905, and is said to have been named James Lillian Theresa Moore

Nanie Campbell

Witnesses To Mark:

{

Subscribed and sworn to before me this 29 day of April , 1905

Orrin M Renfield<br>Notary Public.

---

Choc. New Born 1355
    Boyd Turner Woolridge
    (Born Jan 21, 1905)

**BIRTH AFFIDAVIT.**

DEPARTMENT OF THE INTERIOR.<br>COMMISSION TO THE FIVE CIVILIZED TRIBES.

**IN RE APPLICATION FOR ENROLLMENT,** as a citizen of the Choctaw Nation, of Boyd Turner Woolridge , born on the 21$^{st}$ day of Jany , 1905

Name of Father: Nicholas Woolridge     a citizen of the Choctaw Nation.
Name of Mother: Adeline Woolridge     a citizen of the Choctaw Nation.

Postoffice    Whitefield, Ind. Ter.

AFFIDAVIT OF MOTHER.

**UNITED STATES OF AMERICA, Indian Territory,**
    Western            **DISTRICT.**

    I, Adeline Woolridge , on oath state that I am 27 years of age and a citizen by Blood , of the Choctaw Nation; that I am the lawful wife of Nicholas Woolridge , who is a citizen, by Blood of the Choctaw Nation; that a male child was born to me on 21$^{st}$ day of Jany , 1905; that said child has been named Boyd Turner Woolridge , and was living March 4, 1905.

Adeline Woolridge

Witnesses To Mark:

{

# Applications for Enrollment of Choctaw Newborn
## Act of 1905   Volume XVIII

Subscribed and sworn to before me this 10 day of   April   , 1905

A.L. Beckett

My Com. Expires May 21, 1907                                    Notary Public.

---

**AFFIDAVIT OF ATTENDING PHYSICIAN OR MID-WIFE.**

UNITED STATES OF AMERICA, Indian Territory,
  Western                                  DISTRICT.

I, _____ , a   Physician   , on oath state that I attended on Mrs.   Adeline Woolridge   , wife of   Nicholas Woolridge   on the 21$^{st}$   day of   Jany   , 1905; that there was born to her on said date a   male   child; that said child was living March 4, 1905, and is said to have been named   Boyd Turner Woolridge

T.B. Turner

Witnesses To Mark:

Subscribed and sworn to before me this 27$^{th}$   day of   April   , 1905

J.F. Griffin

Notary Public.

---

7-4504.

Muskogee, Indian Territory, May 3, 1905.

Nicholas Woolridge,
  Whitefield, Indian Territory.

Dear Sir:

Receipt is hereby acknowledged of the affidavit of Adeline Woolridge and T. B. Turner to the birth of Boyd Turner Woolridge, son of Nicholas and Adeline Wollridge[sic], January 21, 1905, and the same have been filed with our records as an application for the enrollment of said child.

Respectfully,

Chairman.

# Applications for Enrollment of Choctaw Newborn
# Act of 1905   Volume XVIII

7 NB 1355.

Muskogee, Indian Territory, June 26, 1905.

Adeline Woolridge,
    Whitefield, Indian Territory.

Dear Madam:

    Receipt is hereby acknowledged of your letter of June 17, 1905, stating that you desire to enroll your baby Boyd Tinner[sic] Woolridge and wish to know how to proceed in the matter.

    In reply to your letter you are advised that the name of your son Boyd Tinner Woolridge has been placed upon a schedule of citizens by blood of the Choctaw Nation prepared for forwarding to the Secretary of the Interior and you will be advised when his enrollment is approved.

                              Respectfully,

                                      Chairman.

---

Choc. New Born 1356
    Simon C. Jackson
    (Born Dec. 7, 1902)
    Green Jackson
    (Born Oct. 26, 1904)

**BIRTH AFFIDAVIT.**

**DEPARTMENT OF THE INTERIOR.**
**COMMISSION TO THE FIVE CIVILIZED TRIBES.**

**IN RE APPLICATION FOR ENROLLMENT,** as a citizen of the Choctaw Nation, of Simon C Jackson, born on the 7 day of December, 1902

Name of Father: Greenwood Jackson    a citizen of the Choctaw Nation.
Name of Mother: Belle Z Jackson    a citizen of the Choctaw Nation.

                      Postoffice    Globe I.T.

## Applications for Enrollment of Choctaw Newborn
## Act of 1905   Volume XVIII

**AFFIDAVIT OF MOTHER.**

UNITED STATES OF AMERICA, Indian Territory, }
Central                           DISTRICT. }

  I, Belle Z Jackson       , on oath state that I am  30   years of age and a citizen by     Intermarriage      , of the    Choctaw     Nation; that I am the lawful wife of    Greenwood Jackson         , who is a citizen, by  Blood    of the      Choctaw   Nation; that a    male    child was born to me on   7    day of   Dec.     , 1902; that said child has been named   Simon C Jackson       , and was living March 4, 1905.

            Belle Z Jackson

Witnesses To Mark:
{

  Subscribed and sworn to before me this  28  day of    April       , 1905

            D A Spears
              Notary Public.

---

**AFFIDAVIT OF ATTENDING PHYSICIAN OR MID-WIFE.**

UNITED STATES OF AMERICA, Indian Territory, }
Central                           DISTRICT. }

  I,   J M Suttle[sic]        , a   Physician       , on oath state that I attended on Mrs.   Belle Z Jackson        , wife of    Greenwood Jackson       on the  7   day of  December     , 1902; that there was born to her on said date a     male    child; that said child was living March 4, 1905, and is said to have been named    Simon C Jackson

            J M Settle

Witnesses To Mark:
{

  Subscribed and sworn to before me this  26  day of    April       , 1905

            D A Spears
              Notary Public.

# Applications for Enrollment of Choctaw Newborn
## Act of 1905 Volume XVIII

BIRTH AFFIDAVIT.

### DEPARTMENT OF THE INTERIOR.
### COMMISSION TO THE FIVE CIVILIZED TRIBES.

IN RE APPLICATION FOR ENROLLMENT, as a citizen of the Choctaw Nation, of Green Jackson, born on the 26 day of October, 1904

Name of Father: Greenwood Jackson a citizen of the Choctaw Nation.
Name of Mother: Belle Z Jackson a citizen of the Choctaw Nation.

Postoffice Globe I.T.

### AFFIDAVIT OF MOTHER.

UNITED STATES OF AMERICA, Indian Territory,
Central DISTRICT.

I, Belle Z Jackson, on oath state that I am 30 years of age and a citizen by Inter-Marriage, of the Choctaw Nation; that I am the lawful wife of Greenwood Jackson, who is a citizen, by Blood of the Choctaw Nation; that a male child was born to me on 26 day of October, 1904; that said child has been named Green Jackson, and was living March 4, 1905.

Belle Z Jackson

Witnesses To Mark:

Subscribed and sworn to before me this 28 day of April, 1905

D A Spears
Notary Public.

### AFFIDAVIT OF ATTENDING PHYSICIAN OR MID-WIFE.

UNITED STATES OF AMERICA, Indian Territory,
Central DISTRICT.

I, Ola Wilson, a mid-wife, on oath state that I attended on Mrs. Belle Z Jackson, wife of Greenwood Jackson on the 26 day of October, 1904; that there was born to her on said date a male child; that said child was living March 4, 1905, and is said to have been named Green Jackson

Ola Wilson

# Applications for Enrollment of Choctaw Newborn
## Act of 1905   Volume XVIII

Witnesses To Mark:

{

    Subscribed and sworn to before me this   26  day of    April      , 1905

                                            D A Spears
                                                Notary Public.

7-4397.

Muskogee, Indian Territory, May 3, 1905.

Greenwood Jackson,
    Globe, Indian Territory.

Dear Sir:

    Receipt is hereby acknowledged of the affidavits of Belle Z. Jackson and J. M. Settle to the birth of Simon C. Jackson; also the affidavits of Belle Z. Jackson and Ola Wilson to the birth of Green Jackson, children of Greenwood and Belle Z. Jackson, December 7, 1902 and October 26, 1904, respectively, and the same have been filed with our records as applications for the enrollment of said children.

                                          Respectfully,

                                                                       Chairman.

---

<u>Choc. New Born 1357</u>
    Jimmie Smith
    (Born Jan. 31, 1904)

Applications for Enrollment of Choctaw Newborn
Act of 1905 Volume XVIII

**NEW-BORN AFFIDAVIT.**

Number..................

## ...Choctaw Enrolling Commission...

IN THE MATTER OF THE APPLICATION FOR ENROLLMENT, as a citizen of the Choctaw Nation, of   Jimmie Lee Smith

born on the  31  day of  January    190 4

Name of father  Will Smith                     a citizen of   United States
Nation final enrollment No.    x
Name of mother   Dora Jones (e[sic] Smith)    a citizen of   Choctaw
Nation final enrollment No.  11338

Postoffice   Non I.T.

**AFFIDAVIT OF MOTHER.**

UNITED STATES OF AMERICA
INDIAN TERRITORY
  Central       DISTRICT

I       Dora Jones (Smith)           , on oath state that I am  17"  years of age and a citizen by  Blood  of the  Choctaw  Nation, and as such have been placed upon the final roll of the  Choctaw  Nation, by the Honorable Secretary of the Interior my final enrollment number being   11338 ; that I am the lawful wife of  Will Smith   , who is a citizen of the  United States  Nation, and as such has been placed upon the final roll of said Nation by the Honorable Secretary of the Interior, his final enrollment number being  x    and that a   Male   child was born to me on the  31$^{st}$ day of  January    190 4; that said child has been named   Jimmie Lee   , and is now living.

Mrs Dora Jones (e Smith)

Witnesseth.
Must be two  ⎱  John Pusley
Witnesses who ⎰
are Citizens.      Nannie Pusley

Subscribed and sworn to before me this  10$^{th}$  day of  Feb.     190 5

Ben F. Gillium
Notary Public.

My commission expires:
  Jan. 24$^{th}$ 1906

## Applications for Enrollment of Choctaw Newborn
## Act of 1905 Volume XVIII

## AFFIDAVIT OF ATTENDING PHYSICIAN OR MIDWIFE

UNITED STATES OF AMERICA
INDIAN TERRITORY
Central    DISTRICT

I,    G. S. Smith    a    Midwife on oath state that I attended on Mrs. Dora Jones (e Smith) wife of Will Smith on the 31st day of January, 1904, that there was born to her on said date a male child, that said child is now living, and is said to have been named Jimmie Lee

*Witness to mark*
*(Name Illegible)*

her
(Mrs.) G. S. x Smith    ~~M.D.~~
mark    *midwife*

WITNESSETH:

Must be two witnesses who are citizens and know the child.
{ John Pusley
  Nannie Pusley

Subscribed and sworn to before me this, the 10th day of February 1905

Ben F. Gillium    Notary Public.

We hereby certify that we are well acquainted with Mrs. G. S. Smith a Midwife and know her to be reputable and of good standing in the community.

{ John Pusley
  Nannie Pusley

7-11338
**BIRTH AFFIDAVIT.**

### DEPARTMENT OF THE INTERIOR.
### COMMISSION TO THE FIVE CIVILIZED TRIBES.

IN RE APPLICATION FOR ENROLLMENT, as a citizen of the Choctaw Nation, of Jimmie Smith, born on the 31 day of January, 1904

Name of Father: William Smith    a citizen of the United States Nation.
Name of Mother: Dora Smith nee Jones    a citizen of the Choc Nation.

Postoffice

## Applications for Enrollment of Choctaw Newborn
## Act of 1905 Volume XVIII

### AFFIDAVIT OF MOTHER.

UNITED STATES OF AMERICA, Indian Territory, }
Central DISTRICT.

I, Dora Smith nee Jones , on oath state that I am 18 years of age and a citizen by blood , of the Choctaw Nation; that I am the lawful wife of William Smith , who is a citizen, ~~by~~ of the United States Nation; that a male child was born to me on 31 day of January , 1904; that said child has been named Jimmie Smith , and was living March 4, 1905.

Dora Smith

Witnesses To Mark:
{

Subscribed and sworn to before me this 27 day of April , 1905

OL Johnson
Notary Public.

---

### AFFIDAVIT OF ATTENDING PHYSICIAN OR MID-WIFE.

UNITED STATES OF AMERICA, Indian Territory, }
Central DISTRICT.

I, Georgeann Smith , a midwife , on oath state that I attended on Mrs. Dora Smith , wife of William Smith on the 31 day of January , 1904; that there was born to her on said date a male child; that said child was living March 4, 1905, and is said to have been named Jimmie Smith

her
Georgeann x Smith
mark

Witnesses To Mark:
{ Clara Wooley
{ JH Elliott

Subscribed and sworn to before me this 28 day of April , 1905

JH Elliott
Notary Public.
My com exp July 8, 1908

## Applications for Enrollment of Choctaw Newborn
## Act of 1905   Volume XVIII

7-4053.

Muskogee, Indian Territory, May 3, 1905.

William Smith,
    Guertie, Indian Territory.

Dear Sir:

    Receipt is hereby acknowledged of the affidavits of Dora Smith and Georgeann Smith to the birth of Jimmie Smith, son of William and Dora Smith, January 31. 1904, and the same have been filed with our records as an application for the enrollment of said child.

    Respectfully,

Chairman.

---

7-N.B. 1357.

Muskogee, Indian Territory, May 8, 1905.

Dora Smith,
    Guertie, Indian Territory.

Dear Madam:

    Receipt is hereby acknowledged of your letter without date, asking if applications have been received for the enrollment of your child, Jemmie[sic] Smith.

    In reply to your letter you are advised that the affidavits heretofore forwarded to the birth of Jimmie Smith, son of William and Dora Smith, have been filed with our records as an application for the enrollment of said child.

    Respectfully,

Commissioner in Charge.

## Applications for Enrollment of Choctaw Newborn
## Act of 1905   Volume XVIII

Choc. New Born 1358
    Insey Fobb
    (Born Sep. 7, 1904)

**BIRTH AFFIDAVIT.**

**DEPARTMENT OF THE INTERIOR.**
**COMMISSION TO THE FIVE CIVILIZED TRIBES.**

**IN RE APPLICATION FOR ENROLLMENT,** as a citizen of the Choctaw Nation, of Insey Fobb, born on the 7 day of Sept, 1904

Name of Father: Lee Fobb      a citizen of the Choctaw Nation.
Name of Mother: Phillis[sic] Fobb      a citizen of the Choctaw Nation.

        Postoffice    Eagletown I.T.

**AFFIDAVIT OF MOTHER.**

UNITED STATES OF AMERICA, Indian Territory,
    Central      **DISTRICT.**

    I, Phillis Fobb, on oath state that I am 38 years of age and a citizen by Blood, of the Choctaw Nation; that I am the lawful wife of Lee Fobb, who is a citizen, by Blood of the Choctaw Nation; that a Female child was born to me on 7th day of Sept, 1904; that said child has been named Insey Fobb, and was living March 4, 1905.

                        her
                      Phillis x Fobb
Witnesses To Mark:        mark
   { *(Name Illegible)*
    David Dyer

    Subscribed and sworn to before me this 26th day of April, 1905

My Commission          Jeff Gardner
expires 23rd Dec 1905        Notary Public.

## Applications for Enrollment of Choctaw Newborn
## Act of 1905 Volume XVIII

### AFFIDAVIT OF ATTENDING PHYSICIAN OR MID-WIFE.

UNITED STATES OF AMERICA, Indian Territory,  
Central DISTRICT.

I, Mela Winship, a midwife, on oath state that I attended on Mrs. Phillis Fobb, wife of Lee Fobb on the 7$^{th}$ day of Sept, 1904; that there was born to her on said date a Female child; that said child was living March 4, 1905, and is said to have been named Insey Fobb

                                          her  
Witnesses To Mark:                Mela x Winship  
   { *(Name Illegible)*                 mark  
    David Dyer

Subscribed and sworn to before me this 26$^{th}$ day of April, 1905

My Commission                    Jeff Gardner  
expires 23$^{rd}$ Dec 1905                    Notary Public.

---

Choc. New Born 1359  
      Clinton Muncrief  
      (Born June 6, 1903)

BIRTH AFFIDAVIT.
### DEPARTMENT OF THE INTERIOR.
### COMMISSION TO THE FIVE CIVILIZED TRIBES.

**IN RE APPLICATION FOR ENROLLMENT,** as a citizen of the Choctaw Nation, of Clinton Muncrief, born on the 6 day of June, 1903

Name of Father: Walter Lee Muncrief     a citizen of the Choctaw Nation.  
Name of Mother: Olivia Muncrief        a citizen of the Choctaw Nation.

                        Postoffice    Comanche I.T.

# Applications for Enrollment of Choctaw Newborn
# Act of 1905   Volume XVIII

### AFFIDAVIT OF MOTHER.

UNITED STATES OF AMERICA, Indian Territory, }
    Southern          DISTRICT.

    I, Olivia Muncrief, on oath state that I am Twenty six years of age and a citizen by marriage, of the Choctaw Nation; that I am the lawful wife of Walter Lee Muncrief, who is a citizen, by blood of the Choctaw Nation; that a male child was born to me on the 6 day of June, 1903; that said child has been named Clinton Muncrief, and was living March 4, 1905.

                                    Olivia Muncrief

Witnesses To Mark:
  { T.A. M$^c$Kenzie
    T. Graham

    Subscribed and sworn to before me this   26   day of   April   , 1905

                                      H.B. Rockett
                                      Notary Public.

---

### AFFIDAVIT OF ATTENDING PHYSICIAN OR MID-WIFE.

UNITED STATES OF AMERICA, Indian Territory, }
........................................................ DISTRICT.

    I, William B Cudgington, a physician, on oath state that I attended on Mrs. WL Moncrief[sic], wife of Walter L Moncrief on the 6 day of June, 1903; that there was born to her on said date a male child; that said child was living March 4, 1905, and is said to have been named Clinton Moncrief

                                  William B Cudgington M.D.

Witnesses To Mark:
  { Tho$^s$ M. Bosson
    Batton Clark

    Subscribed and sworn to before me this   27$^{th}$   day of   April   , 1905

                                Tho$^s$ M. Bosson
My Commission                   Notary Public.
Expires June 30 1905

## Applications for Enrollment of Choctaw Newborn
## Act of 1905   Volume XVIII

Choc. New Born 1360
      John M. Carr
      (Born Dec. 31, 1904)
      Jim Walter Carr
      (Born Aug. 13, 1903)   Died prior to
          March 4, 1905.

**BIRTH AFFIDAVIT.**

### DEPARTMENT OF THE INTERIOR.
### COMMISSION TO THE FIVE CIVILIZED TRIBES.

IN RE APPLICATION FOR ENROLLMENT, as a citizen of the Choctaw Nation, of John M Carr, born on the 31 day of December, 1904

Name of Father: W^m M Carr     *by marriage* a citizen of the Choctaw Nation.
Name of Mother: Alma Carr     a citizen of the Choctaw Nation.

          Postoffice   Utica I.T.

**AFFIDAVIT OF MOTHER.**

UNITED STATES OF AMERICA, Indian Territory,
   Central            DISTRICT.

    I, Alma Carr, on oath state that I am 18 years of age and a citizen by blood, of the Choctaw Nation; that I am the lawful wife of W^m M Carr, who is a citizen, *marriage* by —— of the Choctaw Nation; that a male child was born to me on 31 day of December, 1904; that said child has been named John M. Carr, and was living March 4, 1905.

                          Alma Carr
Witnesses To Mark:

    Subscribed and sworn to before me this 24^th day of April, 1905.

                      W.J. O'Donby
                           Notary Public.

## Applications for Enrollment of Choctaw Newborn
## Act of 1905   Volume XVIII

### AFFIDAVIT OF ATTENDING PHYSICIAN OR MID-WIFE.

UNITED STATES OF AMERICA, Indian Territory,  
Central   DISTRICT.

I, A.J. Wells , a Physician , on oath state that I attended on Mrs. Alma Carr , wife of W$^m$ M Carr on the 31 day of December , 1904; that there was born to her on said date a male child; that said child was living March 4, 1905, and is said to have been named John M. Carr

A.J. Wells, M.D.

Witnesses To Mark:

{

Subscribed and sworn to before me this 24$^{th}$ day of April , 1905

W.J. O'Donby  
Notary Public.

---

### DEPARTMENT OF THE INTERIOR, COMMISSIONER TO THE FIVE CIVILIZED TRIBES.

It appearing from the within affidavits that the applicant, John M. Carr for whose enrollment application was made under the provisions of the Act of Congress approved March 3, 1905 (33 Stats., 1060), died prior to March 4, 1905, I am of the opinion that the application for the enrollment of John M. Carr as a citizen by blood of the Choctaw Nation, should be dismissed and it is so ordered.

Tams Bixby   Commissioner.  
**JAN 25 1907**  
Muskogee, Indian Territory.

---

### DEPARTMENT OF THE INTERIOR.
### COMMISSION TO THE FIVE CIVILIZED TRIBES.

---

In the matter of the death of John M Carr a citizen of the Choctaw Nation, who formerly resided at or near Utica , Ind. Ter., and died on the 13$^{th}$ day of Jan'y , 1905

# Applications for Enrollment of Choctaw Newborn
# Act of 1905   Volume XVIII

### AFFIDAVIT OF RELATIVE.

UNITED STATES OF AMERICA, Indian Territory,
    Central          DISTRICT.

    I, William Madison Carr, on oath state that I am 31 years of age and a citizen by intermarriage, of the Choctaw Nation; that my postoffice address is Utica, Ind. Ter.; that I am the father of John M Carr who was a citizen, by blood, of the Choctaw Nation and that said John M Carr died on the 13 day of Jany, 1905

                                                    William Madison Carr

Witnesses To Mark:

    Subscribed and sworn to before me this 11<sup>th</sup> day of Jan'y, 1907

                                                    Lacey P Bobo
                                                    Notary Public.

### AFFIDAVIT OF ACQUAINTANCE.

UNITED STATES OF AMERICA, Indian Territory,
    Central          DISTRICT.

    I, Alma Carr, on oath state that I am 20 years of age, and a citizen by blood of the Choctaw Nation; that my postoffice address is Utica, Ind. Ter.; that I ~~was personally acquainted with~~ *am the mother of John M. Carr* who was a citizen, by blood, of the Choctaw Nation; and that said John M Carr died on the 13 day of Jan'y, 1905

                                                      Alma Carr

Witnesses To Mark:

    Subscribed and sworn to before me this 11<sup>th</sup> day of Jan'y, 1907

                                                    Lacey P Bobo
                                                    Notary Public.

## DEPARTMENT OF THE INTERIOR,
## COMMISSION TO THE FIVE CIVILIZED TRIBES.

    Record in the matter of the application for enrollment as a citizen by blood of the Choctaw Nation of:

        JIM WALTER CARR                       7-NB-1360.

# Applications for Enrollment of Choctaw Newborn
## Act of 1905   Volume XVIII

**BIRTH AFFIDAVIT.**

### DEPARTMENT OF THE INTERIOR.
### COMMISSION TO THE FIVE CIVILIZED TRIBES.

---

**IN RE APPLICATION FOR ENROLLMENT,** as a citizen of the   Choctaw   Nation, of   Jim Walter Carr   , born on the   13   day of   August   , 1903

*by marriage*

Name of Father: W$^m$ M Carr      a citizen of the   Choctaw   Nation.
Name of Mother: Alma Carr         a citizen of the   Choctaw   Nation.

Postoffice   Utica I.T.

---

**AFFIDAVIT OF MOTHER.**

UNITED STATES OF AMERICA, Indian Territory, }
Central                                      DISTRICT. }

I, Alma Carr, on oath state that I am 18 years of age and a citizen by blood, of the Choctaw Nation; that I am the lawful wife of W$^m$ M Carr, who is a citizen, *marriage* by —— of the Choctaw Nation; that a male child was born to me on 13$^{th}$ day of August, 1903; that said child ~~has been~~ *was* named Jim Walter Carr, and was living March 4, 1905.

Alma Carr

Witnesses To Mark:
{

Subscribed and sworn to before me this 24$^{th}$ day of April, 1905

W.J. O'Donby
Notary Public.

---

**AFFIDAVIT OF ATTENDING PHYSICIAN OR MID-WIFE.**

UNITED STATES OF AMERICA, Indian Territory, }
Central                                      DISTRICT. }

I, A.J. Wells, a Physician, on oath state that I attended on Mrs. Alma Carr, wife of W$^m$ M Carr on the 13 day of August, 1903; that there was born to her on said date a male child; that said child was living March 4, 1905, and is said to have been named Jim Walter Carr

A.J. Wells, M.D.

Witnesses To Mark:
{

## Applications for Enrollment of Choctaw Newborn
## Act of 1905 Volume XVIII

Subscribed and sworn to before me this 24th day of April , 1905

W.J. O'Donby
Notary Public.

## DEPARTMENT OF THE INTERIOR.
## COMMISSION TO THE FIVE CIVILIZED TRIBES.

In the matter of the death of　　　　Jim Walter Carr
a citizen of the　Choctaw　Nation, who formerly resided at or near　Utica　, Ind. Ter., and died on the　18th　day of　August　, 1903

**AFFIDAVIT OF RELATIVE.**

UNITED STATES OF AMERICA, Indian Territory, }
　　Central　　　　　　DISTRICT.

I,　William M Carr　, on oath state that I am　30　years of age and a citizen by　marriage　, of the　Choctaw　Nation; that my postoffice address is　Utica　, Ind. Ter.; that I am　the father　of　Jim Walter Carr　who was a citizen, by blood　, of the　Choctaw　Nation and that said　Jim Walter Carr　died on the　18　day of August　, 1903

William M Carr

Witnesses To Mark:
{

Subscribed and sworn to before me this　8　day of　May　, 1905

*(Name Illegible)*
Notary Public.

**AFFIDAVIT OF ACQUAINTANCE.**

UNITED STATES OF AMERICA, Indian Territory, }
　　Central　　　　　　DISTRICT.

I,　E O M<sup>c</sup>Guire　, on oath state that I am　40　years of age, and a citizen by marriage　of the　Choctaw　Nation; that my postoffice address is　Roberta　, Ind. Ter.; that I was personally acquainted with　Jim Walter Carr　who was a citizen, by blood　, of the　Choctaw　Nation; and that said　Jim Walter Carr　died on the　18　day of August　, 1903

EO McGuire

Witnesses To Mark:
{

## Applications for Enrollment of Choctaw Newborn
## Act of 1905   Volume XVIII

Subscribed and sworn to before me this   8   day of   May   , 1905

*(Name Illegible)*
Notary Public.

*W.F.*
7-NB-1360.

### DEPARTMENT OF THE INTERIOR,
### COMMISSION TO THE FIVE CIVILIZED TRIBES.

In the matter of the application for the enrollment of Jim Walter Carr as a citizen by blood of the Choctaw Nation.

---oOo---

It appears from the record herein that on April 29, 1905 there was filed with the Commission application for the enrollment of Jim Walter Carr as a citizen by blood of the Choctaw Nation.

It further appears from the record herein and the records of the Commission that the applicant was born August 13, 1903; that he is a son of Alma Carr, a recognized and enrolled citizen by blood of the Choctaw Nation whose name appears opposite number 503 upon the final roll of citizens by blood of the Choctaw Nation, approved by the Secretary of the Interior December 12, 1902, and Wm. M. Carr, a noncitizen; and that said applicant died August 18, 1903.

The Act of Congress approved March 3, 1905 (Public No. 212) among other things provides:

"That the Commission to the Five Civilized Tribes is authorized for sixty days after the date of the approval of this act to receive and consider applications for enrollment of children born subsequent to September twenty-fifth, nineteen hundred and two, and prior to March fourth, nineteen hundred and five, and who were living on said latter date, to citizens by blood of the Choctaw and Chickasaw tribes of Indians whose enrollment has been approved by the Secretary of the Interior prior to the date of the approval of this act; and to enroll and make allotments to such children."

It is, therefore, hereby ordered that the application for the enrollment of Jim Walter Carr as a citizen by blood of the Choctaw Nation be dismissed in accordance with the order of the Commission of March 31, 1905.

COMMISSION TO THE FIVE CIVILIZED TRIBES.

Tams Bixby
Chairman.

Muskogee, Indian Territory.
JUN 28 1905

## Applications for Enrollment of Choctaw Newborn
## Act of 1905  Volume XVIII

7-NB-1360.

Muskogee, Indian Territory, June 28, 1905.

William M. Carr,                                      **COPY**
    Utica, Indian Territory.

Dear Sir:

    Inclosed herewith you will find a copy of the order of this Commission, dated June 28, 1905, dismissing the application for the enrollment of Jim Walter Carr as a citizen by blood of the Choctaw Nation.

                        Respectfully,
                            SIGNED

                            *Tams Bixby*
Registered.                              Chairman.
Incl. 7-NB-1360.

---

7-NB-1360.

Muskogee, Indian Territory, June 28, 1905.

Mansfield, McMurray & Cornish,                 **COPY**
    Attorneys for Choctaw and Chickasaw Nations,
        South McAlester, Indian Territory.

Gentlemen:

    Inclosed herewith you will find a copy of the order of this Commission, dated June 28, 1905, dismissing the application for the enrollment of Jim Walter Carr as a citizen by blood of the Choctaw Nation.

                        Respectfully,
                            SIGNED

                             *Tams Bixby*
Registered.                              Chairman.
Incl. 7-NB-1360.

# Applications for Enrollment of Choctaw Newborn
## Act of 1905   Volume XVIII

7-237.

Muskogee, Indian Territory, May 3, 1905.

William M. Carr,
    Utica, Indian Territory.

Dear Sir:

    Receipt is hereby acknowledged of the affidavits of Alma Carr and A. J. Wells to the birth of John M. Carr, son of William M. and Alma Carr, December 31, 1904, and the same have been filed with our records as an application for the enrollment of said child. application for the enrollment of said child.

    Receipt is also acknowledged of the affidavits of Alma Carr and A. J. Wells to the birth of Jim Walter Carr, son of William M. and Alma Carr, August 1903.

    It appears from the affidavits that this child was not living on March 4, 1905, and for the purpose of making the correct date of his death a matter of record there is enclosed herewith blank form for proof of death which please have executed and returned to this office as early as practicable.

    Respectfully,

    Chairman.

---

7-237

Muskogee, Indian Territory, May 18, 1905.

William M. Carr,
    Utica, Indian Territory.

Dear Sir:

    Receipt is hereby acknowledged of your affidavit and the affidavit of E. A. McGuire to the death of your child Jim Walter Carr which occurred August 18, 1903, and the same have been filed with our records as evidence of the death of the above named child.

    Respectfully,

    Chairman.

# Applications for Enrollment of Choctaw Newborn
## Act of 1905    Volume XVIII

7-NB-1360.

Muskogee, Indian Territory, June 1, 1905.

William M. Carr,
    Utica, Indian Territory.

Dear Sir:

    Referring to the application for the enrollment of your infant child, John M. Carr, born December 231, 1904, heretofore filed in this office, it is noted that the applicant is dead.

    In order that this fact may be made a matter of record, you will execute and return to this office the enclosed proof of death.

    In having these affidavits executed care should be exercised to see that all names are written in full, as they appear in the body of the affidavit, and in the event that either of the persons signing the affidavit are unable to write, signatures by mark must be attested by two witnesses. Each affidavit must be executed before a Notary Public and the notarial seal and signature of the officer must be attached to each separate affidavit.

                        Respectfully,

VR 1-7.

---

7-NB-1360

Muskogee, Indian Territory, July 25, 1905.

William M. Carr,
    Utica, Indian Territory.

Dear Sir:

    Referring to the application for the enrollment of your infant child, John M. Carr, born December 31, 1904, heretofore filed in this office, it is noted that the applicant is dead.

    In order that his death may be made a matter of record you are requested to have executed and returned to this office the inclosed proof of death.

    In having these affidavits executed care should be exercised to see that all names are written in full and if either of the persons signing the affidavits are unable to write, signature by mark must be attested by two witnesses. Each affidavit must be executed

# Applications for Enrollment of Choctaw Newborn
## Act of 1905 Volume XVIII

before a Notary Public and the notarial seal and signature of the officer must be attached to each separate affidavit.

You are requested to give this matter your immediate attention.

Respectfully,

LM 25/5

Commissioner.

---

7-NB-1360

Muskogee, Indian Territory, January 25, 1907.

William Madison Carr,
Utica, Indian Territory.

Dear Sir:

You are hereby advised that it appearing from the records of this office that your minor child, John M. Carr died prior to March 4, 1905, the Commissioner to the Five Civilized Tribes, on January 26, 1907, dismissed the application for his enrollment as a new born citizen of the Choctaw Nation.

Respectfully,

Commissioner.

---

7-NB-1360

Muskogee, Indian Territory, January 28, 1907.

Chief Clerk,
Choctaw Land Office,
Atoka, Indian Territory.

Dear Sir:

Referring to Choctaw New Born card No. 1360, John M. Carr you are advised that a red line has been drawn through the name of No. 1 John M. Carr, the stamp "No. 1 Dismissed Jan. 25, 1907" placed thereon and the following notation placed on said card:

"No. 1 died Jan. 13, 1905. Proof of death filed Jan. 22, 1907."

You are therefore directed to make duplicate Choctaw new born roll card of the same number in your possession conform to the information thereon and eliminate the

## Applications for Enrollment of Choctaw Newborn
## Act of 1905 Volume XVIII

name of this person from your list of undetermined applicants for enrollment in the Choctaw Nation.

Respectfully,

Commissioner.

---

Choc. New Born 1361
    Dixon Dyer
    (Born March 2, 1905)

**BIRTH AFFIDAVIT.**

### DEPARTMENT OF THE INTERIOR.
### COMMISSION TO THE FIVE CIVILIZED TRIBES.

**IN RE APPLICATION FOR ENROLLMENT,** as a citizen of the Choctaw Nation, of Dixon Dyer, born on the $2^{nd}$ day of March, 1905

Name of Father: David Dyer      a citizen of the Choctaw Nation.
Name of Mother: Celia Dyer      a citizen of the Choctaw Nation.

Postoffice    Eagletown I.T.

**AFFIDAVIT OF MOTHER.**

UNITED STATES OF AMERICA, Indian Territory,
    Central      DISTRICT.

    I, Celia Dyer, on oath state that I am 40 years of age and a citizen by Blood, of the Choctaw Nation; that I am the lawful wife of David Dyer, who is a citizen, by Blood of the Choctaw Nation; that a male child was born to me on $2^{nd}$ day of March, 1905; that said child has been named Dixon Dyer, and was living March 4, 1905.

                              Celia Dyer

Witnesses To Mark:

    Subscribed and sworn to before me this 26 day of April, 1905

My Commission              Jeff Gardner
expires $23^{rd}$ Dec 1905            Notary Public.

# Applications for Enrollment of Choctaw Newborn
## Act of 1905   Volume XVIII

**AFFIDAVIT OF ATTENDING PHYSICIAN OR MID-WIFE.**

UNITED STATES OF AMERICA, Indian Territory,
Central                    DISTRICT.

   I,   Isabel Homma   , a   midwife   , on oath state that I attended on Mrs.   Celia Dyer   , wife of   David Dyer   on the   2$^{nd}$   day of   March   , 1905; that there was born to her on said date a   male   child; that said child was living March 4, 1905, and is said to have been named   Dixon Dyer

her<br>Isabel x Homma<br>mark

Witnesses To Mark:
{ (Name Illegible)
{ (Name Illegible)

   Subscribed and sworn to before me this   26   day of   April   , 1905

My Commission                    Jeff Gardner
expires 23$^{rd}$ Dec 1905                    Notary Public.

7-676.

Muskogee, Indian Territory, May 3, 1905.

David Dyer,
   Eagletown, Indian Territory.

Dear Sir:

   Receipt is hereby acknowledged of the affidavits of Celia Dyer and Isabel Homma, to the birth of Dixon Dyer, son of David and Celia Dyer, March 2, 1905, and the same have been filed with our records as an application for the enrollment of said child.

Respectfully,

Chairman.

Applications for Enrollment of Choctaw Newborn
Act of 1905   Volume XVIII

Choc. New Born 1362
    Lena Riddle
    (Born Oct. 17, 1904)

# NEW BORN AFFIDAVIT

No ........

## CHOCTAW ENROLLING COMMISSION

IN THE MATTER OF THE APPLICATION FOR ENROLLMENT as a citizen of the Choctaw Nation, of Lena Riddle born on the 17$^{th}$ day of October 190 4

Name of father   L A Riddle   a citizen of   Choctaw   Nation, final enrollment No. 8916
Name of mother   Elizabeth Riddle nee Goins   a citizen of   Choctaw   Nation, final enrollment No. 10111

                          Boswell I.T.                Postoffice.

### AFFIDAVIT OF MOTHER

UNITED STATES OF AMERICA  
    INDIAN TERRITORY  
DISTRICT   Central

    I   Elizabeth Riddle   , on oath state that I am   22 years of age and a citizen by   blood   of the   Choctaw   Nation, and as such have been placed upon the final roll of the   Choctaw   Nation, by the Honorable Secretary of the Interior my final enrollment number being   10111   ; that I am the lawful wife of   L A Riddle   , who is a citizen of the   Choctaw   Nation, and as such has been placed upon the final roll of said Nation by the Honorable Secretary of the Interior, his final enrollment number being   8916   and that a   Female   child was born to me on the   17$^{th}$   day of   October   190 4; that said child has been named   Lena Riddle   , and is now living.

                                    Elizabeth Riddle

WITNESSETH:  
  Must be two witnesses { H.W. Goins  
  who are citizens { Isham Nelson

## Applications for Enrollment of Choctaw Newborn
### Act of 1905   Volume XVIII

Subscribed and sworn to before me this, the   21   day of   Feb   , 190 5

SH Downing
Notary Public.

My Commission Expires:   March 14th 1908

---

*Affidavit of Attending Physician or Midwife*

UNITED STATES OF AMERICA,  
INDIAN TERRITORY,  
Central   DISTRICT

I,   Elizabeth Durant   a   Midwife   on oath state that I attended on Mrs. Elizabeth Riddle   wife of   L A Riddle   on the   17   day of   October   , 190 4, that there was born to her on said date a   Female   child, that said child is now living, and is said to have been named   Lena Riddle

                         her  
Elizabeth x Durant   *Midwife*  
                         mark

Subscribed and sworn to before me this the   21   day of   February   1905

SH Downing
Notary Public.

WITNESSETH:  
Must be two witnesses  { H.W. Goins  
who are citizens and  
know the child.        { Isham Nelson

We hereby certify that we are well acquainted with   Elizabeth Durant   a   Midwife   and know   her   to be reputable and of good standing in the community.

Must be two citizen { H.W. Goins  
witnesses.          { Isham Nelson

---

BIRTH AFFIDAVIT.

### DEPARTMENT OF THE INTERIOR.
### COMMISSION TO THE FIVE CIVILIZED TRIBES.

IN RE APPLICATION FOR ENROLLMENT, as a citizen of the   Choctaw   Nation, of   Lena Riddle   , born on the   17   day of   October   , 1904

Name of Father: Lorrin Riddle         a citizen of the   Choctaw   Nation.  
Name of Mother: Elizabeth Riddle      a citizen of the   Choctaw   Nation.

## Applications for Enrollment of Choctaw Newborn
## Act of 1905   Volume XVIII

Postoffice   Boswell I.T.

---

**AFFIDAVIT OF MOTHER.**

UNITED STATES OF AMERICA, Indian Territory, }
Central   DISTRICT. }

I,   Elizabeth Riddle   , on oath state that I am   22   years of age and a citizen by   blood   , of the   Choctaw   Nation; that I am the lawful wife of   Lorrin Riddle   , who is a citizen, by blood   of the   Choctaw   Nation; that a Female   child was born to me on   17"   day of   October   , 1904; that said child has been named   Lena Riddle   , and was living March 4, 1905.

Elizabeth Riddle

Witnesses To Mark:
{

Subscribed and sworn to before me this   15"   day of   April   , 1905

S H Downing
Notary Public.

---

**AFFIDAVIT OF ATTENDING PHYSICIAN OR MID-WIFE.**

UNITED STATES OF AMERICA, Indian Territory, }
Central   DISTRICT. }

I,   Elizabeth Durant   , a   Midwife   , on oath state that I attended on Mrs.   Elizabeth Riddle   , wife of   Lorrin Riddle   on the   17"   day of   October , 1904; that there was born to her on said date a   Female   child; that said child was living March 4, 1905, and is said to have been named   Lena Riddle

her
Elizabeth x Durant
mark

Witnesses To Mark:
{ D.A. Bridges
{ *(Name Illegible)*

Subscribed and sworn to before me this   15"   day of   April   , 1905

SH Downing
Notary Public.

# Applications for Enrollment of Choctaw Newborn
## Act of 1905  Volume XVIII

Muskogee, Indian Territory, April 20, 1905.

Lorrin Riddle,
    Boswell, Indian Territory.

Dear Sir:

    Receipt is hereby acknowledged of the affidavits of Elizabeth Riddle and Elizabeth Durant to the birth of Lena Riddle, daughter of Lorrin and Elizabeth Riddle, October 17, 1904.

    It is stated in the affidavit of the mother that she is a citizen by blood of the Choctaw Nation, and if this is correct you are requested to state the name under which she was enrolled, the names of her parents, and if she has made selection of the lands of the Choctaw and Chickasaw Nations, please give her roll number as the same appears upon her allotment certificate.

    This matter should receive immediate attention in order that proper disposition may be made of the application for the enrollment of your child.

Respectfully,

Chairman.

---

Boswell, I. T. May 1, 1905.

Commission to the Five Civilized Tribes,
    Muskogee, I. T.

Your letter received in regards to Elizabeth Riddle affidavit. Will say she is a Choctaw citizen by blood of the Choctaw Nation, enrolled as Elizabeth Goins We were married after the enrollment. Her father's name is Jim Goins. Her mother's name do not appear on the rolls as she has been dead about twenty years.

    Elizabeth Riddle (nee) Goins roll number on allotment certificate is 10111. She selected her land in the Choctaw Nation. I hope this will meet your approval.

Your respt.
Lorin[sic] A. Riddle,
Boswell,
I.T.

Applications for Enrollment of Choctaw Newborn
Act of 1905 Volume XVIII

Choc. New Born 1363
  Willie Alexander Hutchinson
  (Born July 21, 1904)

**NEW-BORN AFFIDAVIT.**

Number..............

## Choctaw Enrolling Commission.

IN THE MATTER OF THE APPLICATION FOR ENROLLMENT, as a citizen of the Choctaw Nation, of Willie A Hutchinson

born on the 21 day of July 190 4

Name of father Ollie Hutchinson    a citizen of Choctaw
Nation final enrollment No 9778
Name of mother Matilda Hutchinson    a citizen of white
Nation final enrollment No ..............

    Postoffice  Wade I.T.

**AFFIDAVIT OF MOTHER.**

UNITED STATES OF AMERICA,
 INDIAN TERRITORY,
Central    DISTRICT

  I Matilda Hutchinson         on oath state that I am 25 years of age and a citizen by white of the .............. Nation, and as such have been placed upon the final roll of the .............. Nation, by the Honorable Secretary of the Interior my final enrollment number being ..............; that I am the lawful wife of Ollie Hutchinson, who is a citizen of the Choctaw Nation, and as such has been placed upon the final roll of said Nation by the Honorable Secretary of the Interior, his final enrollment number being 9778 and that a male child was born to me on the 21st day of July 190 4; that said child has been named Willie A Hutchinson, and is now living.

            Matilda Hutchinson

WITNESSETH:
 Must be two  William W Hardage
 Witnesses who
 are Citizens.  Andrew C. Hardage

  Subscribed and sworn to before me this 15th day of January 190 5

          P. L. Cain
            Notary Public.

My commission expires March 1907

Applications for Enrollment of Choctaw Newborn
Act of 1905   Volume XVIII

## Affidavit of Attending Physician or Midwife.

UNITED STATES OF AMERICA
INDIAN TERRITORY
Central        DISTRICT

I, Hannah Walker    a    Midwife on oath state that I attended on Mrs. Matilda Hutchinson    wife of    Ollie Hutchinson on the  21st  day of  July  , 190 4 , that there was born to her on said date a  Male child, that said child is now living, and is said to have been named  Willie A. Hutchinson

Hannah Walker    M.D.

Subscribed and sworn to before me this, the  19th  day of  January   190 5

P. L. Cain
Notary Public.

WITNESSETH:
Must be two witnesses who are citizens and know the child.
{ William W Hardage
  Andrew C. Hardage

We hereby certify that we are well acquainted with   Hannah Walker   a   Midwife   and know   her   to be reputable and of good standing in the community.

{ William W Hardage
  Andrew C. Hardage

BIRTH AFFIDAVIT.

### DEPARTMENT OF THE INTERIOR.
### COMMISSION TO THE FIVE CIVILIZED TRIBES.

**IN RE APPLICATION FOR ENROLLMENT**, as a citizen of the   Choctaw   Nation, of   Willie Alexander Hutchinson   , born on the   21 day of July   , 1904

Name of Father: Ollie Hutchinson         a citizen of the   Choctaw   Nation.
Name of Mother: Matilda Hutchinson     a citizen of the   ~~Choctaw~~   Nation.

Postoffice    Wade I.T.

# Applications for Enrollment of Choctaw Newborn
# Act of 1905   Volume XVIII

### AFFIDAVIT OF MOTHER.

UNITED STATES OF AMERICA, Indian Territory, }
   Central            DISTRICT.

   I,   Matilda Hutchinson   , on oath state that I am   24   years of age and a citizen by _____, of the _____ Nation; that I am the lawful wife of Ollie Hutchinson   , who is a citizen, by blood   of the   Choctaw   Nation; that a   male   child was born to me on   21   day of   July   , 1904; that said child has been named   Willie Alexander Hutchinson   , and was living March 4, 1905.

                                        Matilda Hutchinson

Witnesses To Mark:
   {

   Subscribed and sworn to before me this   17th   day of   April   , 1905

                                        P. L. Cain
                                        Notary Public.

---

### AFFIDAVIT OF ATTENDING PHYSICIAN OR MID-WIFE.

UNITED STATES OF AMERICA, Indian Territory, }
   Central            DISTRICT.

   I,   Hannah Walker   , a midwife   , on oath state that I attended on Mrs.   Matilda Hutchinson   , wife of   Ollie Hutchinson   on the   21   day of   July   , 1904; that there was born to her on said date a   male   child; that said child was living March 4, 1905, and is said to have been named   Willie Alexander Hutchinson

                                        Hannah Walker

Witnesses To Mark:
   {

   Subscribed and sworn to before me this   17th   day of   April   , 1905

                                        P. L. Cain
                                        Notary Public.

# Applications for Enrollment of Choctaw Newborn
## Act of 1905   Volume XVIII

7-3430

Muskogee, Indian Territory, May 4, 1905.

Ollie Hutchinson,
    Wade, Indian Territory.

Dear Sir:

    Receipt is hereby acknowledged of your letter of April 17, 1905, transmitting affidavits and your letter of May 2, 1905, with reference to the affidavits of Matilda Hutchinson and Hannah Walker to the birth of Willie Alexander Hutchinson, and Clare Gertrue[sic] Hutchinson, children of Ollie and Matilda Hutchinson, April 10, 1903 and July 21, 1904, and the same have been filed with our records as applications for the enrollment of said children.

                        Respectfully,

                                      Chairman.

---

<u>Choc. New Born 1363</u>
    Jim Hutchinson
    (Born March 9, 1903)
    Albert Jerry Hutchinson
    (Born Feb. 18, 1905)

**NEW-BORN AFFIDAVIT.**

                Number..................

## Choctaw Enrolling Commission.

    IN THE MATTER OF THE APPLICATION FOR ENROLLMENT, as a citizen of the Choctaw Nation, of Jim Hutchinson

born on the 9th day of March 1903

Name of father     Lewis S Hutchinson     a citizen of     Choctaw
Nation final enrollment No   9777
Name of mother     Lillie Lee Hutchinson     a citizen of     Choctaw
Nation final enrollment No ................

                        Postoffice     Durant

## Applications for Enrollment of Choctaw Newborn
## Act of 1905  Volume XVIII

### AFFIDAVIT OF MOTHER.

UNITED STATES OF AMERICA,  
   INDIAN TERRITORY,  
Central    DISTRICT

    I     Lillie Lee Hutchinson     on oath state that I am 25 years of age and a citizen by marriage of the Choctaw Nation, and as such have been placed upon the final roll of the Choctaw Nation, by the Honorable Secretary of the Interior my final enrollment number being ................; that I am the lawful wife of Lewis S. Hutchinson, who is a citizen of the Choctaw Nation, and as such has been placed upon the final roll of said Nation by the Honorable Secretary of the Interior, his final enrollment number being 9777 and that a male child was born to me on the 9 day of March 190 3; that said child has been named Jim Hutchinson, and is now living.

Lillie Lee Hutchinson

WITNESSETH:  
  Must be two Witnesses who are Citizens.    *(Name Illegible)*  
                           E.J. Nail

Subscribed and sworn to before me this 16 day of January 190 5

James Bower<br>Notary Public.

My commission expires Sept 23 1907

---

## Affidavit of Attending Physician or Midwife.

UNITED STATES OF AMERICA  
INDIAN TERRITORY  
Central    DISTRICT

    I, B.W. Stover a Practicing Physician on oath state that I attended on Mrs. Lillie Hutchinson wife of Lewis S. Hutchinson on the 9 day of March, 190 3, that there was born to her on said date a Male child, that said child is now living, and is said to have been named Jim Hutchinson

B.W. Stover     M.D.

Subscribed and sworn to before me this, the 16 day of January 190 5

James Bower<br>Notary Public.

WITNESSETH:  
  Must be two witnesses who are citizens and know the child.    Jesse Robinson  
                               E. J. Nail

# Applications for Enrollment of Choctaw Newborn
## Act of 1905   Volume XVIII

We hereby certify that we are well acquainted with .................................................................
a................................................ and know ............................... to be reputable and of good standing in the community.

{ Jesse Robinson
E.J. Nail

**BIRTH AFFIDAVIT.**

## DEPARTMENT OF THE INTERIOR.
## COMMISSION TO THE FIVE CIVILIZED TRIBES.

IN RE APPLICATION FOR ENROLLMENT, as a citizen of the   Chocktaw[sic]   Nation, of   Albert Jerry Hutchison   , born on the 18$^{th}$ day of February , 1905

Name of Father: L.S. Hutchison          a citizen of the   Chocktaw   Nation.
Name of Mother: Lillie Hutchison        a citizen of the   Chocktaw   Nation.

Postoffice   Durant, Ind. Ter.

**AFFIDAVIT OF MOTHER.**

UNITED STATES OF AMERICA, Indian Territory, }
Central                DISTRICT.

I,   Lillie Hutchison   , on oath state that I am   nineteen   *(19)*   years of age and a citizen by   intermarriage   , of the   Chocktaw Nation; that I am the lawful wife of   L.S. Hutchison   , who is a citizen, by   blood   of the   Chocktaw Nation; that a   male   child was born to me on 18$^{th}$   day of   February   , 1905; that said child has been named   Albert Jerry Hutchison   , and was living March 4, 1905.

Lillie x Hutchison

Witnesses To Mark:
{ A.W. Willis
Sidney G. Hogan

Subscribed and sworn to before me this   4$^{th}$   day of   April   , 1905.

Johan Simon
Notary Public.

## Applications for Enrollment of Choctaw Newborn
## Act of 1905    Volume XVIII

### AFFIDAVIT OF ATTENDING PHYSICIAN OR MID-WIFE.

UNITED STATES OF AMERICA, Indian Territory,  
Central    DISTRICT.

I,    W.F. Clifton M.D.    , a    Physician    , on oath state that I attended on Mrs.    Lillie Hutchison    , wife of    L.S. Hutchison    on the  $18^{th}$    day of February    , 1905; that there was born to her on said date a    male    child; that said child was living March 4, 1905, and is said to have been named Albert Jerry Hutchison

W.F. Clifton B.S.M.D.

Witnesses To Mark:
{ A.W. Willis
{ Sidney G. Hogan

Subscribed and sworn to before me this    $4^{th}$    day of    April    , 1905

Johan Simon  
Notary Public.

---

BIRTH AFFIDAVIT.

### DEPARTMENT OF THE INTERIOR.
### COMMISSION TO THE FIVE CIVILIZED TRIBES.

---

IN RE APPLICATION FOR ENROLLMENT, as a citizen of the    Choctaw    Nation, of Jim Hutchison    , born on the  $9^{th}$    day of March    , 1903

Name of Father: Louis S. Hutchison            a citizen of the    Choctaw    Nation.  
Name of Mother: Lillie Hutchison              a citizen of the    Choctaw    Nation.

Postoffice    Durant, Ind. Ter.

---

### AFFIDAVIT OF MOTHER.

UNITED STATES OF AMERICA, Indian Territory,  
Central    DISTRICT.

I,    Lillie Hutchison    , on oath state that I am    nineteen *(19)*    years of age and a citizen by    intermarriage    , of the    Choctaw    Nation; that I am the lawful wife of    Louis S. Hutchison    , who is a citizen, by    blood    of the    Choctaw    Nation; that a    male    child was born to me on  $9^{th}$    day of    March A.D. , 1903; that said child has been named    Jim Hutchison    , and was living March 4, 1905.

*her x mark*  
Lillie  Hutchison

# Applications for Enrollment of Choctaw Newborn
# Act of 1905   Volume XVIII

Witnesses To Mark:
{ C.K. Hart
{ J.M. Nance

    Subscribed and sworn to before me this   5   day of   Apl. A.D.   , 1905

*(Name Illegible)*
Notary Public.

---

**AFFIDAVIT OF ATTENDING PHYSICIAN OR MID-WIFE.**

UNITED STATES OF AMERICA, Indian Territory,
    Central        DISTRICT.

    I,   B. W. Stover   , a   physician   , on oath state that I attended on Mrs.   Lillie Hutchison   , wife of   Louis S. Hutchison   on the 9   day of March   , 1903; that there was born to her on said date a   male   child; that said child was living March 4, 1905, and is said to have been named Jim Hutchison

                        B. W. Stover

Witnesses To Mark:
{

    Subscribed and sworn to before me this   19   day of   Apl. A.D.   , 1905

*(Name Illegible)*
Notary Public.

---

Choc. New Born 1365
    Bennie Wall[sic]
    (Born Feb. 1, 1905)[sic]

Applications for Enrollment of Choctaw Newborn
Act of 1905   Volume XVIII

**NEW-BORN AFFIDAVIT.**

Number..................

**...Choctaw Enrolling Commission...**

IN THE MATTER OF THE APPLICATION FOR ENROLLMENT, as a citizen of the Choctaw Nation, of Bennie Walls

born on the 1$^{st}$ day of __February__ 190 4

Name of father   Jessie Walls          a citizen of   Choctaw
Nation final enrollment No.   12427
Name of mother   Pink Walls            a citizen of   Choctaw
Nation final enrollment No.   4475

Postoffice   Enterprise IT

**AFFIDAVIT OF MOTHER.**

UNITED STATES OF AMERICA
INDIAN TERRITORY
   Western      DISTRICT

I       Pink Walls               , on oath state that I am 27 years of age and a citizen by marriage of the Choctaw Nation, and as such have been placed upon the final roll of the Choctaw Nation, by the Honorable Secretary of the Interior my final enrollment number being   4475 ; that I am the lawful wife of   Jessie Walls   , who is a citizen of the   Choctaw   Nation, and as such has been placed upon the final roll of said Nation by the Honorable Secretary of the Interior, his final enrollment number being   12427   and that a   Male   child was born to me on the  1$^{st}$ day of   February   190 4; that said child has been named   Bennie Walls   , and is now living.

                                                her
                                        Pink Walls x
Witnesseth.                                   mark

Must be two   ⎱   T.J. Walls
Witnesses who ⎰
are Citizens.      Susan Neal

Subscribed and sworn to before me this   5   day of   Jan   190 5

                                John M. Lentz
                                     Notary Public.

My commission expires:   Nov. 27 1907

# Applications for Enrollment of Choctaw Newborn
# Act of 1905   Volume XVIII

## AFFIDAVIT OF ATTENDING PHYSICIAN OR MIDWIFE

UNITED STATES OF AMERICA
INDIAN TERRITORY
Western   DISTRICT

I,   D. S. Billington   a   practicing physician on oath state that I attended on Mrs. Pink Walls   wife of Jessie Walls on the   1st   day of   February , 190 4, that there was born to her on said date a   male child, that said child is now living, and is said to have been named   Bennie Walls

                          D.S. Billington   *M.D.*

Subscribed and sworn to before me this, the   5   day of January   190 5

WITNESSETH:            John M Lentz   Notary Public.
Must be two witnesses who are citizens { T.J. Walls
                  Susan Neal

We hereby certify that we are well acquainted with   D.S. Billington a   practicing physician   and know   him   to be reputable and of good standing in the community.

    T.J. Walls

    Susan Neal

---

**BIRTH AFFIDAVIT.**
### DEPARTMENT OF THE INTERIOR.
### COMMISSION TO THE FIVE CIVILIZED TRIBES.

**IN RE APPLICATION FOR ENROLLMENT**, as a citizen of the   Choctaw   Nation, of Bennie Walls   , born on the   1st   day of   February , 1905[sic]

Name of Father:  Jessie Walls        a citizen of the   Choctaw   Nation.
Name of Mother: Pink Walls        a citizen of the   Choctaw   Nation.

                Postoffice   Enterprise Ind. Ter.

# Applications for Enrollment of Choctaw Newborn
## Act of 1905   Volume XVIII

**AFFIDAVIT OF MOTHER.**

UNITED STATES OF AMERICA, Indian Territory, }
　　Western　　　　　　　　DISTRICT. }

　　I,　Pink Walls　, on oath state that I am　25　years of age and a citizen by Marriage　, of the　Choctaw　Nation; that I am the lawful wife of　Jessie Walls　, who is a citizen, by Blood　of the　Choctaw　Nation; that a　male　child was born to me on　1$^{st}$　day of　February　, 1905[sic]; that said child has been named　Bennie Walls　, and was living March 4, 1905.

　　　　　　　　　　　　　　　　　　　　　her
　　　　　　　　　　　　　　　　Pink Walls  x
Witnesses To Mark:　　　　　　　　　　　mark
　{ James T. Killebrew　Enterprise IT
　 *(Name Illegible)*　　　- - - - - - -

　　Subscribed and sworn to before me this　27　day of　April　, 1905

My commission　　　　　　　　John M Lentz
Expires Nov 27 1907　　　　　　　　Notary Public.

---

**AFFIDAVIT OF ATTENDING PHYSICIAN OR MID-WIFE.**

UNITED STATES OF AMERICA, Indian Territory, }
　　Western　　　　　　　　DISTRICT. }

　　I,　D.S. Billington　, a Physician　, on oath state that I attended on Mrs.　Pink Walls　, wife of　Jessie Walls　on the　1$^{st}$　day of　February　, 1905; that there was born to her on said date a　male　child; that said child was living March 4, 1905, and is said to have been named　Bennie Walls

　　　　　　　　　　　　　　D$^r$ D.S. Billington
Witnesses To Mark:
　{ James T. Killebrew
　 *(Name Illegible)*

　　Subscribed and sworn to before me this　27　day of　April　, 1905

My commission　　　　　　　　John M Lentz
Expires Nov 27 1907　　　　　　　　Notary Public.

## Applications for Enrollment of Choctaw Newborn
## Act of 1905   Volume XVIII

BIRTH AFFIDAVIT.

## DEPARTMENT OF THE INTERIOR.
## COMMISSION TO THE FIVE CIVILIZED TRIBES.

IN RE APPLICATION FOR ENROLLMENT, as a citizen of the Choctaw Nation, of Bennie Walls, born on the 1st day of February, 1904

Name of Father: Jessie Walls    a citizen of the Choctaw Nation.
Name of Mother: Pink Walls    a citizen of the Choctaw Nation.

Postoffice    Enterprise Ind. Ter.

### AFFIDAVIT OF MOTHER.

UNITED STATES OF AMERICA, Indian Territory,
Western    DISTRICT.

I, Pink Walls, on oath state that I am 25 years of age and a citizen by marriage, of the Choctaw Nation; that I am the lawful wife of Jessie Walls, who is a citizen, by blood of the Choctaw Nation; that a male child was born to me on 1st day of February, 1904; that said child has been named Bennie Walls, and was living March 4, 1905.

her
Pink x Walls
mark

Witnesses To Mark:
 Noah Mouser
 H.A. Billington

Subscribed and sworn to before me this 29 day of August, 1905

My commission            John M Lentz
Expires Nov 27 1907        Notary Public.

### AFFIDAVIT OF ATTENDING PHYSICIAN OR MID-WIFE.

UNITED STATES OF AMERICA, Indian Territory,
Western    DISTRICT.

I, D.S. Billington, a physician, on oath state that I attended on Mrs. Pink Walls, wife of Jessie Walls on the 1st day of February, 1904; that there was born to her on said date a male child; that said child was living March 4, 1905, and is said to have been named Bennie Walls

D.S. Billington

# Applications for Enrollment of Choctaw Newborn
## Act of 1905    Volume XVIII

Witnesses To Mark:
   { Noah Mouser
      H.A. Billington

      Subscribed and sworn to before me this   29   day of     August      , 1905

My commission                           John M Lentz
Expires Nov 27 1907                       Notary Public.

---

                                                                   7-4475

                        Muskogee, Indian Territory, May 4, 1905.

Jesse Walls,
      Enterprise, Indian Territory.

Dear Sir:

      Receipt is hereby acknowledged of the affidavits of Pink Walls and D. S. Billington to the birth of Bennie Walls, son of Jessie and Pink Walls, February 1, 1905, and the same have been filed with our records as an application for the enrollment of said child.

                                    Respectfully,

                                              Chairman.

---

                                                       7-NB-1365.

                     Muskogee, Indian Territory, June 14, 1905.

Jesse Walls,
      Enterprise, Indian Territory.

Dear Sir:

      There is enclosed herewith for execution application for the enrollment of your infant child, Bennie Walls.

      In the affidavits of January 5, 1905, heretofore filed in this office the date of the applicant's birth is given as February 1, 1904, while in those of April 27, 1905, this date is given as February 1, 1905.

      In the enclosed application the date of birth is left blank. Please insert the correct date, and when the affidavits are properly executed return them to this office.

## Applications for Enrollment of Choctaw Newborn
## Act of 1905   Volume XVIII

Respectfully,

Chairman.

DeB--2/1?.

7-NB-1365

Muskogee, Indian Territory, July 25, 1905.

Jesse Walls,
    Enterprise, Indian Territory.

Dear Sir:

    Your attention is called to a communication addressed to you under date of June 14, 1905, with which was enclosed, for execution, application for the enrollment of your infant child, Danie[sic] Walls.

    In said letter you were advised of the fact that in the affidavits of January 5, 1905, heretofore filed in this office, the date of birth of applicant was given as February 1, 1904, while those of April 27, 1905, give the date of birth as February 1, 1905. No reply to this letter has been received.

    You are requested to give this matter your immediate attention as no further action can be taken relative to the enrollment of said child until the evidence requested is supplied.

Respectfully,

Commissioner.

*(Letter below typed as given.)*

7-NB-1365

Enterprise Ind. Ter.

August 18, 1905.

Commission to the Five Civilized Tribes
    Muskogee, Ind. Ter.

Gentlemen:

    The correct date of the Birth Bennie Walls is February 1$^{st}$ 1904

Very Respt

Jessy Walls

# Applications for Enrollment of Choctaw Newborn
## Act of 1905   Volume XVIII

7-NB-1365

Muskogee, Indian Territory, August 24, 1905.

Jesse Walls,
    Enterprise, Indian Territory.

Dear Sir:

    Receipt is hereby acknowledged of your letter of August 8, 1905, stating that the correct date of the birth of your child Bennie Walls is February 1, 1904.

    In reply you are advised that it will be necessary for you to have the inclosed affidavits executed by the mother and the physician show the correct date of the birth of your child Bennie Walls before further consideration can be given the application for enrollment. Please give this matter your immediate attention.

                        Respectfully,

B C                                                                              Commissioner.

---

7-NB-1365.

Muskogee, Indian Territory, September 5, 1905.

Jesse Walls,
    Enterprise, Indian Territory.

Dear Sir:

    Receipt is hereby acknowledged of the affidavits of Pink Walls, the mother, and D. S. Billington, the attending physician, to the birth of your infant child, Bennie Walls, February 1, 1904, offered in support of the application for the enrollment of said child as a citizen by blood of the Choctaw Nation.

    You are advised that said affidavits have been filed with the record in this case.

                        Respectfully,

                                        Acting Commissioner.

# Applications for Enrollment of Choctaw Newborn
## Act of 1905   Volume XVIII

Choctaw NB 1365

Muskogee, Indian Territory, October 13, 1905.

Jess[sic] Walls,
    Enterprise, Indian Territory.

Dear Sir:

    Receipt is hereby acknowledged of your letter of October 6, asking if Bennie Walls is approved and if you may file for him before you receive notice of his approval.

    In reply to your letter you are advised that the name of Bennie Walls has not yet been placed upon a schedule of new born citizens of the Choctaw Nation, but you will be notified as soon as this office is advised of the approval of his enrollment. Pending such approval no selection of allotment can be made for said child.

                Respectfully,

                              Commissioner.

---

7-NB-1365

Muskogee, Indian Territory, February 28, 1906.

Jess[sic] Walls,
    Enterprise, Indian Territory.

Dear Sir:

    Receipt is hereby acknowledged of your letter of February 20, 1906, asking if the enrollment of your child Bennie Walls has been approved.

    In reply to your letter you are advised that the name of your child Bennie Walls has been placed upon a schedule of new born citizens of the Choctaw Nation which has been forwarded the Secretary of the Interior, but this office has not yet been notified of Departmental action thereon. You will be notified when the enrollment of this child is approved by the Secretary of the Interior.

                Respectfully,

                            Acting Commissioner.

# Applications for Enrollment of Choctaw Newborn
## Act of 1905   Volume XVIII

Choc. New Born 1366
    Mack Ott
    (Born March 8, 1904)

        Cancelled and transferred to
            Chickasaw No. N.B. 516.

**New Born**
Choctaw                        7-NB. 1366

Mack Ott
Born March 8 1904

Act of March 3 - 1905

Cancelled and transferred
to Chickasaw No. N.B. 516.

---

Choc. New Born 1367
    Edward Oakes
    (Born May 31, 1903)

        Cancelled and transferred to
        Choc. N.B. 1126.

**New Born**
Choctaw                        7-NB. 1367

Edward Oakes
Born May 31 - 1903

Act of Congress approved Mar 3 - 05

Cancelled and transferred
to Choctaw N.B. 1126.

Applications for Enrollment of Choctaw Newborn
Act of 1905   Volume XVIII

Choc. New Born 1368
    Lena Bell Perkins
    (Born Sep. 28, 1904)
    Laura Perkins
    (Born Apr. 5, 1905) Born subsequent
        to March 4, 1905.

---

1368

## NEW BORN
### CHOCTAW
### ENROLLMENT

LENA BELL PERKINS
(BORN SEPTEMBER 28, 1904)

LAURA PERKINS
(BORN APRIL 5, 1905) BORN SUBSEQUENT
TO MARCH 4, 1905.

As Citizen of the
CHOCTAW NATION
Act of Congress
Approved March 3, 1905

LAURA PERKINS TRANSFERRED TO N. B. 382 UNDER ACT OF APRIL 26, 1906.
NO. 2  DECLINE TO RECEIVER[sic] OR CONSIDER NOVEMBER 16, 1905
COPY OF DECISION FORWARDED ATTORNEYS FOR CHOCTAW AND CHICKASAW NATIONS.

NOVEMBER 16, 1905
COPY OF DECISION FORWARDED APPLICANT
NOVEMBER 16, 1905
RECORD FORWARDED DEPARTMENT. NOVEMBER 16, 1905
ACTION APPROVED BY SECRETARY OF INTERIOR
JANUARY 2, 1906
COPY OF DECISION FORWARDED ATTORNEYS FOR CHOCTAW AND CHICKASAW NATIONS. JAN 22, 1906
NOTICE OF DEPARTMENTAL ACTION MAILED APPLICANT'S FATHER. JANUARY 22, 1906.

NOTICE OF DEPARTMENTAL ACTION MAILED APPLICANT'S FATHER. JANUARY 22, 1906.

1368

## Applications for Enrollment of Choctaw Newborn
### Act of 1905 Volume XVIII

BIRTH AFFIDAVIT.

## Department of the Interior,
COMMISSION TO THE FIVE CIVILIZED TRIBES.

IN RE APPLICATION FOR ENROLLMENT, as a citizen of the Choctaw Nation, of Lena Bell Perkins, born on the 28th day of September, 190 3

Name of Father: Noah Perkins     a citizen of the Choctaw Nation.
Name of Mother: Nellie Perkins     a citizen of the Choctaw Nation.

Post-Office: Caney, Ind. Ter.

### AFFIDAVIT OF MOTHER.

UNITED STATES OF AMERICA,
   INDIAN TERRITORY,
Central     District.

I, Nellie Perkins, on oath state that I am 23 years of age and a citizen by Blood, of the Choctaw Nation; that I am the lawful wife of Noah Perkins, who is a citizen, by Blood of the Choctaw Nation; that a girl child was born to me on 28th day of September, 190 3, that said child has been named Lena Bell Perkins, and is now living.

Nellie Perkins

WITNESSES TO MARK:

Subscribed and sworn to before me this 16th day of January, 190 .

Sol. J. Homer
*Notary Public.*

### AFFIDAVIT OF ATTENDING PHYSICIAN OR MID-WIFE.

UNITED STATES OF AMERICA,
   INDIAN TERRITORY,
Central     District.

birth
I, Serena Perkins, a n attendant at, on oath state that I attended on Mrs. Nellie Perkins, wife of Noah Perkins on the 28th day of September, 190 3; that there was born to her on said date a Female child; that said child is now living and is said to have been named Lena Bell Perkins

Applications for Enrollment of Choctaw Newborn
Act of 1905 Volume XVIII

Serena Perkins

WITNESSES TO MARK:

Subscribed and sworn to before me this 16th day of January , 190 .

Sol. J. Homer
*Notary Public.*

# NEW BORN AFFIDAVIT

No ............

## CHOCTAW ENROLLING COMMISSION

IN THE MATTER OF THE APPLICATION FOR ENROLLMENT as a citizen of the Choctaw Nation, of Lena Perkins born on the 28 day of December[sic] 190 4[sic]

Name of father Noah Perkins    a citizen of Choctaw Nation, final enrollment No. 9720
Name of mother Nellie Perkins    a citizen of Choctaw Nation, final enrollment No. 9721

Caney I.T.    Postoffice.

**AFFIDAVIT OF MOTHER**

UNITED STATES OF AMERICA
INDIAN TERRITORY
DISTRICT Central

I Nellie Perkins , on oath state that I am 22 years of age and a citizen by blood of the Choctaw Nation, and as such have been placed upon the final roll of the Choctaw Nation, by the Honorable Secretary of the Interior my final enrollment number being 9721 ; that I am the lawful wife of Noah Perkins , who is a citizen of the Choctaw Nation, and as such has been placed upon the final roll of said Nation by the Honorable Secretary of the Interior, his final enrollment number being 9720 and that a Female child was born to me on the 28 day of December 190 4; that said child has been named Lena Perkins , and is now living.

Nellie Perkins

# Applications for Enrollment of Choctaw Newborn
## Act of 1905   Volume XVIII

WITNESSETH:

Must be two witnesses who are citizens { Marcus Washington
Allington Jones

Subscribed and sworn to before me this, the 16 day of February , 190 5

A Denton Phillips
Notary Public.

My Commission Expires:

---

*Affidavit of Attending Physician or Midwife*

UNITED STATES OF AMERICA,
INDIAN TERRITORY,
Central DISTRICT

I, Sallie Lewis a mid wife on oath state that I attended on Mrs. Nellie Perkins wife of Noah Perkins on the 28 day of December[sic] , 190 4[sic], that there was born to her on said date a Female child, that said child is now living, and is said to have been named Lena Perkins

Sallie Lewis      M. D.

Subscribed and sworn to before me this the 15 day of February 1905

A Denton Phillips
Notary Public.

WITNESSETH:

Must be two witnesses who are citizens and know the child. { J.A. Lewis
N.A. Perkins

We hereby certify that we are well acquainted with Sallie Lewis a Midwife and know her to be reputable and of good standing in the community.

Must be two citizen witnesses. { J.A. Wade
Loring Robinson

## Applications for Enrollment of Choctaw Newborn
## Act of 1905   Volume XVIII

BIRTH AFFIDAVIT.

### DEPARTMENT OF THE INTERIOR.
### COMMISSION TO THE FIVE CIVILIZED TRIBES.

IN RE APPLICATION FOR ENROLLMENT, as a citizen of the   Choctaw   Nation, of Lena Bell Perkins   , born on the   28   day of   Sept   , 1903

Name of Father: Noah Perkins   a citizen of the   Choctaw   Nation.
Name of Mother: Nellie Perkins   a citizen of the   Choctaw   Nation.

Postoffice   Caney, Ind. Ter.

### AFFIDAVIT OF MOTHER.

UNITED STATES OF AMERICA, Indian Territory,
Central   DISTRICT.

I,   Nellie Perkins   , on oath state that I am   23   years of age and a citizen by   blood   , of the   Choctaw   Nation; that I am the lawful wife of   Noah Perkins   , who is a citizen, by  blood   of the   Choctaw   Nation; that a female   child was born to me on   28   day of   September   , 1903; that said child has been named   Lena Bell Perkins   , and was living March 4, 1905.

Nellie Perkins

Witnesses To Mark:
{

Subscribed and sworn to before me this   19   day of   June   , 1905

R.R. Hall
Notary Public.

### AFFIDAVIT OF ATTENDING PHYSICIAN OR MID-WIFE.

UNITED STATES OF AMERICA, Indian Territory,
Central   DISTRICT.

I,   Serena Perkins   , a   Midwife   , on oath state that I attended on Mrs.   Nellie Perkins   , wife of   Noah Perkins   on the   28   day of   September , 1903; that there was born to her on said date a   female   child; that said child was living March 4, 1905, and is said to have been named   Lena Bell Perkins

Serena Perkins

Witnesses To Mark:
{

## Applications for Enrollment of Choctaw Newborn
## Act of 1905   Volume XVIII

Subscribed and sworn to before me this 19<sup>th</sup> day of June , 1905

R.R. Hall
Notary Public.

---

*(The letter below typed as given.)*

(COPY)

7-N.B. 1368.

Commission to Five Civilized Tribes,

Dear Gentlemen:

The affidavits you received on April 25, 1905 from the Principal Chief of the Choctaw Nation was to the birth of Lena Bell Perkins, daughter of Noah and Nellie Perkins, born September 28, 1903,-- the name Lena Belle is the name of one child.

In having the affidavits executed care should be exercised to see that all names are written in full, as they appear in the body of the affidavits and in the event filled by Sol J. Homer, Notery Bublic at Caddo, I. T. made mistake in dating, said December 28, 1904. By that is mistake, September 28, 1903, is correct date the child was born on. After I sent the affidavits to the Principal Chief of the Choctaw Nation, I heard that it was not right, that it ought to be sent to the Commission, so I went and had another affidavits filled by Notary Bublic at Caney, and in giving the correct date which was different from the firs date caused missunderstanding.

But remember September 28, 1903, was the birth of Lena Belle Perkins, name of one child.

You said the affidavits was received three days after the expiration of sixty days. It ought to have reached you before because I had the first affidavits filled and sent to the Principal Chief in month of January 1905.

I hope you will understand this letter and have the child enrolled for us.

From yours respected friend

Noah Perkins,

C oney, I. T.

# Applications for Enrollment of Choctaw Newborn
## Act of 1905 Volume XVIII

7 N.B. 1368.

Muskogee, Indian Territory, May 8, 1905.

Noah Perkins,
    Caney, Indian Territory.

Dear Sir:

    Receipt is hereby acknowledged of the affidavits of Nellie Perkins and Serena Perkins to the birth of Lena Bell Perkins, September 28, 1903.

    It appears from our records that application has heretofore been made to this Commission for the enrollment of Lena Perkins, child of Noah and Nellie Perkins, born December 28, 1904.

    You are requested to advise this office you have two children, one Lena Bell Perkins born September 28, 1903, and the other, Lena Perkins., born December 28, 1904.

    Respectfully,

    Commissioner in Charge.

---

7-N.B. 1368.

Muskogee, Indian Territory, May 15, 1905.

Noah Perkins,
    Caney, Indian Territory.

Dear Sir:

    Receipt is hereby acknowledged of your letter without date in the matter of the enrollment of Lena, or Lena Belle Perkins, in which you state that the application of September 1904, should be Laura Perkins instead of Lena, and you presume this change can be made in this office.

    You are advised that on April 25, 1905, there were received from the Principal Chief of the Choctaw Nation affidavits to the birth of Lena Perkins, daughter of Noah and Nellie Perkins, December 28, 1904.

    There were also received at the General Office of the Commission, May 5, 1905, in an envelope postmarked Caney, Indian Territory, and bearing date May 4, 1905, affidavits to the birth of Lena Bell Perkins, daughter of Noah and Nellie Perkins, September 28, 1903.

## Applications for Enrollment of Choctaw Newborn
## Act of 1905   Volume XVIII

These affidavits were received three days after the expiration of the sixty days provided by the act of Congress of March 3, 1905, within which the Commission could receive applications for the enrollment of children born to citizens of the Choctaw and Chickasaw Nations, but it was believed that Lena and Lena Belle Perkins was the same child, and that an error had been made in the date of birth, on May 8, 1905, a letter was addressed to you asking an explanation.

You are now advised that it is not very clear from your letter whether you have one child named Laura Perkins born September 28, 1903, and one named Lena Belle Perkins born December 28, 1904, but if this is correct you are advised that the affidavits to the birth of Lena Belle Perkins were forwarded after the expiration of the time within which the Commission could receive applications for the enrollment of children and it is therefore without authority to enroll said child.

Respectfully,

Chairman.

---

7 N.B. 1368.

Muskogee, Indian Territory, June 1, 1905.

Noah Perkins,
    Caney, Indian Territory.

Dear Sir:

Receipt is hereby acknowledged of your letter without date relative to the enrollment of your child, Lena Belle Perkins.

It is not yet clear from your letter whether you have one child named Lena Bell and another child named Laura Perkins, or whether this is the same child and the error was in her name.

You are therefore requested to advise this office at once whether you have two children, on named Lena Bell Perkins and the other Laura Perkins, or only one child, and it you have only one child, please state the correct name of said child.

This matter should receive your immediate attention.

Respectfully,

Commissioner in Charge.

# Applications for Enrollment of Choctaw Newborn
## Act of 1905   Volume XVIII

*(The letter below typed as given.)*

(COPY)   7-N.B. 1368.

June 3, 1905

Commission to the Five Civilized Tribes

Sir.

I have one child names Lena Bell Perkins Born on Sept. 28, 1903.
And also one name Laura Perkins-Born April 5, 1905.

Ypurs res.

Nosh Perkins

---

7 NB 1368

Muskogee, Indian Territory, June 9, 1905.

Noah Perkins,
    Kaney[sic], Indian Territory.

Dear Sir:

Receipt is hereby acknowledged of your letter of June 3, 1905, giving he names and dates of the birth of your two children Lena Bell and Laura Perkins and this information has been made a matter of record.

Respectfully,

Chairman.

---

7-NB-1368.

Muskogee, Indian Territory, June 14, 1905.

Noah Perkins,
    Caney, Indian Territory.

Dear Sir:

There is enclosed herewith for execution application for the enrollment of your infant child, Lena Bell Perkins, born September 28, 1903. The affidavits heretofore filed in this office show that the applicant was living on February 16, 1905, and in order that the child be enrolled it is necessary for her to be living on March 4, 1905.

## Applications for Enrollment of Choctaw Newborn
## Act of 1905   Volume XVIII

The mother's affidavit of February 16, 1905, and the midwife's of February 15, 1905, above referred to give the applicant as Lena Perkins and the date of birth as December 28, 1904, while the affidavits of January 16, 1905, give her name as Lena Bell Perkins and the date of birth as September 28, 1903.

In the enclosed application the name and date of birth given in the latter affidavits are inserted in compliance with your letter of June 3, 1905. You will please have these affidavits executed and return them promptly to this office as no further action can be taken until they have been filed.

In having these affidavits executed care should be exercised to see that all names are written in full, as they appear in the body of the affidavit, and in the event either of the persons signing the affidavits is unable to write, signature by mark must be attested by two witnesses. Each affidavit must be executed before a Notary Public and the notarial seal and signature of the officer must be attached to each separate affidavit.

Respectfully,

Chairman.

DeB--DeB--1/14.

---

7 NB 1368

Muskogee, Indian Territory, June 21, 1905.

Noah Perkins,
    Caney, Indian Territory.

Dear Sir:

Receipt is hereby acknowledged of the affidavits of Nellie Perkins and Serena Perkins to the birth of Lena Bell Perkins, daughter of Noah and Nellie Perkins, September 28, 1903, and the same have been filed with our records in the matter of the enrollment of said child.

Respectfully,

Chairman.

# Applications for Enrollment of Choctaw Newborn
## Act of 1905  Volume XVIII

7-NB-1368

Muskogee, Indian Territory, February 2, 1906.

Noah Perkins,
    Caney, Indian Territory.

Dear Sir:

    Receipt is hereby acknowledged of your letter of January 1906, in which you ask if your child Lena Bell Perkins has been enrolled and if you can file on land for her now.

    In reply to your letter you are advised that Lena Bell Perkins has been enrolled as a new born citizen of the Choctaw Nation and her enrollment as such approved by the Secretary of the Interior and selection of allotment can now be made for her in accordance with the rules and regulations governing the selection of allotments and designation of homesteads in the Choctaw and Chickasaw Nations.

                  Respectfully,

                              Acting Commissioner.

---

*Noah Perkins*
*Caney I.T.*

| COMMISSION TO FIVE TRIBES | | | |
|---|---|---|---|
| No. | Received | Book | Page |
| 1905 | MAY 5 1905 | | |

*Commission To The Five Civilized Tribes*
*Muscogee*
*Ind. Ter.*

Applications for Enrollment of Choctaw Newborn
Act of 1905   Volume XVIII

Choc. New Born 1369
          Harriet Peter
          (Born Feb. 20, 1903)

**NEW-BORN AFFIDAVIT.**

Number.................

## Choctaw Enrolling Commission.

IN THE MATTER OF THE APPLICATION FOR ENROLLMENT, as a citizen of the Choctaw   Nation, of          Harriet Peter

born on the   20   day of   Feb       190 3

Name of father   Thompson Peter          a citizen of   Choctaw
Nation final enrollment No   11543
Name of mother   Sarah Peter              a citizen of   Choctaw
Nation final enrollment No   11286

                    Postoffice    Atoka IT

**AFFIDAVIT OF MOTHER.**

UNITED STATES OF AMERICA,  ⎫
   INDIAN TERRITORY,         ⎬
   Cent       DISTRICT       ⎭

I         Sara[sic] Peter              on oath state that I am   22   years of age and a citizen by   blood     of the   Choctaw     Nation, and as such have been placed upon the final roll of the    Choctaw    Nation, by the Honorable Secretary of the Interior my final enrollment number being    11286     ; that I am the lawful wife of     Thompson Peter          , who is a citizen of the    Choctaw    Nation, and as such has been placed upon the final roll of said Nation by the Honorable Secretary of the Interior, his final enrollment number being   11543    and that a    Female    child was born to me on the   20   day of   Feb      190 3 ; that said child has been named    Harriet Peter        , and is now living.

                                      Sara x Peter
                                          mark

WITNESSETH:
 Must be two   ⎫  Calvin Lewis
 Witnesses who ⎬
 are Citizens. ⎭  JW Jones

       Subscribed and sworn to before me this    19   day of   Jan       190 5

                              JW Jones
                                      Notary Public.

My commission expires    Oct 14$^{th}$ 1907

Applications for Enrollment of Choctaw Newborn
Act of 1905   Volume XVIII

## Affidavit of Attending Physician or Midwife.

UNITED STATES OF AMERICA }
INDIAN TERRITORY
  Cent           DISTRICT

I, Kitsy Wilson    a    midwife on oath state that I attended on Mrs. Sarah Peter   wife of   Thompson Peter on the   20   day of   Feb   , 190 3 , that there was born to her on said date a   Female child, that said child is now living, and is said to have been named   Harriet Peter

                              her
                      Kitsy x Wilson      Midwife
                          mark

Subscribed and sworn to before me this, the   19   day of   Jan   190 5

                      JW Jones
                        Notary Public.

WITNESSETH:
Must be two witnesses   { I.A. Folsom
who are citizens and         her
know the child.              Batsey x Frazier
                                 mark

We hereby certify that we are well acquainted with   Kitsey Wilson   a   midwife   and know   her   to be reputable and of good standing in the community.

                    Eastmon Jacob
                    Petter[sic] Hokuby

BIRTH AFFIDAVIT.

### DEPARTMENT OF THE INTERIOR.
### COMMISSION TO THE FIVE CIVILIZED TRIBES.

IN RE APPLICATION FOR ENROLLMENT, as a citizen of the   Choctaw   Nation, of   Harriet Peter   , born on the 20th   day of   February   , 1903

Name of Father: Thompson Peter     a citizen of the   Choctaw   Nation.
Name of Mother: Sarah Peter        a citizen of the   Choctaw   Nation.

                Postoffice    Atoka, I. T.

# Applications for Enrollment of Choctaw Newborn
## Act of 1905   Volume XVIII

### AFFIDAVIT OF MOTHER.

UNITED STATES OF AMERICA, Indian Territory, }
Central                    DISTRICT.

I, Sarah Peter, on oath state that I am 23 years of age and a citizen by blood, of the Choctaw Nation; that I am the lawful wife of Thompson Peter, who is a citizen, by blood of the Choctaw Nation; that a female child was born to me on 20$^{th}$ day of February, 1903; that said child has been named Harriet Peter, and was living March 4, 1905.

                        her
                    Sarah x Peter
Witnesses To Mark:        mark
{ Richard Shanafelt
{ M.C. Blair

Subscribed and sworn to before me this 1$^{st}$ day of May, 1905

                W.H. Angell
                    Notary Public.

---

### AFFIDAVIT OF ATTENDING PHYSICIAN OR MID-WIFE.

UNITED STATES OF AMERICA, Indian Territory, }
Central                    DISTRICT.

I, Kitsy Wilson, a midwife, on oath state that I attended on Mrs. Sarah Peter, wife of Thompson Peter on the 20$^{th}$ day of February, 1903; that there was born to her on said date a female child; that said child was living March 4, 1905, and is said to have been named Harriet Peter

                        her
                    Kitsy x Wilson
Witnesses To Mark:        mark
{ Richard Shanafelt
{ M.C. Blair

Subscribed and sworn to before me this 1$^{st}$ day of May, 1905

                W.H. Angell
                    Notary Public.

## Applications for Enrollment of Choctaw Newborn
## Act of 1905   Volume XVIII

Choc. New Born 1370
  Rena Shaw
  (Born Dec. 19, 1904)

**NEW-BORN AFFIDAVIT.**

Number..................

**...Choctaw Enrolling Commission...**

IN THE MATTER OF THE APPLICATION FOR ENROLLMENT, as a citizen of the Choctaw   Nation, of   Rena Shaw

born on the 19$^{th}$   day of   December   190 4

Name of father  Keith Shaw           a citizen of   Choctaw
Nation final enrollment No. 3561       *Shaw*
Name of mother  Sena Thompson   *now*   a citizen of   Choctaw
Nation final enrollment No. 3064

                              Postoffice       Idabel IT

**AFFIDAVIT OF MOTHER.**

UNITED STATES OF AMERICA
INDIAN TERRITORY
   Central   DISTRICT

I   Sena Thompson   , on oath state that I am 25 years of age and a citizen by  blood  of the  Choctaw   Nation, and as such have been placed upon the final roll of the   Choctaw  Nation, by the Honorable Secretary of the Interior my final enrollment number being   3064 ; that I am the lawful wife of   Keith Shaw  , who is a citizen of the   Choctaw    Nation, and as such has been placed upon the final roll of said Nation by the Honorable Secretary of the Interior, his final enrollment number being   3561   and that a   female    child was born to me on the 19$^{th}$   day of   December   190 4; that said child has been named   Rena Shaw  , and is now living.

                              her
                         Sena x Thompson
Witnesseth.                   mark
  Must be two  ⎫  Arlington King
  Witnesses who ⎬
  are Citizens. ⎭  Frank M$^c$Afee

# Applications for Enrollment of Choctaw Newborn
## Act of 1905  Volume XVIII

Subscribed and sworn to before me this   21   day of   Jan   190 5

W A Shoney
Notary Public.

My commission expires:   Jan 10, 1909

---

## AFFIDAVIT OF ATTENDING PHYSICIAN OR MIDWIFE

UNITED STATES OF AMERICA
INDIAN TERRITORY
   Central   DISTRICT

I,   Bessie Shaw   a   Midwife on oath state that I attended on Mrs._____wife of   Keith Shaw   on the   19$^{th}$   day of   December  , 190 4 , that there was born to her on said date a female   child, that said child is now living, and is said to have been named   Rena Shaw

her
Bessie Shaw  x
mark

Subscribed and sworn to before me this, the   21$^{st}$   day of Jan   190 5

WITNESSETH:   W.A. Shoney   Notary Public.

Must be two witnesses who are citizens
{ Arlington King
  Frank M$^c$Afee

We hereby certify that we are well acquainted with   Bessie Shaw   a   midwife   and know   her   to be reputable and of good standing in the community.

Arlington King   _____

Frank McAfee    _____

---

BIRTH AFFIDAVIT.

## DEPARTMENT OF THE INTERIOR.
## COMMISSION TO THE FIVE CIVILIZED TRIBES.

---

IN RE APPLICATION FOR ENROLLMENT, as a citizen of the   Choctaw   Nation, of   Rena Shaw   , born on the   19 day of   Dec  , 1904

Name of Father: Keith Shaw         a citizen of the   Choctaw   Nation.

*Sena Shaw*
Name of Mother: Sena Thompson   *now*   a citizen of the   Choctaw   Nation.

# Applications for Enrollment of Choctaw Newborn
# Act of 1905    Volume XVIII

Postoffice   Idabel I T

### AFFIDAVIT OF MOTHER.

UNITED STATES OF AMERICA, Indian Territory, }
............................................................ DISTRICT. }

I, Sena Thompson *now* Sena Shaw, on oath state that I am 25 years of age and a citizen by blood, of the Choctaw Nation; that I am the lawful wife of Keith Shaw, who is a citizen, by blood of the Choctaw Nation; that a female child was born to me on 19 day of Dec, 1904; that said child has been named Rena Shaw, and was living March 4, 1905.

                          her
                       Sena x Thompson *now Sena Shaw*

Witnesses To Mark:                mark
{ W.E. Frazier
{ CA Denison

Subscribed and sworn to before me this 7 day of June, 1905

                    G.G. Merry
                    Notary Public.

### AFFIDAVIT OF ATTENDING PHYSICIAN OR MID-WIFE.

UNITED STATES OF AMERICA, Indian Territory, }
............................................................ DISTRICT. }

I, Bessie Shaw, a midwife, on oath state that I attended on Mrs. Sena Thompson *now Sena Shaw*, wife of Keith Shaw on the 19 day of Dec, 1904; that there was born to her on said date a female child; that said child was living March 4, 1905, and is said to have been named Rena Shaw

                    her
                Bessie x Shaw

Witnesses To Mark:              mark
{ W.E. Frazier
{ CA Denison

Subscribed and sworn to before me this 7 day of June, 1905

                  G.G. Merry
                  Notary Public.

# Applications for Enrollment of Choctaw Newborn
## Act of 1905   Volume XVIII

7--NB--1370

Muskogee, Indian Territory, June 1, 1905.

Keith Shaw,
    Idabel, Indian Territory.

Dear Sir:

    There is enclosed you herewith for execution application for the enrollment of your infant child, Rena Shaw, born December 19, 1904.

    The affidavits heretofore filed with the Commission show the child was living January 21, 1905. It is necessary, for the child to be enrolled, that she was living on March 4, 1905.

    In having these affidavits executed care should be exercised to see that all names are written in full, as they appear in the body of the affidavit, and in the event that either of the persons signing the affidavit are unable to write, signatures by mark must be attested by two witnesses. Each affidavit must be executed before a Notary Public and the notarial seal and signature of the officer must be attached to each separate affidavit.

    This matter should receive your immediate attention as no further action can be taken relative to the enrollment of said child until the Commission has been furnished with these affidavits.

    Respectfully,

Enc. FVK-3

Commissioner in Charge.

---

7 NB 1370

Muskogee, Indian Territory, June 12, 1905.

Keith Shaw,
    Idabel, Indian Territory.

Dear Sir:

    Receipt is hereby acknowledged of the affidavits of Sena Thompson and Bessie Shaw to the birth of Rena Shaw, daughter of Keith Shaw and Sena Thompson, December 19, 1904, and the same have been filed in the matter of the enrollment of said child.

    Respectfully,

Chairman.

# Applications for Enrollment of Choctaw Newborn
## Act of 1905 Volume XVIII

Choc. New Born 1371
Rosie Lee Shield
(Born Nov. 17, 1904)

# NEW BORN AFFIDAVIT

No ...........

## CHOCTAW ENROLLING COMMISSION

IN THE MATTER OF THE APPLICATION FOR ENROLLMENT as a citizen of the Choctaw Nation, of Rosie Lee Shealds[sic] born on the 17th day of November 190 4

Name of father  Jack Shealds   a citizen of ———— Nation, final enrollment No. ————
Name of mother  Nancy Shealds   a citizen of   Choctaw   Nation, final enrollment No. 11936

Atoka I.T.              Postoffice.

### AFFIDAVIT OF MOTHER

UNITED STATES OF AMERICA }
INDIAN TERRITORY }
DISTRICT  Central }

I   Nancy Shealds  , on oath state that I am  39  years of age and a citizen by  blood  of the  Choctaw  Nation, and as such have been placed upon the final roll of the  Choctaw  Nation, by the Honorable Secretary of the Interior my final enrollment number being  11936  ; that I am the lawful wife of  Jack Shealds  , who is a citizen of the  ————  Nation, and as such has been placed upon the final roll of said Nation by the Honorable Secretary of the Interior, his final enrollment number being  ———  and that a  Female  child was born to me on the  17th  day of November  190 4; that said child has been named  Rosie Lee Shealds  , and is now living.

                                her
WITNESSETH:                    Nancy x Shealds
Must be two witnesses { Ben Moses    mark
who are citizens      { Eddie Wilson

## Applications for Enrollment of Choctaw Newborn
## Act of 1905   Volume XVIII

Subscribed and sworn to before me this, the   2$^d$   day of   March   , 190 5

A.E. Folsom
Notary Public.

My Commission Expires:
Jan 9-1909

---

## AFFIDAVIT OF ATTENDING PHYSICIAN OR MIDWIFE

UNITED STATES OF AMERICA
INDIAN TERRITORY
  Central      DISTRICT

I,   Jack Shealds   *The ~~a~~ Father*
on oath state that I attended on Mrs.   Nancy Shealds   ~~my~~ wife of   Jack Shealds
on the   17$^{th}$   day of   November , 190 4, that there was born to her on said date a   Female
child, that said child is now living, and is said to have been named   Rosie Lee Shealds

Jack Shields *The Father*   ~~M.D~~.

WITNESSETH:
Must be two witnesses who are citizens and know the child.
{ Ben Moses
  Eddie Wilson

Subscribed and sworn to before me this, the   2$^d$   day of   March       190 5

A E Folsom   Notary Public.

We hereby certify that we are well acquainted with   Jack Shealds
~~a~~   The Father   and know   him   to be reputable and of good standing in the community.

{ Ben Moses
  Eddie Wilson

## Applications for Enrollment of Choctaw Newborn
## Act of 1905   Volume XVIII

*(The affidavit below types as given.)*

DEPARTMENT OF THE INTERIOR
COMMISSION

DEPARTMENT OF THE INTERIOR
COMMISSION TO THE FIVE CIVILIZED TRIBES

I Charles Moses of lawful age being first duly sworn, depose and say that I am a citizen by blood of the Choctaw Nation, and reside at Atoka I T, that I am acquainted with Nancy Shields and Jack Shields, that Nancy Shields is the Mother and Jack Shields is the Father, of Rosa Lee Shields; That Rosa Lee Shields, was born on *or about* the 17th day of Novemember, *1904* and that she was living on the 4th day of March 1905, that he lives in the same neighborhood and knows the facts, as above *(illegible)*, and from his own knowledge.

Charles Moses

Subscribed in my presense and sworn to before me this the 2nd day of Nov, 1o5.

EA Newman
Notary Public

---

**BIRTH AFFIDAVIT.**

DEPARTMENT OF THE INTERIOR.
**COMMISSION TO THE FIVE CIVILIZED TRIBES.**

IN RE APPLICATION FOR ENROLLMENT, as a citizen of the   Choctaw   Nation, of Rosie Lee Shield   , born on the   17   day of   Nov   , 1904

Name of Father: Jack Shield         a citizen of the   ———Nation.
Name of Mother: Nancy Shield     a citizen of the   Choctaw   Nation.

Postoffice   Atoka, Ind. Ter.

**AFFIDAVIT OF MOTHER.**

UNITED STATES OF AMERICA, Indian Territory,
Central        DISTRICT.

I, Nancy Shield   , on oath state that I am   39   years of age and a citizen by blood   , of the   Choctaw   Nation; that I am the lawful wife of   Jack Shield   , who is a citizen, by   ———   of the   ———   Nation; that a   female   child was

## Applications for Enrollment of Choctaw Newborn
## Act of 1905   Volume XVIII

born to me on   17   day of   Nov   , 1904; that said child has been named   Rosie Lee Shield   , and was living March 4, 1905.

her<br>Nancy x Shields[sic]<br>mark

Witnesses To Mark:
{ JM Humphreys
{ EA Newman

Subscribed and sworn to before me this   2<sup>nd</sup>   day of   November   , 1905

EA Newman<br>Notary Public.

---

**AFFIDAVIT OF ATTENDING PHYSICIAN OR MID-WIFE.**

UNITED STATES OF AMERICA, Indian Territory,
   Central               DISTRICT.

I,   Bill Colbert   , a ................, on oath state that I attended on Mrs.   Nancy Shield   , wife of   Jack Shield   on the   17 day of   Nov   , 1904; that there was born to her on said date a   female   child; that said child was living March 4, 1905, and is said to have been named   Rosie Lee Shield  *and there was no one present except Jack Shields*[sic] *and myself*.

Bill Colbert

Witnesses To Mark:
{ EA Newman

Subscribed and sworn to before me this   2<sup>nd</sup>   day of   November   , 1905

EA Newman<br>Notary Public.

---

7--NB--1371

Muskogee, Indian Territory, June 1, 1905.

Jack Shield,
   Atoka, Indian Territory.

Dear Sir:

There is enclosed you herewith for execution application for the enrollment of your infant child, Rosie Lee Shield, born November 17, 1904.

# Applications for Enrollment of Choctaw Newborn
# Act of 1905   Volume XVIII

The affidavits heretofore filed with the Commission show the child was living on March 2, 1905. It is necessary, for the child to be enrolled, that she was living on March 4, 1905.

It further appears from the affidavits heretofore filed that you attended your wife at the birth of this child, and you are advised that before said child can be finally enrolled, it will be necessary that you furnish the Commission with the affidavits of two disinterested persons to the effect that said child was born November 17, 1904, and was living on March 4, 1905.

In having these affidavits executed care should be exercised to see that all names are written in full, as they appear in the body of the affidavit, and in the event that either of the persons signing the affidavit are unable to write, signatures by mark must be attested by two witnesses. Each affidavit must be executed before a Notary Public and the notarial seal and signature of the officer must be attached to each separate affidavit.

    Respectfully,

    Chairman.

Enc. FVK-4

---

7-NB-1371

Muskogee, Indian Territory, July 28, 1905.

Jack Shield,
    Atoka, Indian Territory.

Dear Sir:

Your attention is called to a communication addressed to you by the Commission to the Five Civilized Tribes under date of June 1, 1905, with which there was inclosed for execution application for the enrollment of your infant child, Rosie Lee Shields[sic], born November 17, 1904.

In said letter you were advised that the affidavits heretofore filed with the Commission to the Five Civilized Tribes, show the child was living March 2, 1905, and that it was necessary for her to be enrolled that she was living March 4, 1905; you were further advised that if you attended your wife at the time of the birth of the applicant, that it was necessary for you to supply the affidavits of two disinterested persons to the effect that said child was born, November 17, 1904, and was living March 4, 1905. No reply to this letter has been received.

The matter should receive your immediate attention as no further action can be taken relative to the enrollment of said child until the evidence requested is supplied.

# Applications for Enrollment of Choctaw Newborn
## Act of 1905   Volume XVIII

Respectfully,

Commissioner.

7-NB-1371

Muskogee, Indian Territory, November 7, 1905.

E. A. Newman,
    Atoka, Indian Territory.

Dear Sir:

    Receipt is hereby acknowledged of your letter of November 2, 1905, inclosing affidavits of Nancy Shields[sic], Bill Colbert, and Charles Moses to the birth of Rosie Lee Shields, child of Jack and Nancy Shields and the same have been filed with the record in this case.

Respectfully,

Commissioner.

---

Choc. New Born 1372
    Lilia Stiles
    (Born May 12, 1903)

**NEW-BORN AFFIDAVIT.**

Number...............

...Choctaw Enrolling Commission...

    IN THE MATTER OF THE APPLICATION FOR ENROLLMENT, as a citizen of the Choctaw Nation, of Lilia Stiles born on the 12th day of May 190 3

Name of father   Harvey Stiles    a~citizen of   Choctaw   *non*
Nation final enrollment No. ———
Name of mother   Mattie Stiles  (Nee Battles)    a citizen of   Choctaw
Nation final enrollment No.   8285

# Applications for Enrollment of Choctaw Newborn
## Act of 1905   Volume XVIII

Postoffice   Hartshorne, Ind. Ter.

**AFFIDAVIT OF MOTHER.**

UNITED STATES OF AMERICA
INDIAN TERRITORY
Central   DISTRICT

I Mattie Ott *(Nee Battles & Stiles)*, on oath state that I am 34 years of age and a citizen by blood of the Choctaw Nation, and as such have been placed upon the final roll of the Choctaw Nation, by the Honorable Secretary of the Interior my final enrollment number being 8285 ; that I am the lawful *divorced* wife of Harvey Stiles, who is a *non* citizen of the Choctaw Nation, and as such has been placed upon the final roll of said Nation by the Honorable Secretary of the Interior, his final enrollment number being ——— and that a Female child was born to me on the 12$^{th}$ day of May 190 3; that said child has been named Lilia Stiles, and is now living.

Mattie Ott *(nee Stiles & Battles)*

Witnesseth.
Must be two Witnesses who are Citizens.   Eastman Wade
   Stephen Ott

Subscribed and sworn to before me this 6$^{th}$ day of March 190 5

Wm J Hulsey
Notary Public.

My commission expires:   1908

---

## AFFIDAVIT OF ATTENDING PHYSICIAN OR MIDWIFE

UNITED STATES OF AMERICA
INDIAN TERRITORY
Central   DISTRICT

I, Sarah Wade a midwife on oath state that I attended on Mrs. Mattie Ott *(nee Stiles) divorced* wife of Harvey Stiles on the 12$^{th}$ day of May , 190 3 , that there was born to her on said date a Female child, that said child is now living, and is said to have been named Lilia Stiles

*Witness to mark*
*Eastman Wade*
*Stephen Ott*

her
Sarah x Wade
mark

Subscribed and sworn to before me this, the 6$^{th}$ day of March 190 5

Wm J Hulsey   Notary Public.

# Applications for Enrollment of Choctaw Newborn
## Act of 1905   Volume XVIII

WITNESSETH:

Must be two witnesses who are citizens { Stephen Ott

Eastman Wade

We hereby certify that we are well acquainted with Sarah Wade a midwife and know her to be reputable and of good standing in the community.

Eastman Wade _____X_____

Stephen Ott _____X_____

(Copy)

Hulsey & Patterson
   Attorneys
Hartshorne, I. T.

May 18th 1905.

Commission to the Five Civilized Tribes,
   Muskogee,   I. T.

Gentlemen:-

In reference to he[sic] application for the enrollment of Lena[sic] Stiles daughter of Mattie Ott (nee Stiles), we wish to state that we are now informed that Mattie Ott (nee Stiles) is enrolled as Mattie Battles, she having formerly been the lawful wife of one Battles.

With this information you will please advise whether or not the information is now sufficient for the enrollment of Lena Stiles.

Very respectfully yours,
(Signed) Hulsey and Patterson

## Applications for Enrollment of Choctaw Newborn
## Act of 1905   Volume XVIII

7-N.B. 1372.

Muskogee, Indian Territory, May 24, 1905.

Hulsey & Patterson,
    Attorneys at Law,
        Hartshorne, Indian Territory.

Gentlemen:

Receipt is hereby acknowledged of your letter of May 18th, in the matter of the enrollment of Lena Stiles, in which you state you are informed that Mattie Ott, the mother of said child, was enrolled as Mattie Battles, and this information has been made a matter of record in this case and the child's mother has been identified as a citizen by blood of the Choctaw Nation.

Respectfully,

Chairman.

---

Choc. New Born 1373
    Georgie Lee Scroggins
    (Born Sep. 24, 1904)

# NEW BORN AFFIDAVIT

No _____

## CHOCTAW ENROLLING COMMISSION

IN THE MATTER OF THE APPLICATION FOR ENROLLMENT as a citizen of the Choctaw Nation, of Gorgie[sic] Lee Scroggins born on the 24 day of September 190 4

Name of father  George Scroggins    a citizen of  _____  Nation,
final enrollment No. ————
Name of mother  Lucinda Scroggins    a citizen of  Choctaw  Nation,
final enrollment No.  14071

Caney I.T.    Postoffice.

## Applications for Enrollment of Choctaw Newborn
## Act of 1905 Volume XVIII

**AFFIDAVIT OF MOTHER**

UNITED STATES OF AMERICA  
   INDIAN TERRITORY  
DISTRICT   Central

I   Lucinda Scroggins, on oath state that I am 25 years of age and a citizen by blood of the Choctaw Nation, and as such have been placed upon the final roll of the Choctaw Nation, by the Honorable Secretary of the Interior my final enrollment number being 14071; that I am the lawful wife of George W Scroggins, who is a citizen of the United States Nation, and as such has been placed upon the final roll of said Nation by the Honorable Secretary of the Interior, his final enrollment number being .................. and that a Male child was born to me on the 24 day of September 190 4; that said child has been named Gorgie Lee Scroggins, and is now living.

                                              Lucinda Scroggins

WITNESSETH:  
Must be two witnesses who are citizens { Robert Jackson  
Robt. O. Sumter

    Subscribed and sworn to before me this, the 2 day of March, 190 5

                                            A Denton Phillips  
                                                    Notary Public.

My Commission Expires:  
   Dec 17-1905

### *Affidavit of Attending Physician or Midwife*

UNITED STATES OF AMERICA,  
   INDIAN TERRITORY,  
  Central   DISTRICT

I, J H Armstrong a M.D. on oath state that I attended on Mrs. Lucinda Scroggins wife of George W Scroggins on the 24 day of September, 190 4, that there was born to her on said date a male child, that said child is now living, and is said to have been named Gorgie Lee Scroggins

                                      J H Armstrong    M. D.

    Subscribed and sworn to before me this the 3 day of March 1905

                                              A Denton Phillips  
                                                    Notary Public.

## Applications for Enrollment of Choctaw Newborn
## Act of 1905   Volume XVIII

WITNESSETH:

Must be two witnesses who are citizens and know the child.
{ Robert Jackson
  Robt. O. Sumter

We hereby certify that we are well acquainted with ................................ a ........................................ and know ............................ to be reputable and of good standing in the community.

Must be two citizen witnesses. { Robert Jackson
                                 Robt O Sumter

BIRTH AFFIDAVIT.

## DEPARTMENT OF THE INTERIOR.
## COMMISSION TO THE FIVE CIVILIZED TRIBES.

IN RE APPLICATION FOR ENROLLMENT, as a citizen of the   Choctaw   Nation, of Georgie Lee Scroggins  , born on the 24 day of Sept , 1904

Name of Father: George Scroggins     a citizen of the   non      Nation.
Name of Mother: Lucinda Scroggins    a citizen of the   Choctaw  Nation.

Postoffice   Caney IT

### AFFIDAVIT OF MOTHER.

UNITED STATES OF AMERICA, Indian Territory, }
Central                        DISTRICT.    }

I, Lucinda Scroggins , on oath state that I am 25 years of age and a citizen by blood , of the Choctaw Nation; that I am the lawful wife of George Scroggins , who is a *non* citizen, by —— of the ——— Nation; that a male child was born to me on 24 day of Sept , 1904; that said child has been named Georgie Lee Scroggins , and was living March 4, 1905.

Lucinda Scroggins

Witnesses To Mark:
{

Subscribed and sworn to before me this 26 day of June , 1905

A Denton Phillips
Notary Public.

# Applications for Enrollment of Choctaw Newborn
## Act of 1905   Volume XVIII

**AFFIDAVIT OF ATTENDING PHYSICIAN OR MID-WIFE.**

UNITED STATES OF AMERICA, Indian Territory, }
Central                     DISTRICT.

I, J. H. Armstrong, a physician, on oath state that I attended on Mrs. Lucinda Scroggins, wife of George Scroggins on the 24 day of Sept, 1904; that there was born to her on said date a male child; that said child was living March 4, 1905, and is said to have been named Georgie Lee Scroggins

J H Armstrong M.D.

Witnesses To Mark:
{

Subscribed and sworn to before me this 26 day of June, 1905

A Denton Phillips
Notary Public.

7-N.B. 1373.

Muskogee, Indian Territory, May 24, 1905.

William Fronterhouse,
   Caney, Indian Territory.

Dear Sir:

Receipt is hereby acknowledged of your letter of May 19, asking for a blank for the enrollment of a child, George Lee Scroggins, son of George and Lucinda Scroggins, and stating that you are guardian of said child.

In reply to your letter you are advised that application has heretofore been made to this Commission for the enrollment of Georgie Lee Scroggins, son of George and Lucinda Scroggins, as a citizen by blood of the Choctaw Nation.

Respectfully,

Chairman.

## Applications for Enrollment of Choctaw Newborn
## Act of 1905   Volume XVIII

7-NB-1373

Muskogee, Indian Territory, June 1, 1905.

George Scroggins,
    Caney, Indian Territory.

Dear Sir:

    There is enclosed you herewith for execution application for the enrollment of your infant child, Georgie Lee Scroggins, born September 24, 1904.

    The affidavits heretofore filed with the Commission show the child was living on March 2, 1905. It is necessary, for the child to be enrolled, that he was living on March 4, 1905.

    In having these affidavits executed care should be exercised to see that all names are written in full, as they appear in the body of the affidavit, and in the event that either of the persons signing the affidavit are unable to write, signatures by mark must be attested by two witnesses. Each affidavit must be executed before a Notary Public and the notarial seal and signature of the officer must be attached to each separate affidavit.

        Respectfully,

        Chairman.

Enc. FVK-6

---

7 NB 1373

Muskogee, Indian Territory, June 24, 1905.

William Fronterhouse,
    Caney, Indian Territory.

Dear Sir:

    Receipt is hereby acknowledged of your letter of June 20, 1905, in which you state that George Scroggins died October 5, 1904, and you have been appointed guardian of Georgie Lee Scroggins and you ask if it will be proper for you to execute the affidavit forwarded with our letter of June 1, 1905, in the matter of the enrollment of said Georgie Lee Scroggins.

    In reply to your letter you are advised that the affidavits on the blank forwarded with our letter of June 1, 1905, should be executed, the one by the mother and the other by the attending physician or midwife and it will be proper for you to have the same signed and sworn to by the persons named and return them to this office as early as

## Applications for Enrollment of Choctaw Newborn
## Act of 1905   Volume XVIII

practicable in order that disposition may be made of the application for the enrollment of this child.

The letter of the Commission of June 1, 1905, enclosed with your letter is herewith returned.

Respectfully,

EB 3-23

Chairman.

---

7 NB 1373

Muskogee, Indian Territory, June 30, 1905.

George Scroggins,
    Caney, Indian Territory.

Dear Sir:

Receipt is hereby acknowledged of the affidavits of Lucinda Scroggins and J. H. Armstrong to the birth of Georgie Lee Scroggins son of George and Lucinda Scroggins, September 24, 1904, and the same have been filed with our records in the matter of the enrollment of said child.

Respectfully,

Chairman.

---

Choc. New Born 1374
    Roy Zion
    (Born Jan. 15, 1905)
    Floyd Zion
    (Born May 31, 1903)

Applications for Enrollment of Choctaw Newborn
Act of 1905   Volume XVIII

**NEW-BORN AFFIDAVIT.**

Number............

...Choctaw Enrolling Commission...

IN THE MATTER OF THE APPLICATION FOR ENROLLMENT, as a citizen of the Choctaw    Nation, of    Roy Zion

born on the  15$^{th}$  day of  January    190 5

Name of father  W E Zion                         a citizen of   — —
Nation final enrollment No. ———
Name of mother  Susan Zion                       a citizen of    Choctaw
Nation final enrollment No.  10885

                                        Postoffice    Matoy I.T.

**AFFIDAVIT OF MOTHER.**

UNITED STATES OF AMERICA
INDIAN TERRITORY
 Central        DISTRICT

I    Susan Zion             , on oath state that I am  23  years of age and a citizen by  blood  of the  Choctaw   Nation, and as such have been placed upon the final roll of the  Choctaw  Nation, by the Honorable Secretary of the Interior my final enrollment number being  10885 ; that I am the lawful wife of  W.E. Zion  , who is a citizen of the  —— ——  Nation, and as such has been placed upon the final roll of said Nation by the Honorable Secretary of the Interior, his final enrollment number being  ——  and that a  Male  child was born to me on the  15$^{th}$  day of  January   190 5; that said child has been named  Roy Zion  , and is now living.

                                        Susan Zion

Witnesseth.
  Must be two  ⎫   Albert Matoy
  Witnesses who ⎬
  are Citizens. ⎭   Frank Battiest

       Subscribed and sworn to before me this  4$^{th}$   day of  March    190 5

                           A.E. Folsom
                                  Notary Public.

My commission expires:
      Jan 9-1909

# Applications for Enrollment of Choctaw Newborn
## Act of 1905  Volume XVIII

## AFFIDAVIT OF ATTENDING PHYSICIAN OR MIDWIFE

UNITED STATES OF AMERICA
INDIAN TERRITORY
  Central   DISTRICT

I, W.T. Linsey[sic] a Practicing Physician on oath state that I attended on Mrs. Susan Zion wife of W.E. Zion on the 15th day of January, 1905, that there was born to her on said date a male child, that said child is now living, and is said to have been named Roy Zion

W.T. Lindsey   M.D.

WITNESSETH:

Must be two witnesses who are citizens and know the child.
{ Albert Matoy
  Frank Battiest

Subscribed and sworn to before me this, the 7th day of March 1905

J.H.P. Smith   Notary Public.

We hereby certify that we are well acquainted with Dr W.T. Linsey[sic] a Practicing Physician and know him to be reputable and of good standing in the community.

{ Albert Matoy
  Frank Battiest

**NEW-BORN AFFIDAVIT.**

Number..............

### ...Choctaw Enrolling Commission...

IN THE MATTER OF THE APPLICATION FOR ENROLLMENT, as a citizen of the Choctaw Nation, of Floyd Zion

born on the 31st day of May 1903

Name of father  W E Zion                    a citizen of  ~~Choctaw~~
Nation final enrollment No. ———
Name of mother  Susan Zion                  a citizen of  Choctaw
Nation final enrollment No. 10885

Postoffice  Maytoy[sic] I.T.

# Applications for Enrollment of Choctaw Newborn
## Act of 1905   Volume XVIII

### AFFIDAVIT OF MOTHER.

UNITED STATES OF AMERICA  
INDIAN TERRITORY  
Central   DISTRICT

I   Susan Zion   , on oath state that I am 23 years of age and a citizen by blood of the Choctaw Nation, and as such have been placed upon the final roll of the Choctaw Nation, by the Honorable Secretary of the Interior my final enrollment number being   10885 ; that I am the lawful wife of   W.E. Zion   , who is a citizen of the Choctaw Nation, and as such has been placed upon the final roll of said Nation by the Honorable Secretary of the Interior, his final enrollment number being ................ and that a Male child was born to me on the 31$^{st}$ day of May 190 3; that said child has been named   Floyd Zion  , and is now living.

Susan Zion

Witnesseth.

Must be two Witnesses who are Citizens. } Albert Matoy  
Frank Battiest

Subscribed and sworn to before me this 4$^{th}$ day of March 190 5

A.E. Folsom  
Notary Public.

My commission expires:  
Jan 9-1909

---

## AFFIDAVIT OF ATTENDING PHYSICIAN OR MIDWIFE

UNITED STATES OF AMERICA  
INDIAN TERRITORY  
Central   DISTRICT

I,   W.T. Linsey[sic]   a   Practicing Physician on oath state that I attended on Mrs. Susan Zion wife of W.E. Zion on the 31$^{st}$ day of May, 190 3, that there was born to her on said date a male child, that said child is now living, and is said to have been named   Floyd Zion

W.T. Lindsey   M.D.

WITNESSETH:

Must be two witnesses who are citizens and know the child. { Albert Matoy  
Frank Battiest

Subscribed and sworn to before me this, the 7$^{th}$ day of March 190 5

J.H.P. Smith   Notary Public.

## Applications for Enrollment of Choctaw Newborn
## Act of 1905   Volume XVIII

      We hereby certify that we are well acquainted with    D$^r$ W.T. Linsey[sic] a   Practicing Physician   and know   him   to be reputable and of good standing in the community.

                                    Albert Matoy

                                    Frank Battiest

**BIRTH AFFIDAVIT.**

### DEPARTMENT OF THE INTERIOR.
### COMMISSION TO THE FIVE CIVILIZED TRIBES.

      **IN RE APPLICATION FOR ENROLLMENT,** as a citizen of the   Choctaw   Nation, of Roy Zion   , born on the 15   day of  Jan.  , 1905

Name of Father: W.E. Zion           a citizen of the   U.S.   Nation.
Name of Mother: Susan Zion       a citizen of the  Choctaw  Nation.

                            Postoffice   Matoy I.T.

### AFFIDAVIT OF MOTHER.

**UNITED STATES OF AMERICA, Indian Territory,**
   Central               **DISTRICT.**

      I,  Susan Zion  , on oath state that I am  23  years of age and a citizen by Blood  , of the  Choctaw  Nation; that I am the lawful wife of  W.E. Zion  , who is a citizen, by ——of the  US  Nation; that a  mail[sic]  child was born to me on  15  day of  Jan  , 1905; that said child has been named  Roy Zion  , and was living March 4, 1905.

                                    Susan Zion

Witnesses To Mark:

      Subscribed and sworn to before me this  26  day of  April  , 1905

                                J.H.P. Smith
                                Notary Public.

## Applications for Enrollment of Choctaw Newborn
## Act of 1905   Volume XVIII

#### AFFIDAVIT OF ATTENDING PHYSICIAN OR MID-WIFE.

UNITED STATES OF AMERICA, Indian Territory,  
Central       DISTRICT.

I, W.T. Lindsey, a Doctor, on oath state that I attended on Mrs. Susan Zion, wife of W.E. Zion on the 15 day of Jan, 1905; that there was born to her on said date a male child; that said child was living March 4, 1905, and is said to have been named Roy Zion

D$^r$. W. T. Lindsey

Witnesses To Mark:
{

Subscribed and sworn to before me this 26 day of April, 1905

J.H.P. Smith  
Notary Public.

---

BIRTH AFFIDAVIT.

### DEPARTMENT OF THE INTERIOR.
### COMMISSION TO THE FIVE CIVILIZED TRIBES.

IN RE APPLICATION FOR ENROLLMENT, as a citizen of the Choctaw Nation, of Floyd Zion, born on the 31 day of May, 1903

Name of Father: W.E. Zion      a citizen of the   U.S.    Nation.  
Name of Mother: Susan Zion     a citizen of the   Choctaw Nation.

Postoffice   Matoy I.T.

---

#### AFFIDAVIT OF MOTHER.

UNITED STATES OF AMERICA, Indian Territory,  
Central       DISTRICT.

I, Susan Zion, on oath state that I am 23 years of age and a citizen by Blood, of the Choctaw Nation; that I am the lawful wife of W.E. Zion, who is a citizen, by US of the ——— Nation; that a male child was born to me on 31 day of May, 1903; that said child has been named Floyd Zion, and was living March 4, 1905.

Susan Zion

Witnesses To Mark:
{

# Applications for Enrollment of Choctaw Newborn
## Act of 1905   Volume XVIII

Subscribed and sworn to before me this  26  day of    April     , 1905

                                            J.H.P. Smith
                                            Notary Public.

---

### AFFIDAVIT OF ATTENDING PHYSICIAN OR MID-WIFE.

UNITED STATES OF AMERICA, Indian Territory, }
   Central                       DISTRICT. }

     I,   W.T. Lindsey    , a  Doctor    , on oath state that I attended on Mrs.   Susan Zion   , wife of   W.E. Zion    on the   31 day of   May    , 1905[sic]; that there was born to her on said date a    male    child; that said child was living March 4, 1905, and is said to have been named   Floyd Zion

                                       D$^r$. W. T. Lindsey

Witnesses To Mark:
  {

Subscribed and sworn to before me this  26  day of    April     , 1905

                                            J.H.P. Smith
                                            Notary Public.

---

BIRTH AFFIDAVIT.
### DEPARTMENT OF THE INTERIOR.
### COMMISSION TO THE FIVE CIVILIZED TRIBES.

     IN RE APPLICATION FOR ENROLLMENT, as a citizen of the     Choctaw      Nation, of   Floyd Zion     , born on the  31   day of  May    , 1903

Name of Father: W.E. Zion            a citizen of the   non citizen  Nation.
Name of Mother: Susan Zion    Roll 10885      a citizen of the   Choctaw    Nation.

                             Postoffice     Matoy I.T.

# Applications for Enrollment of Choctaw Newborn
# Act of 1905   Volume XVIII

### AFFIDAVIT OF MOTHER.

UNITED STATES OF AMERICA, Indian Territory,
................................................. DISTRICT.

I, ........................., on oath state that I am ................ years of age and a citizen by ...................., of the ............................ Nation; that I am the lawful wife of ...................., who is a citizen, by .................... of the ............................ Nation; that a ................ child was born to me on ........ day of ................, 1......, that said child has been named ............................................., and was living March 4, 1905.

Witnesses To Mark:
{ ........................................
  ........................................

Subscribed and sworn to before me this ........ day of ................, 1905.

.................................................................
Notary Public.

---

### AFFIDAVIT OF ATTENDING PHYSICIAN OR MID-WIFE.

UNITED STATES OF AMERICA, Indian Territory,
................................................. DISTRICT.

I, W.T. Lindsey, a Physician, on oath state that I attended on Mrs. Susan Zion, wife of W.E. Zion on the 31 day of May, 1903; that there was born to her on said date a male child; that said child was living March 4, 1905, and is said to have been named Floyd Zion

D$^r$. W. T. Lindsey

Witnesses To Mark:
{

Subscribed and sworn to before me this 14 day of May, 1905

J.H.P. Smith
Notary Public.

## Applications for Enrollment of Choctaw Newborn
## Act of 1905   Volume XVIII

7-NB-1374.

Muskogee, Indian Territory, June 2, 1905.

W. E. Zion,
    Matoy, Indian Territory.

Dear Sir:

There is enclosed you herewith for execution application for the enrollment of your infant child, Floyd Zion.

In the affidavits of March 4, 1905, the date of the applicant's birth is given as May 31, 1903 while in those of April 26, 1905, your wife gives the date as May 31, 1903, and the physician gives it as May 31, 1905. In the enclosed application the date of birth is left blank. Please insert the correct date and, when the affidavit is properly executed, return it to this office.

In having the affidavit executed care should be exercised to see that all names are written in full, as they appear in the body of the affidavit. Signature by mark must be attested by two witnesses. Each affidavit must be executed before a Notary Public and the notarial seal and signature of the officer must be attached to each separate affidavit.

                Respectfully,

VR 2-7.                                                      [sic]

---

7 NB 1374

Muskogee, Indian Territory, June 19, 1905.

W. E. Zion,
    Matoy, Indian Territory.

Dear Sir:

Receipt is hereby acknowledged of the affidavit of W. T. Lindsay[sic] to the birth of Floyd Zion, son of W. E. and Susan Zion, May 31, 1903, and the same has been filed with our records in the matter of the enrollment of said child.

                Respectfully,

                              Chairman.

Applications for Enrollment of Choctaw Newborn
Act of 1905   Volume XVIII

Choc. New Born 1375
    Beulah V. Platt
    (Born Jan. 25, 1904)

# NEW BORN AFFIDAVIT

No ........

## CHOCTAW ENROLLING COMMISSION

IN THE MATTER OF THE APPLICATION FOR ENROLLMENT as a citizen of the Choctaw Nation, of  Bulah[sic] V. Platt  born on the 25 day of January 190 4

Name of father  B.F. Platt  a citizen of  U. S.  ~~Nation~~, final enrollment No. ———
Name of mother  Elizabeth F. Platt  a citizen of  Choctaw  Nation, final enrollment No..  5250

Antlers I.T.  Postoffice.

### AFFIDAVIT OF MOTHER

UNITED STATES OF AMERICA }
INDIAN TERRITORY }
DISTRICT   Central

I  Elizabeth F. Platt  , on oath state that I am  33  years of age and a citizen by  blood  of the  Choctaw  Nation, and as such have been placed upon the final roll of the  Choctaw  Nation, by the Honorable Secretary of the Interior my final enrollment number being  5250  ; that I am the lawful wife of  B.F. Platt , who is a citizen of the  U. S.  ~~Nation~~, and as such has been placed upon the final roll of said Nation by the Honorable Secretary of the Interior, his final enrollment number being ............... and that a  Female  child was born to me on the  25<sup>th</sup>  day of  January  190 4; that said child has been named  Bulah V. Platt  , and is now living.

WITNESSETH:      Elizabeth F. Platt
  Must be two witnesses { Dennis Impson
  who are citizens    { Elba Gardner

## Applications for Enrollment of Choctaw Newborn
## Act of 1905   Volume XVIII

Subscribed and sworn to before me this, the  25   day of   February   , 190 5

A J Arnote
Notary Public.

My Commission Expires:  May 16" 1907

### *Affidavit of Attending Physician or Midwife*

UNITED STATES OF AMERICA,  
INDIAN TERRITORY,  
Central   DISTRICT

I,   Mildred Benham   a   Mid-wife   on oath state that I attended on Mrs. Elizabeth F. Platt   wife of   B.F. Platt   on the  25   day of   January  , 190 4, that there was born to her on said date a   Female child, that said child is now living, and is said to have been named   Bulah V. Platt

Mildred Benham   *midwife*

Subscribed and sworn to before me this the   25   day of   February   1905

AJ Arnote
Notary Public.

WITNESSETH:

Must be two witnesses who are citizens and know the child.
{ Dennis Impson  
  Elba Gardner

We hereby certify that we are well acquainted with   Mildred Benham   a   midwife   and know   her   to be reputable and of good standing in the community.

Must be two citizen witnesses.
{ Dennis Impson  
  Elba Gardner

BIRTH AFFIDAVIT.

### DEPARTMENT OF THE INTERIOR.
### COMMISSION TO THE FIVE CIVILIZED TRIBES.

IN RE APPLICATION FOR ENROLLMENT, as a citizen of the   Choctaw   Nation, of   Beulah Viola Platt   , born on the  25th   day of   January  , 1904

Name of Father:  B.F. Platt         a citizen of the United States Nation.  
Name of Mother:  Elizabeth F. Platt     a citizen of the   Choctaw   Nation.

# Applications for Enrollment of Choctaw Newborn
## Act of 1905   Volume XVIII

Postoffice   Antlers, Ind Ter

### AFFIDAVIT OF MOTHER.

UNITED STATES OF AMERICA, Indian Territory,
Central   DISTRICT.

I, Elizabeth F. Platt, on oath state that I am 33 years of age and a citizen by blood, of the Choctaw Nation; that I am the lawful wife of B. F. Platt, who is a citizen, ~~by~~ _____ of the United States ~~Nation~~; that a female child was born to me on 25th day of January, 1904; that said child has been named Beulah Viola Platt, and was living March 4, 1905.

Elizabeth F. Platt

Witnesses To Mark:
{

Subscribed and sworn to before me this 29th day of April, 1905

Wirt Franklin
Notary Public.

### AFFIDAVIT OF ATTENDING PHYSICIAN OR MID-WIFE.

UNITED STATES OF AMERICA, Indian Territory,
Central   DISTRICT.

I, Mildred Benham, a mid-wife, on oath state that I attended on Mrs. Elizabeth F. Platt, wife of B. F. Platt on the 25th day of January, 1904; that there was born to her on said date a female child; that said child was living March 4, 1905, and is said to have been named Beulah Viola Platt

Mildred Benham

Witnesses To Mark:
{

Subscribed and sworn to before me this 29th day of April, 1905

Wirt Franklin
Notary Public.

## Applications for Enrollment of Choctaw Newborn
### Act of 1905   Volume XVIII

7-NB-1375

Muskogee, Indian Territory, July 6, 1905.

Elizabeth F. Platt,
   Antlers, Indian Territory.

Dear Madam:

   Receipt is hereby acknowledged of your letter of June 26, 1905, addressed to the United States Indian Agent which has been by him referred to this office for appropriate action. Therein you ask when you can file for your youngest child.

   In reply to your letter you are advised that the name of your child Bulah[sic] Viola Platt has been placed upon a schedule of citizens by blood of the Choctaw Nation of the Choctaw Nation prepared for forwarding to the Secretary of the Interior, but pending the approval of her enrollment no selection of allotment could be made in her behalf.

Respectfully,

Commissioner.

---

Choc. New Born 1376
   Oweta Stallings
   (Born Jan. 4, 1904)

**NEW-BORN AFFIDAVIT.**

Number............

## Choctaw Enrolling Commission.

IN THE MATTER OF THE APPLICATION FOR ENROLLMENT, as a citizen of the Choctaw   Nation, of   Oweta Stallings

born on the   4   day of   January   190 4

Name of father   Jared A Stallings         a citizen of   Choctaw
Nation final enrollment No   303
Name of mother   Carrie M Stallings        a citizen of   Choctaw
Nation final enrollment No   9339

Postoffice   Durant I.T.

211

## Applications for Enrollment of Choctaw Newborn
## Act of 1905   Volume XVIII

### AFFIDAVIT OF MOTHER.

UNITED STATES OF AMERICA,  
INDIAN TERRITORY,  
Central    DISTRICT

I    Carrie M Stallings    on oath state that I am  24  years of age and a citizen by  blood  of the  Choctaw  Nation, and as such have been placed upon the final roll of the  Choctaw  Nation, by the Honorable Secretary of the Interior my final enrollment number being  9339  ; that I am the lawful wife of  Jared A Stallings  *(deceased)* , who is a citizen of the  Choctaw  Nation, and as such has been placed upon the final roll of said Nation by the Honorable Secretary of the Interior, his final enrollment number being  303  *Ind Mar.*  and that a  Female  child was born to me on the  4  day of  January  190 4 ; that said child has been named  Oweta Stallings  , and is now living.

Carrie Maye Stallings

WITNESSETH:  
Must be two Witnesses who are Citizens.    EM Wilson  
                                           G.W. Seeley

Subscribed and sworn to before me this  14  day of  January  190 5

James Bower  
Notary Public.

My commission expires  Sept 23- 1907

---

## Affidavit of Attending Physician or Midwife.

UNITED STATES OF AMERICA  
INDIAN TERRITORY  
Central    DISTRICT

I,  Emma J Ross  a  midwife on oath state that I attended on Mrs. Carrie M Stallings wife of Jared A Stallings *(deceased)* on the  4  day of  January  , 190 4 , that there was born to her on said date a  Female  child, that said child is now living, and is said to have been named  Oweta Stallings

Emma J Ross    M.D.

Subscribed and sworn to before me this, the  14  day of  January  190 5

James Bower  
Notary Public.

WITNESSETH:  
Must be two witnesses who are citizens and know the child.    EM Wilson  
                                                              G.W. Seeley

## Applications for Enrollment of Choctaw Newborn
## Act of 1905   Volume XVIII

We hereby certify that we are well acquainted with   Emma J Ross   a   midwife   and know   her   to be reputable and of good standing in the community.

$\left\{\begin{array}{l}\text{EM Wilson}\\ \text{G.W. Seeley}\end{array}\right.$

**BIRTH AFFIDAVIT.**

### DEPARTMENT OF THE INTERIOR.
### COMMISSION TO THE FIVE CIVILIZED TRIBES.

**IN RE APPLICATION FOR ENROLLMENT,** as a citizen of the   Choctaw   Nation, of   Oweta Stallings   , born on the   4$^{th}$   day of   Jany   , 1904

Name of Father:  Jared A Stallings          a citizen of the   Choctaw   Nation.  *Inter Mar*
Name of Mother:  Carrie M. Stallings       a citizen of the   Choctaw   Nation.

Postoffice   Durant, I.T.

**AFFIDAVIT OF MOTHER.**

UNITED STATES OF AMERICA, Indian Territory, $\Big\}$
Central                 DISTRICT.

I,   Carrie M. Stallings   , on oath state that I am   25   years of age and a citizen by   Blood   , of the   Choctaw   Nation; that I am the lawful wife of   Jared A Stallings   , who is a citizen, by   Inter Mar   of the   Choctaw   Nation; that a   female   child was born to me on   4$^{th}$   day of   Jany   , 1904; that said child has been named   Oweta Stallings   , and was living March 4, 1905.

Carrie M Stallings

Witnesses To Mark:
$\left\{\begin{array}{l}\text{H.G. Dearing}\\ \text{John Benton}\end{array}\right.$

Subscribed and sworn to before me this   3$^{d}$   day of   May   , 1905

E E Fuller
Notary Public.

## Applications for Enrollment of Choctaw Newborn
## Act of 1905   Volume XVIII

### AFFIDAVIT OF ATTENDING PHYSICIAN OR MID-WIFE.

UNITED STATES OF AMERICA, Indian Territory, }
Central   DISTRICT.

I, Emma J Ross, a Grand mother, on oath state that I attended on Mrs. Carrie M Stallings, wife of Jared A. Stallings on the 4$^{th}$ day of Jany, 1905[sic]; that there was born to her on said date a female child; that said child was living March 4, 1905, and is said to have been named Oweta Stallings

Emma J Ross

Witnesses To Mark:
{ H.G. Dearing
{ John Benton

Subscribed and sworn to before me this 3$^d$ day of May, 1905

E E Fuller
Notary Public.

---

BIRTH AFFIDAVIT.

### DEPARTMENT OF THE INTERIOR.
### COMMISSION TO THE FIVE CIVILIZED TRIBES.

IN RE APPLICATION FOR ENROLLMENT, as a citizen of the Choctaw Nation, of Oweta Stallings, born on the 4 day of Jan, 1904

Name of Father: Jared A Stallings   (*W 303*)   a citizen of the Choctaw Nation.
Name of Mother: Carrie M. Stallings   (*R 9339*)   a citizen of the Choctaw Nation.

Postoffice   Durant, I.T.

---

### AFFIDAVIT OF MOTHER.

UNITED STATES OF AMERICA, Indian Territory, }
Central   DISTRICT.

I, Carrie M. Stallings, on oath state that I am 24 years of age and a citizen by blood, of the Choctaw Nation; that I am the lawful wife of Jared A Stallings (*deceased*), who is a citizen, by marriage of the Choctaw Nation; that a female child was born to me on 4 day of Jan, 1904; that said child has been named Oweta Stallings, and was living March 4, 1905.

Carrie M Stallings

## Applications for Enrollment of Choctaw Newborn
## Act of 1905   Volume XVIII

Witnesses To Mark:
{
    Subscribed and sworn to before me this   7$^{th}$   day of     June     , 1905

                                    Wm J Hulsey
                                    Notary Public.

---

### AFFIDAVIT OF ATTENDING PHYSICIAN OR MID-WIFE.

UNITED STATES OF AMERICA, Indian Territory, }
                              DISTRICT.

    I,   Emma J Ross   , a midwife   , on oath state that I attended on Mrs.   Carrie M Stallings   , wife of   Jared A. Stallings   *(deceased)*   on the  4 day of  Jan  , 1904; that there was born to her on said date a   Female   child; that said child was living March 4, 1905, and is said to have been named  Oweta Stallings

                                    Emma J Ross

Witnesses To Mark:
{
    Subscribed and sworn to before me this   13 day of     June    , 1905

                                    E E Fuller
                                  Notary Public.

---

                                                7--NB--1376.

                Muskogee, Indian Territory, June 1, 1905.

Carrie M. Stallings,
        Durant, Indian Territory.

Dear Madam:

    There is enclosed you herewith for execution application for the enrollment of your infant child, Oweta Stallings, born January 4, 1904.

    The affidavits heretofore filed with the Commission show the child was living on the fourteenth of January, 1905. It is necessary, for the child to be enrolled, that she was living on March 4, 1905.

    In having these affidavits executed care should be exercised to see that all names are written in full, as they appear in the body of the affidavit, and in the event that either

## Applications for Enrollment of Choctaw Newborn
## Act of 1905   Volume XVIII

of the persons signing the affidavit are unable to write, signatures by mark must be attested by two witnesses. Each affidavit must be executed before a Notary Public and the notarial seal and signature of the officer must be attached to each separate affidavit.

Respectfully,

Chairman.

Enc. FVK-7

---

Choctaw N B 1376

Muskogee, Indian Territory, June 28, 1905.

Carrie M. Stallings,
    Care Hulsey & Patterson,
        Hartshorne, Indian Territory.

Dear Madam:

    Receipt is hereby acknowledged of your affidavit and the affidavit of Emma J. Ross to the birth of Oweta Stallings, daughter of Jared A. and Carrie M. Stallings, January 4, 1904, and the same have been filed with the record in the matter of the enrollment of said child.

Respectfully,

Chairman.

---

7-NB-1376

Muskogee, Indian Territory, August 11, 1905.

Carrie M. Stallings,
    Durant, Indian Territory.

Dear Madam:

    Receipt is hereby acknowledged of your letter of August 4, 1905, asking if your baby Oweta Stallings has been approved.

    In reply to your letter you are advised that the name of your child Oweta Stallings has been placed upon a schedule of citizens by blood of the Choctaw Nation which has been forwarded the Secretary of the Interior and you will be notified when her enrollment is approved by the Department.

Respectfully,

Acting Commissioner.

## Applications for Enrollment of Choctaw Newborn
## Act of 1905   Volume XVIII

Choc. New Born 1377
    Virla Etna Taylor
    (Born June 24, 1904)

7-NB
1377

*(Letter below typed as given.)*

**TURNER McGILBERRY,**　　　　　　**H. M. MOORE,**
COUNTY AND PROBATE JUDGE.　　　　COUNTY CLERK AND TREAS.
OFFICE OF
**SANS BOIS COUNTY COURT.**

KENTA, I. T., _____ 190

Marriage Certificate

This is to certify that John Taylor of Sans Bois County in the Choctaw Nation and Maude Deenent of Sans Bois County in the Choctaw Nation were at McCurtain in said county by me joined together in the Holy Bonds of Matrimona of the 20th day of December 1902.

                                            Turner McGilberry
Recorded in my office the 20th　　　Co Judge Sans Bois County
day of December 1902　　　　　　　　Choctaw Nation
            J.W. Nigers
            Co Clerk

I do hereby certify that the above is a true and correct coppy of the Original on Record Book A Page 106 in the Records of Sans Bois County Choctaw Nation

                                        H.M. Moore
This the 24 day of　　　　　　　　　Co Clerk S.B. Co. CN
June A D 1905
    Kinta I.T.

# Applications for Enrollment of Choctaw Newborn
## Act of 1905   Volume XVIII

## AFFIDAVIT OF ATTENDING PHYSICIAN OR MIDWIFE

UNITED STATES OF AMERICA
INDIAN TERRITORY
Western       DISTRICT

I, D. S. Billington   a   practicing physician on oath state that I attended on Mrs. Maud Taylor   wife of John Taylor on the 24th day of June, 190 4, that there was born to her on said date a female child, that said child is now living, and is said to have been named Viola Etna Taylor

D.S. Billington   M.D.

Subscribed and sworn to before me this, the   5   day of January   190 5

WITNESSETH:                              John M Lentz   Notary Public.
Must be two witnesses   { T.J. Walls
who are citizens            { Jess Walls

We hereby certify that we are well acquainted with   D.S. Billington M.D. a practicing physician and know him to be reputable and of good standing in the community.

Jess Walls

T. J. Walls

**NEW-BORN AFFIDAVIT.**

Number..............

...Choctaw Enrolling Commission...

IN THE MATTER OF THE APPLICATION FOR ENROLLMENT, as a citizen of the Choctaw   Nation, of   Viola Etna Taylor

born on the 24th day of   June   190 4

Name of father   John Taylor            a citizen of   Choctaw
Nation final enrollment No.   8277
Name of mother   Maude Taylor          a citizen of   white
Nation final enrollment No. ..................

Postoffice   Enterprise I.T.

# Applications for Enrollment of Choctaw Newborn
## Act of 1905   Volume XVIII

### AFFIDAVIT OF MOTHER.

UNITED STATES OF AMERICA
INDIAN TERRITORY
Western   DISTRICT

I   Maude Taylor   , on oath state that I am 18 years of age and a citizen by white of the _____ Nation, and as such have been placed upon the final roll of the _____ Nation, by the Honorable Secretary of the Interior my final enrollment number being ——— ; that I am the lawful wife of   John Taylor   , who is a citizen of the   Choctaw   Nation, and as such has been placed upon the final roll of said Nation by the Honorable Secretary of the Interior, his final enrollment number being   8377   and that a   female   child was born to me on the 24th   day of   June   190 4; that said child has been named   Viola Etna Taylor   , and is now living.

Maud[sic] Taylor

Witnesseth.

Must be two Witnesses who are Citizens.   } T.J. Walls
Jess Walls

Subscribed and sworn to before me this   25   day of   Jan   190 5

John M Lentz
Notary Public.

My commission expires:   Nov 29 1907

---

BIRTH AFFIDAVIT.

### DEPARTMENT OF THE INTERIOR.
### COMMISSION TO THE FIVE CIVILIZED TRIBES.

---

**IN RE APPLICATION FOR ENROLLMENT,** as a citizen of the   Choctaw   Nation, of Virla[sic] Etna Taylor   , born on the   24   day of   June   , 1904

Name of Father: John Taylor   a citizen of the   Choctaw   Nation.
Name of Mother: Maud Taylor   a citizen of the   Choctaw   Nation.

Postoffice   Enterprise, Ind Ter

---

### AFFIDAVIT OF MOTHER.

UNITED STATES OF AMERICA, Indian Territory,
Western   DISTRICT.   }

I,   Maud Taylor   , on oath state that I am   18   years of age and a citizen by Marriage   , of the   Choctaw   Nation; that I am the lawful wife of   John Taylor   , who is a citizen, by   blood   of the   Choctaw   Nation; that a   Female

# Applications for Enrollment of Choctaw Newborn
## Act of 1905   Volume XVIII

child was born to me on   24   day of   June   , 1904; that said child has been named Virla Etna Taylor   , and was living March 4, 1905.

Maud Taylor

Witnesses To Mark:
{ B.F. Graves
  J.H. Graves

Subscribed and sworn to before me this   24 day of   April   , 1905
My commission
expires Nov 27 1907                John M Lentz
                                   Notary Public.

---

**AFFIDAVIT OF ATTENDING PHYSICIAN OR MID-WIFE.**

UNITED STATES OF AMERICA, Indian Territory,
   Western                  DISTRICT.

I,   D.S. Billington   , a   Physician   , on oath state that I attended on Mrs.   Maud Taylor   , wife of   John Taylor   on the   24   day of   June   , 1904; that there was born to her on said date a   Female   child; that said child was living March 4, 1905, and is said to have been named   Virla Etna Taylor

D$^r$ D.S. Billington

Witnesses To Mark:
{ B.F. Graves
  J.H. Graves

Subscribed and sworn to before me this   24 day of   April   , 1905
My commission
expires Nov 27 1907                John M Lentz
                                   Notary Public.

---

Muskogee, Indian Territory, May 1, 1905.

John Taylor,
   Enterprise, Indian Territory,

Dear Sir:

Receipt is hereby acknowledged of the affidavits of Maud Taylor and D. S. Billington to the birth of Virla Etna Taylor, daughter of John and Maud Taylor, June 24, 1904.

## Applications for Enrollment of Choctaw Newborn
## Act of 1905   Volume XVIII

It is stated in the affidavit of the mother that you are a citizen by blood of the Choctaw Nation and if this is correct you are requested to state the names of your parents and if you have selected an allotment of the lands of the Choctaw and Chickasaw Nations give your roll number as it appears upon your allotment certificate.

This matter should have immediate attention in order that disposition may be made of the application for the enrollment of the above child.

Respectfully,

Chairman.

---

*(The letter below typed as given.)*

7 NB 1377

(COPY)

Enterprise, I. T.

May-9-1905

I received your letter telling me I must Identify my self be fore I could Enrole my baby Viola Etna Taylor

My mothers name is Mary (Allen) Taylor my fathers name is General Taylor I have got my Certificate miss placed and I cant recolect the no. of it I guess you can find the no. of it by going to the record book  If this is not all righ I guess I can send and get another certificate

Resp
John Taylor

---

7 NB 1377

Muskogee, Indian Territory, May 18, 1905.

John Taylor,
    Enterprise, Indian Territory.

Dear Sir:

Receipt is hereby acknowledged of your letter of May 9, 1905, giving information relative to your identification in the matter of the application for the enrollment of your child Virla Etna Taylor and this information has been made a matter of record.

# Applications for Enrollment of Choctaw Newborn
## Act of 1905   Volume XVIII

Respectfully,

Chairman.

7--NB--1377

Muskogee, Indian Territory, June 1, 1905.

John Taylor,
    Enterprise, Indian Territory.

Dear Sir:

    Referring to the application for the enrollment of your infant child, Virla Etna Taylor, born June 24, 1904, it is noted from the affidavits heretofore filed in this office that the applicant claims through you.

    In this event it will be necessary for you to file in this office, either the original or a certified copy of the license and certificate of your marriage to the applicant's mother, Maude Taylor.

Respectfully,

Chairman.

Enc. FVK-9

7-NB-1377

Muskogee, Indian Territory, July 6, 1905.

John Taylor,
    Enterprise, Indian Territory.

Dear Sir:

    Receipt is hereby acknowledged of your letter of June 28, 1905, transmitting a certified copy of the marriage certificate of yourself and Maude Deenent, which you offer in support of the application for the enrollment of your child Virla Etna Taylor and the same has been filed with the record in this case.

Respectfully,

Commissioner.

# Applications for Enrollment of Choctaw Newborn
## Act of 1905   Volume XVIII

Choc. New Born 1378
  Nora Coley
  (Born July 28, 1904)

## NEW-BORN AFFIDAVIT.

Number..............

### ...Choctaw Enrolling Commission...

IN THE MATTER OF THE APPLICATION FOR ENROLLMENT, as a citizen of the Choctaw Nation, of Nora Coley

born on the 28 day of __July__ 190 4

Name of father  David Coley    a citizen of  Choctaw
Nation final enrollment No.  12537
Name of mother  Lovina Coley   a citizen of  Choctaw
Nation final enrollment No.  12538

Postoffice   Kinta I.T.

### AFFIDAVIT OF MOTHER.

UNITED STATES OF AMERICA
INDIAN TERRITORY
Western        DISTRICT

I   Lovina Coley   , on oath state that I am 25 years of age and a citizen by blood of the Choctaw Nation, and as such have been placed upon the final roll of the Choctaw Nation, by the Honorable Secretary of the Interior my final enrollment number being  12538 ; that I am the lawful wife of  David Coley  , who is a citizen of the Choctaw Nation, and as such has been placed upon the final roll of said Nation by the Honorable Secretary of the Interior, his final enrollment number being  12537  and that a  Female  child was born to me on the  28  day of  July  190 4; that said child has been named  Nora Coley  , and is now living.

Lovina Coley

Witnesseth.
  Must be two
  Witnesses who    Calvin Lewis
  are Citizens.    Wesly M$^c$Coy

## Applications for Enrollment of Choctaw Newborn
## Act of 1905 Volume XVIII

Subscribed and sworn to before me this 6th day of Jan 190 5

L.C. Tuey

Notary Public.

My commission expires: Jan 17-1907

## AFFIDAVIT OF ATTENDING PHYSICIAN OR MIDWIFE

UNITED STATES OF AMERICA
INDIAN TERRITORY
Western    DISTRICT

I, Lucinda Cooper  a  midwife on oath state that I attended on Mrs. Lovina Coley wife of David Coley on the 28 day of July , 190 4 , that there was born to her on said date a Female child, that said child is now living, and is said to have been named Nora Coley

Lucinda Cooper

Subscribed and sworn to before me this, the 6 day of Jan. 190 5

L.C. Tuey    Notary Public.

WITNESSETH:
Must be two witnesses who are citizens { Calvin Lewis
Wesly M<sup>c</sup>Coy

We hereby certify that we are well acquainted with Lucinda Cooper a midwife and know her to be reputable and of good standing in the community.

Calvin Lewis    _____

Wesly M<sup>c</sup>Coy    _____

BIRTH AFFIDAVIT.

## DEPARTMENT OF THE INTERIOR.
### COMMISSION TO THE FIVE CIVILIZED TRIBES.

IN RE APPLICATION FOR ENROLLMENT, as a citizen of the Choctaw Nation, of Nora Coley , born on the 28 day of July , 1904

Name of Father: David Coley (R 12537)    a citizen of the Choctaw Nation.
Name of Mother: Lovina Coley (R 12538)    a citizen of the Choctaw Nation.

Postoffice    Kinta IT

# Applications for Enrollment of Choctaw Newborn
## Act of 1905   Volume XVIII

**AFFIDAVIT OF MOTHER.**

UNITED STATES OF AMERICA, Indian Territory, }
   Western               DISTRICT.

   I, Lovina Coley, on oath state that I am 25 years of age and a citizen by blood, of the Choctaw Nation; that I am the lawful wife of David Coley, who is a citizen, by blood of the Choctaw Nation; that a female child was born to me on 28 day of July, 1904; that said child has been named Nora Coley, and was living March 4, 1905.

Lovina Coley

Witnesses To Mark:
{

   Subscribed and sworn to before me this 5th day of June, 1905

*(Name Illegible)*<br>Notary Public.

---

**AFFIDAVIT OF ATTENDING PHYSICIAN OR MID-WIFE.**

UNITED STATES OF AMERICA, Indian Territory, }
   Western               DISTRICT.

   I, Lucinda Cooper, a midwife, on oath state that I attended on Mrs. Lovina Coley, wife of David Coley on the 28 day of July, 1904; that there was born to her on said date a female child; that said child was living March 4, 1905, and is said to have been named Nora Coley

Lucinda Cooper

Witnesses To Mark:
{

   Subscribed and sworn to before me this 5th day of June, 1905

*(Name Illegible)*<br>Notary Public.

# Applications for Enrollment of Choctaw Newborn
## Act of 1905  Volume XVIII

COMMISSIONERS:
TAMS BIXBY,
THOMAS B. NEEDLES,
C.R. BRECKINBRIDGE.

WM. O. BEALL
Secretary

**DEPARTMENT OF THE INTERIOR,
COMMISSIONER TO THE FIVE CIVILIZED TRIBES.**

$W^m O.B.$

REFER IN REPLY TO THE FOLLOWING:

7--NB--1378

ADDRESS ONLY THE
COMMISSION TO THE FIVE CIVILIZED TRIBES.

Muskogee, Indian Territory, June 1, 1905.

David Coley,
    Kinta, Indian Territory.

Dear Sir:

    There is enclosed you herewith for execution application for the enrollment of your infant child, Nora Coley, born July 28, 1904.

    The affidavits heretofore filed with the Commission show the child was lviing on January 6, 1905. It is necessary, for the child to be enrolled, that she was living on March 4, 1905.

    In having these affidavits executed care should be exercised to see that all names are written in full, as they appear in the body of the affidavit, and in the event that either of the persons signing the affidavit are unable to write, signatures by mark must be attested by two witnesses. Each affidavit must be executed before a Notary Public and the notarial seal and signature of the officer must be attached to each separate affidavit.

    Respectfully,

    T.B. Needles
    Commissioner in Charge.

Enc. FVK-9

## Applications for Enrollment of Choctaw Newborn
## Act of 1905 Volume XVIII

7-NB-1378.

Muskogee, Indian Territory, June 9, 1905.

David Coley,
    Kinta, Indian Territory.

Dear Sir:

    Receipt is hereby acknowledged of the affidavits of Louvina[sic] Coley and Lucinda Cooper to the birth of Nora Coley, daughter of David and Louvina Coley, July 28, 1904, and the same have been filed with our records in the matter of the enrollment of said child.

Respectfully,

Chairman.

---

Choc. New Born 1379
    Frank Going
        (Born Sep. 23, 1904)

**1379**

## NEW BORN
### CHOCTAW
### ENROLLMENT

FRANK GOING
(BORN SEPTEMBER 23, 1904)

As Citizen of the
CHOCTAW NATION
Act of Congress
Approved March 3, 1905

DECISION RENDERED OCTOBER 19, 1906
REFUSED, OCTOBER 19, 1906
NOTICE OF DECISION FORWARDED APPLICANT
OCTOBER 19, 1906

## Applications for Enrollment of Choctaw Newborn
## Act of 1905   Volume XVIII

COPY OF DECISION FORWARDED ATTORNEYS FOR
CHOCTAW AND CHICKASAW NATIONS OCTOBER 19, 190
1906
RECORD FORWARDED DEPARTMENT. OCTOBER 19, 1906
ACTION APPROVED BY SECRETARY OF INTERIOR
FEBRUARY 27, 1907
NOTICE OF DEPARTMENTAL ACTION FORWARDED
ATTORNEYS FOR CHOCTAW AND CHICKASAW NATIONS
APRIL 3, 1907

NOTICE OF DEPARTMENTAL ACTION MAILED
APPLICANT. APRIL 3, 1907

### 1379

(COPY-DeB)

NEW BORN AFFIDAVIT
Number _____

CHOCTAW ENROLLING COMMISSION.

IN THE MATTER OF THE APPLICATION FOR ENROLLMENT, as a citizen of the Choctaw Nation, of Frank Going born on the 23 day of Sept 1904. Name of father Peter Going, a citizen of Choctaw Nation, final enrollment No. 1088
Name of mother, Lizzie Going a citizen of Choctaw Nation; final enrollment No. 5967.

Postoffice   Smithville

AFFIDAVIT OF MOTHER.

UNITED STATES OF AMERICA

INDIAN TERRITORY

Central    DISTRICT.

I, Lizzie Going, on oath state that I am 35 years of age and a citizen by blood of the Choctaw Nation, and as such have been placed upon the final roll of the Choctaw Nation, by the Honorable Secretary of the Interior my final enrollment No. being 5967; that I am the lawful wife of Peter Going, who is a citizen of the Choctaw Nation, and as such has been placed upon the final roll of said Nation by the Honorable Secretary of the Interior, his final enrollment No. being 1088 and that a mail[sic] child was born to me on the 23 day of Sept 1904; that said child has been named Frank Going, and is now living.

## Applications for Enrollment of Choctaw Newborn
## Act of 1905    Volume XVIII

her<br>
Lizzie x Going<br>
mark

Witnesseth.
Must be two        ( Vinson Going
witnesses who   (
are citizens.       ( Osborne Going
(SEAL)

    Subscribed and sworn to before me this 21 day of Jan 1905.

C. L. Lester<br>
Notary Public.

My Commission expires:  Oct 15, 1905.

---

### AFFIDAVIT OF ATTENDING PHYSICIAN OR MIDWIFE

UNITED STATES OF AMERICA

INDIAN TERRITORY

_____ DISTRICT

    I, Sissie Naslit a midwife on oath state that I attended on Mrs. Lizzie Going, wife of Peter Going, on the 23 day of Sept 1904, that there was born to her on said date a mail[sic] child, that said child is now living and is said to have been named Frank Going

Sissie Naslit.

    Subscribed and sworn to before me this, the 21 day of Jan 1905.

C. L. Lester<br>
Notary Public.

WITNESSETH;

Must be two witnesses     ( Osborne Going
                                        (
  who are citizens.       ( _____
    Atoka
(SEAL)

    We hereby certify that we are well acquainted with Sissie Naslit, a midwife and know her to be reputable and of good standing in the community.

Osborne Going                                                                    Vinson Going

# Applications for Enrollment of Choctaw Newborn
## Act of 1905    Volume XVIII

Must be two citizen witnesses.

(Endorsed on back- 7-2073      NEW BORN      1379
IN THE MATTER OF THE BIRTH of Frank Going.
Choctaw Commission No. 699.                    Born Sept. 23, 1904.
Act of Congress approved March 30, 1905.
DEPARTMENT OF THE INTERIOR, COMMISSION TO THE FIVE CIVILIZED TRIBES.    F I L E D   MAY 5, 1905. Tams Bixby, Chairman.
CHOCTAW 1379.                                    RECEIVED APR 25 1905.

DEPARTMENT OF THE INTERIOR,
COMMISSIONER TO THE FIVE CIVILIZED TRIBES.

Siloam Springs, Arkansas, August 27, 1906.

- - - - - - - -   - - - - - - - -

In the matter of the death of Frank Going, Choctaw New Born, on Choctaw Card Number 1379.

Testimony taken as Smithville, Indian Territory, June 18, 1906.

PETER GOING, being duly sworn, testified as follows:

Through Interpreter Jacob Homer.

BY THE COMMISSIONER:

Q  What is your name?  A  Peter Going.
Q  How old are you?  A  About 27 years old.
Q  What is your post office address?  A  Smithville, I. T.
Q  Are you a citizen by blood of the Choctaw Nation?  A  Yes, sir.
Q  Are you a married man, if so state the name of your wife?  A  Lizzie Going.
Q  Have you any children been born to you and Lizzie Going, if so mention them in the order of their births?  A  Yes; Lesina, Frank and another Little one.
Q  Are all these children living at the present time, if not state the names of the deceased ones?  A  Frank is dead.
Q  Have any of these children been enrolled by the Dawes Commission and approved by the Secretary of the Interior?  A  Only Lesina has been enrolled; I wanted to make application for the enrollment of Frank, but I saw notice that that would not be good, so I never done anything more about it.
Q  When was Frank Going born?  A  He was born September 23, 1904.
Q  You state that Frank Going is dead: how old was he at the time of his death?  A  He was about 12 days old, he only lived a few days.
Q  State the date of his death, if you know?  A  He died October 5, 1904.

## Applications for Enrollment of Choctaw Newborn
## Act of 1905  Volume XVIII

Q Have you any form of record of the birth and death of your child, Frank Going?
A No, sir.
Q How do you fix these dates in your mind?
A I just remember, I know when all my children were born.
Q How long has Frank Going been dead now?
A Going on two years, two years in October.
Q The records of the Commission to the Five Civilized Tribes show that on the 21st day of January 1905, Lizzie Going, as mother, made affidavit, before C. L. Lester, Notary Public, that Frank Going was born on the 23rd day of September 1903 and was living at the time of the execution of said affidavit (same is exhibited witness): Were you present when this was sworn to, and cognizant of the statements set forth in same?
A Yes, Lester came round to see me about it and that was before I got my notice, and he fixed up that paper that the child was then living, but I told him that the child was dead.
Q How long had Frank Going been dead at the time of the execution of this affidavit?
A He had been dead two or three months.
Q And you state that you informed C. L. Lester at the time that the child was not living and had been dead some time? A Yes, sir, I told him that the child was dead, but he said he guessed it would be enrolled all right and went on and fixed the papers.
Q You may state again the dates of the birth and death, respectively, of Frank Going?
A He was born September 23, 1904, and died October 5, 1904.

Witness Excused.

---

Testimony taken five miles southeast of Smithville, Indian Territory Indian Territory, June 19?[ 1906.

SOPHIA GOING, being duly sworn, testified, through interpreter Jacob Homer, as follows:

BY THE COMMISSIONER:

Q What is your name? A Sophia Going.
Q What is your age? A About 33.
Q What is your post office address? A Smithville, I. T.
Q Are you a citizen by blood of the Choctaw Nation?
A Yes, sir.
Q Are you acquainted with Peter Going, a citizen by blood of the Choctaw Nation?
A Yes, sir.
Q What is the name of his wife? A Lizzie Going.
Q Have Peter and Lizzie Going any children, if so name them in the order of their births?
A Lesina, Frank and another Little one, not yet named.
Q Do you know the date of Frank Going's birth, if so please state it.
A He was born the 23rd day of September 1904.
Q Is Frank Going now living? A No, sir.
Q When did he die?
A He died the 5th day of October 1904.

# Applications for Enrollment of Choctaw Newborn
## Act of 1905  Volume XVIII

Q How old was this child at the time of his death?
A He was something like two weeks old when he died.
Q How do you fix in your mind that Frank Going was born the 23rd day of September 1904 and died October 5, 1904?
A I just remember it, I have not forgot it yet; we have all been living together so I remember it well. We were living in the same house when that child died.
Q Were you related to this child, if so state relationship?
A My husband is the grandfather of that child and I guess I am the step-grandmother.
Q How many years has Frank Going been dead?
A It will be two years this coming October 1906 since that child died.
Q You state positively and under oath that Frank Going was born September 23, 1904, and died October 5th, 1904, when about two weeks, and that he was not living on March 4, 1905? A Yes, sir.

Witness Excused.

Testimony taken at same place and on same date as above.

LIZZIE GOING, being duly sworn, testified as follows:

Through Interpreter Jacob Homer.

BY THE COMMISSIONER:

Q What is your name? A Lizzie Going.
Q How old are you? A About 36.
Q What is your post office address? A Smithville, I. T.
Q Are you a citizen by blood of the Choctaw Nation?
A Yes, sir.
Q What is your husband's name? A Peter Going.
Q State the names of the children of yourself and Peter Going?
A Lesina, Frank and another one not named.
Q Are any of your children dead at the present time?
A Yes, Frank is dead.
Q How old was Frank when he died? A He was about two weeks old.
Q When did Frank Going die? A I do not know.
Q In what year did he die?
A I do not know, it has been over a year since he died.
Q Do you remember appearing before C. L. Lester on the 21st day of January 1905 and making affidavit relative to the birth of Frank Going?
A Yes, sir, Lester came over here and I made affidavit.
Q Was Frank Going living at the time Lester came over here and you made affidavit?
A No, sir, he was dead.
Q State as near as you can how long Frank Going had been dead when you made this affidavit before C. L. Lester?
A I do not know.

## Applications for Enrollment of Choctaw Newborn
## Act of 1905   Volume XVIII

Q  Were you aware when you executed this affidavit that you were affirming that your child, Frank Going was alive on that date?

    This question was repeated to witness through Interpreter, but she positively refused to answer.

Q  Do you state under oath that Frank Going died when about two weeks old, and that he was not living on the date you made affidavit before c. L. Lester in regard to his birth-- January 21, 1905?
A  Yes, sir.

Witness Excused.

---

    W. P. Covington, being duly sworn, states that the above and foregoing is a full and correct transcript of his stenographic notes taken in said case on the dates and at places set forth.

WP Covington

Subscribed and sworn to before, me, this   6   day of     Sept    1906

Lacey P Bobo<br>Notary Public.

---

7-NB-1379.
O.L.J.

DEPARTMENT OF THE INTERIOR,<br>COMMISSIONER TO THE FIVE CIVILIZED TRIBES.

-----

    In the matter of the application for the enrollment of Frank Going as a citizen by blood of the Choctaw Nation.

D E C I S I O N.

    It appears from the record herein that on April 25, 1905, application was made to the Commission to the Five Civilized Tribes for the enrollment of Frank Going as a citizen by blood of the Choctaw Nation.
    It further appears from the record herein that said applicant was born on September 23, 1904, and is the son of Peter Going, whose name appears as number 1088 upon the final roll of citizens by blood of the Choctaw Nation approved by the Secretary of the Interior December 12, 1902, and Lizzie Going, whose name appears as number 5967 upon the final roll of citizens by blood of the Choctaw Nation approved by the Secretary of the Interior January 16, 1903; and that said applicant died on October 5, 1904.

## Applications for Enrollment of Choctaw Newborn
## Act of 1905   Volume XVIII

The Act of Congress approved March 3, 1905 (33 Stats., 1070), provides:

"That the Commission to the Five Civilized Tribes is authorized for sixty days after the date of the approval of this act to receive and consider applications for enrollment of children born subsequent to September twenty-fifth, nineteen hundred and two, and prior to March fourth, nineteen hundred and five, and who were living on said latter date, to citizens by blood of the Choctaw and Chickasaw tribes of Indians whose enrollment has been approved by the Secretary of the Interior prior to the date of the approval of this act; and to enroll and make allotments to such children."

I am of the opinion that inasmuch as said applicant was not living on March 4, 1905, I am without authority to receive or consider any application for the enrollment of Frank Going as a citizen by blood of the Choctaw Nation, and that I should decline to receive the same, and it is so ordered.

Tams Bixby   Commissioner.

Muskogee, Indian Territory.
OCT 19 1906

---

7-NB-1379.

Muskogee, Indian Territory, October 19, 1906

Peter Going,   **COPY**
    Smithville, Indian Territory.

Dear Sir:

Inclosed herewith you will find a copy of the decision of the Commissioner to the Five Civilized Tribes, rendered October 19, 1906, declining to receive or consider the application for the enrollment of Frank Going as a citizen by blood of the Choctaw Nation.

The decision, with the record of proceedings in the case, is this day transmitted to the Secretary of the Interior for review. The final decision of the Secretary will be made known to you as soon as this office is informed of the same.

Respectfully,

Commissioner.

Registered.
Incl. 7-NB-1379.

## Applications for Enrollment of Choctaw Newborn
## Act of 1905 Volume XVIII

7-NB-1379.

Muskogee, Indian Territory, October 19, 1906

Mansfield, McMurray & Cornish,
    Attorneys for Choctaw and Chickasaw Nations,
        McAlester, Indian Territory.

Gentlemen:

    Inclosed herewith you will find a copy of the decision of the Commissioner to the Five Civilized Tribes, rendered October 19, 1906, declining to receive or consider the application for the enrollment of Frank Going as a citizen by blood of the Choctaw Nation.

    The decision, with the record of proceedings in the case, is this day transmitted to the Secretary of the Interior for review. The final decision of the Secretary will be made known to you as soon as this office is informed of the same.

Respectfully,

Commissioner.

Incl. 7-NB-1379.

---

Muskogee, Indian Territory, October 19, 1906

The Honorable,
    The Secretary of the Interior     **COPY**

Sir:

    There is transmitted herewith record of proceedings in the matter of the application for the enrollment of Frank Going as a citizen by blood of the Choctaw Nation, including the decision of the Commissioner to the Five Civilized Tribes, dated October 19, 1906, declining to receive or consider said application.

Respectfully,

Commissioner.

2 Incl. 7-NB-1379.

## Applications for Enrollment of Choctaw Newborn
## Act of 1905   Volume XVIII

*944/409*

Refer in reply to the following:
LAND                DEPARTMENT OF THE INTERIOR,
92796-1906.         OFFICE OF INDIAN AFFAIRS,
                            WASHINGTON.

C O P Y                                         February 20, 1907.

The Honorable,
      The Secretary of the Interior.

Sir:

  There is enclosed record of proceedings in the matter of the application for the enrollment of Frank Going as a citizen of the Choctaw Nation, including decision of the Commissioner to the Five Civilized Tribes, dated October 19, 1906, adverse to the applicant.

  The record shows that application was made on April 25, 1905 to the Commissioner to the Five Civilized Tribes for the enrollment of this applicant as a citizen of the Choctaw Nation. The record further shows that the applicant was born September 23, 1904, and died October 5, 1904; that he is the son of Peter Going and Lizzie Going, whose names appear on the final roll of citizens by blood of the Choctaw Nation.

  Inasmuch as the applicant was not living on March 4, 1906, the Office concurs in the decision of Commissioner Bixby denying the enrollment of Frank Going as a citizen of the Choctaw Nation, under the provisions of the Act of Congress approved April 26, 1906, (34 Stat. L., 137).

       Very respectfully,

         C. F. Larrabee

LMM-LC..                                        Acting Commissioner.

---

                 Y.P.
     DEPARTMENT OF THE INTERIOR.
        WASHINGTON.  O.K.

LRS
D.C. 12051-1907.
  I. T. D.
4594, 4604, 4606, 4608, - 1907.
4642, 4650, 4668, 4702,  "
4716, 4722, 4724, 4728,  "

DIRECT .                                        February 27, 1907.

# Applications for Enrollment of Choctaw Newborn
## Act of 1905 Volume XVIII

Commissioner to the Five Civilized Tribes,
    Muskogee, Indian Territory.

Sir:

Your decisions in the following Choctaw citizenship cases adverse to the applicants are hereby affirmed. Copies of Indian Office letters submitting your reports and recommending that the decisions be affirmed are inclosed:

| Title of Case. | Date of Your Letter of transmittal. |
|---|---|
| Tom Isaac, ( Miss. Choc.), | December 15, 1906. |
| Viney King et al., (Freedmen), | October 19, 1906. |
| Frank Going, | October 19, 1906. |
| James Morris | October 19, 1906. |
| Floy E. Davis et al., | January 16, 1907. |
| Sousan Jackson et al., | January 29, 1907. |
| Lillie Henderson, | January 16, 1907. |
| Claudia A. Plato et al., | December 24, 1906. |
| Beatrice Bottoms, | January 9, 1907. |
| William H. Mitchell et al., | January 9, 1907. |
| Thedia D. Blake et al., | November 22, 1906. |
| Cora A. Pyle, | January 9, 1907. |

A copy hereof and all the papers in the above mentioned cases have been sent to the Indian Office.

            Respectfully,

12 inc. and 24                    Jesse E. Wilson
inc. for Ind. Of.
                        Assistant Secretary.

AF??
2-28-07.

## Applications for Enrollment of Choctaw Newborn
## Act of 1905   Volume XVIII

7-NB-1379

Muskogee, Indian Territory, April 3, 1907.

Peter Going,
    Smithville, Indian Territory.

Dear Sir:

You are hereby advised that on February 27, 1907, the Secretary of the Interior affirmed the decision of the Commissioner to the Five Civilized Tribes, rendered October 19, 1906, declining to receive or consider the application for the enrollment of Frank Going as a citizen by blood of the Choctaw Nation.

Respectfully,

*Geo. D. Rodgers.*

Acting Commissioner.

---

7-NB-1379

Muskogee, Indian Territory, April 3, 1907.

Mansfield, McMurray & Cornish,
    Attorneys for Choctaw and Chickasaw Nations,
        South McAlester, Indian Territory.

Gentlemen:

You are hereby advised that on February 27, 1907, the Secretary of the Interior affirmed the decision of the Commissioner to the Five Civilized Tribes, rendered October 19, 1906, declining to receive or consider the application for the enrollment of Frank Going as a citizen by blood of the Choctaw Nation.

Respectfully,

*Geo. D. Rodgers.*

Acting Commissioner.

# Applications for Enrollment of Choctaw Newborn
## Act of 1905  Volume XVIII

7-NB-1379.

Muskogee, Indian Territory, June 1, 1905.

Peter Going,
    Smithville, Indian Territory.

Dear Sir:

    There is enclosed you herewith for execution application for the enrollment of your infant child, Frank Going, born September 23, 1904.

    The affidavits heretofore filed with the Commission show the child was living on January 5, 1905. It is necessary for the child to be enrolled, that he was living on March 4, 1905.

    In having these affidavits executed care should be exercised to see that all names are written in full, as they appear in the body of the affidavit, and in the event that either of the persons signing the affidavit are unable to write, signatures by mark must be attested by two witnesses. Each affidavit must be executed before a Notary Public and the notarial seal and signature of the officer must be attached to each separate affidavit.

    Respectfully,

    Chairman.

Enc. FVK-11

---

7-NB-1379

Muskogee, Indian Territory, July 28, 1905.

Peter Going,
    Smithville, Indian Territory.

Dear Sir:

    Your attention is called to a communictaion[sic] addressed to you by the Commission to the Five Civilized Tribes, under date of June 1, 1905, with which there was inclosed for execution application for the enrollment of your infant child, Frank Going, born September 23, 1904.

    In said letter you were advised that the affidavits heretofore filed with the Commission to the Five Civilized Tribes show the child was living on January 5, 1905, and that it was necessary for the child to be enrolled that he was living March 4, 1905; you were requested to have the affidavit properly executed and returned to this office. No reply to this letter has been received.

## Applications for Enrollment of Choctaw Newborn
## Act of 1905   Volume XVIII

The matter should receive your immediate attention as no further action can be taken relative to the enrollment of said child until the evidence requested is supplied.

              Respectfully,

              Commissioner.

---

Choc. New Born 1380
  Fredie Robertson
  (Born March 5, 1903)

**NEW-BORN AFFIDAVIT.**

    Number..................

### ...Choctaw Enrolling Commission...

  IN THE MATTER OF THE APPLICATION FOR ENROLLMENT, as a citizen of the Choctaw Nation, of Fredie Robertson born on the 5 day of __March__ 190 3

Name of father  David Robertson    a citizen of   Choctaw
Nation final enrollment No. ..................
Name of mother  Irene Robertson    a citizen of   Choctaw
Nation final enrollment No. 8107

           Postoffice    Chant, I.T.

**AFFIDAVIT OF MOTHER.**

UNITED STATES OF AMERICA
INDIAN TERRITORY
 Central    DISTRICT

   I  Irene Robertson   , on oath state that I am 24 years of age and a citizen by Blood of the Choctaw Nation, and as such have been placed upon the final roll of the Choctaw Nation, by the Honorable Secretary of the Interior my final enrollment number being 8107 ; that I am the lawful wife of David Robertson , who is a citizen of the Choctaw Nation, and as such has been placed upon the final roll of said Nation by the Honorable Secretary of the Interior, his final enrollment number being .................. and that a Male child was born to me on the

# Applications for Enrollment of Choctaw Newborn
## Act of 1905 Volume XVIII

5th day of March 190 3; that said child has been named Fredie Robertson and is now living.

Irene Robertson

Witnesseth.

Must be two Witnesses who are Citizens. } Floyd Nevins

Swinney M<sup>c</sup>Gee

Subscribed and sworn to before me this 17 day of Jan 190 5

Jas A Rogers
Notary Public.

My commission expires: 11/18/06

## AFFIDAVIT OF ATTENDING PHYSICIAN OR MIDWIFE

UNITED STATES OF AMERICA
INDIAN TERRITORY
Central DISTRICT

I, Polly L Bernard a Midwife on oath state that I attended on Mrs. Irene Robertson wife of David Robertson on the 5th day of March , 190 3 , that there was born to her on said date a male child, that said child is now living, and is said to have been named Fredie Robertson

Polly L Bernard

Subscribed and sworn to before me this, the 17th day of January 190 5

Jas A Rogers    Notary Public.

WITNESSETH:

Must be two witnesses who are citizens { Floyd Nevins

Swinney M<sup>c</sup>Gee

We hereby certify that we are well acquainted with Mrs Polly L Bernard a Midwife and know her to be reputable and of good standing in the community.

Floyd Nevins _____

Swinney McGee _____

## Applications for Enrollment of Choctaw Newborn
## Act of 1905   Volume XVIII

BIRTH AFFIDAVIT.

## DEPARTMENT OF THE INTERIOR.
## COMMISSION TO THE FIVE CIVILIZED TRIBES.

IN RE APPLICATION FOR ENROLLMENT, as a citizen of the   Choctaw   Nation, of Fredie Robertson   , born on the 5$^{th}$   day of March   , 1903

Name of Father: David Robertson  Roll 7.W. 729  a citizen of the   Choctaw   Nation.
Name of Mother: Irene Robertson   " 8107   a citizen of the   Choctaw   Nation.

Postoffice   Chant I.T.

### AFFIDAVIT OF MOTHER.

UNITED STATES OF AMERICA, Indian Territory, }
Central   DISTRICT.

I,   Irene Robertson   , on oath state that I am   24   years of age and a citizen by   blood   , of the   Choctaw   Nation; that I am the lawful wife of   David Robertson   , who is a citizen, by   marriage   of the   Choctaw   Nation; that a   male   child was born to me on   5$^{th}$   day of   March   , 1903; that said child has been named   Fredie Robertson   , and was living March 4, 1905.

Irene Robertson

Witnesses To Mark:
{ Roy Parke
{ C.M. Avery

Subscribed and sworn to before me this   24   day of   July   , 1905

My Com Ex 2/2/08   Frank E. Parke
Notary Public.

### AFFIDAVIT OF ATTENDING PHYSICIAN OR MID-WIFE.

UNITED STATES OF AMERICA, Indian Territory, }
Central   DISTRICT.

I,   Polly L Bernard   , a   midwife   , on oath state that I attended on Mrs.   Irene Robertson   , wife of   David Robertson   on the   5$^{th}$   day of March   , 1903; that there was born to her on said date a   male   child; that said child was living March 4, 1905, and is said to have been named Fredie Robertson

her
Polly L x Bernard
mark

## Applications for Enrollment of Choctaw Newborn
## Act of 1905   Volume XVIII

Witnesses To Mark:
{ Roy Parke
{ C.M. Avery

Subscribed and sworn to before me this  24   day of    July      , 1905

My Com Ex 2/2/08                    Frank E. Parke
                                                    Notary Public.

---

7--NB--1380

Muskogee, Indian Territory, June 1, 1905.

David Robertson,
     Chant, Indian Territory.

Dear Sir:

There is enclosed you herewith for execution application for the enrollment of your infant child, Fredie Robertson, born March 5, 1903.

The affidavits heretofore filed with the Commission show the child was living on January 17, 1905. It is necessary, for the child to be enrolled, that he was living on March 4, 1905.

In having these affidavits executed care should be exercised to see that all names are written in full, as they appear in the body of the affidavit, and in the event that either of the persons signing the affidavit are unable to write, signatures by mark must be attested by two witnesses. Each affidavit must be executed before a Notary Public and the notarial seal and signature of the officer must be attached to each separate affidavit.

Respectfully,

Chairman.

FVK-15

## Applications for Enrollment of Choctaw Newborn
## Act of 1905   Volume XVIII

7-NB-1380

Muskogee, Indian Territory, July 28, 1905.

David Robertson,
    Chant, Indian Territory.

Dear Sir:

    Receipt is hereby acknowledged of the affidavits of Irene Robertson and Polly L. Bernard to the birth of Fredie Robertson, son of David and Irene Robertson, March 5, 1903, and the same have been filed with the records of this office in the matter of the enrollment of said child.

        Respectfully,

                Commissioner.

---

Choc. New Born 1381
    Louisa Riddle
    (Born Jan. 1, 1905)

**NEW-BORN AFFIDAVIT.**

    Number..................

...Choctaw Enrolling Commission...

    IN THE MATTER OF THE APPLICATION FOR ENROLLMENT, as a citizen of the Choctaw       Nation, of       Louisa Riddle

born on the   1$^{st}$   day of   January       190 5

Name of father   Coleman Riddle           a citizen of   Choctaw
Nation final enrollment No.   13056      *Byington)*
Name of mother   Nancy Riddle   *(nee*         a citizen of   Choctaw
Nation final enrollment No.   13807

                Postoffice   Quinton I.T.

# Applications for Enrollment of Choctaw Newborn
## Act of 1905   Volume XVIII

### AFFIDAVIT OF MOTHER.

UNITED STATES OF AMERICA
INDIAN TERRITORY
Western        DISTRICT

I   Nancy Riddle  *(nee Byington)*   , on oath state that I am 29 years of age and a citizen by  blood  of the  Choctaw  Nation, and as such have been placed upon the final roll of the  Choctaw  Nation, by the Honorable Secretary of the Interior my final enrollment number being  13807 ; that I am the lawful wife of  Coleman Riddle  , who is a citizen of the  Choctaw  Nation, and as such has been placed upon the final roll of said Nation by the Honorable Secretary of the Interior, his final enrollment number being  13056  and that a  Female  child was born to me on the  1st  day of  January  190 5; that said child has been named  Louisa  , and is now living.

Nancy Riddle

Witnesseth.

Must be two Witnesses who are Citizens.
- Andrew C. Bullard
- James H Bickle

Subscribed and sworn to before me this  17th  day of  Feb   190 5

Guy A. Curry<br>Notary Public.

My commission expires:
Apr 27 - 1907

---

## AFFIDAVIT OF ATTENDING PHYSICIAN OR MIDWIFE

UNITED STATES OF AMERICA
INDIAN TERRITORY
Western        DISTRICT

I,   Lizzie Reed   a   midwife on oath state that I attended on Mrs.  Nancy Riddle   wife of  Coleman Riddle  on the  1st  day of  January , 190 5, that there was born to her on said date a  male[sic] child, that said child is now living, and is said to have been named  Louisa Riddle

Lizzie Reed

Subscribed and sworn to before me this, the   17th   day of  February    190 5

Guy A. Curry    Notary Public.

WITNESSETH:

Must be two witnesses who are citizens
- Andrew C. Bullard
- James H Bickle

## Applications for Enrollment of Choctaw Newborn
## Act of 1905   Volume XVIII

We hereby certify that we are well acquainted with   Lizzie Reed   a   midwife   and know   her   to be reputable and of good standing in the community.

Andrew C. Bullard

James H Bickle

**BIRTH AFFIDAVIT.**

### DEPARTMENT OF THE INTERIOR.
### COMMISSION TO THE FIVE CIVILIZED TRIBES.

IN RE APPLICATION FOR ENROLLMENT, as a citizen of the   Choctaw   Nation, of Louisa Riddle   , born on the   1st   day of   January   , 1905

Name of Father: Coleman Riddle   a citizen of the   Choctaw   Nation.
Name of Mother: Nancy Riddle (nee Byington)   a citizen of the   Choctaw   Nation.

Postoffice

**AFFIDAVIT OF MOTHER.**

UNITED STATES OF AMERICA, Indian Territory,
Western   DISTRICT.

I,   Nancy Riddle   , on oath state that I am   28   years of age and a citizen by blood   , of the   Choctaw   Nation; that I am the lawful wife of   Coleman Riddle , who is a citizen, by blood   of the   Choctaw   Nation; that a   female   child was born to me on   1st   day of   January   , 1905; that said child has been named Louisa Riddle   , and was living March 4, 1905.

Nancy Riddle

Witnesses To Mark:

Subscribed and sworn to before me this   29th   day of   March   , 1905

Guy A. Curry
Notary Public.

My commission expires Apr 27-1907

# Applications for Enrollment of Choctaw Newborn
## Act of 1905   Volume XVIII

**AFFIDAVIT OF ATTENDING PHYSICIAN OR MID-WIFE.**

UNITED STATES OF AMERICA, Indian Territory, }
Western                          DISTRICT.

I,   Lizzie Reed   , a  midwife   , on oath state that I attended on Mrs.   Coleman Robertson  , wife of  Coleman Robertson   on the 1$^{st}$   day of January   , 1905; that there was born to her on said date a    Female    child; that said child was living March 4, 1905, and is said to have been named  Louisa Riddle

Lizzie Reed

Witnesses To Mark:
{

Subscribed and sworn to before me this 29$^{th}$   day of   March   , 1905

Guy A. Curry<br>Notary Public.

My commission expires Apr 27-1907

---

7-N.B. 1381.

Muskogee, Indian Territory, May 22, 1905.

Coleman Riddle,
    Quinton, Indian Territory.

Dear Sir:

Receipt is hereby acknowledged of the affidavits of Nancy Riddle and Lizzie Reed to the birth of Louisa Riddle, daughter of Coleman and Nancy Riddle, January 1, 1905, and the same have been filed with our records in the matter of the enrollment of said child.

Respectfully,

Chairman.

Applications for Enrollment of Choctaw Newborn
Act of 1905   Volume XVIII

7-NB-1381

Muskogee, Indian Territory, August 19, 1905.

Coleman Riddle,
    Quinton, Indian Territory.

Dear Sir:

Receipt is hereby acknowledged of your letter of August 15, 1905, asking if you can file for your child, Louisa Riddle, who was born January 1, 1905, and died July 15, 1905.

In reply to your letter you are advised that the enrollment of your child, Louisa Riddle was approved by the Secretary of the Interior on August 2, 1905, and selection of allotment may now be made in her behalf, but if this child died July 15, 1905, it will be necessary that an administrator be appointed by the United States Court in order to make selection of her allotment.

Respectfully,

Acting Commissioner.

---

Choc. New Born 1382
    Levi Pickens
    (Born Feb. 2, 1904)

## NEW BORN AFFIDAVIT

No _____

### CHOCTAW ENROLLING COMMISSION

IN THE MATTER OF THE APPLICATION FOR ENROLLMENT as a citizen of the Choctaw Nation, of   Levi Pickens   born on the $2^d$ day of  February  190 4

Name of father  Jefferson Pickens    a citizen of   Choctaw   Nation, final enrollment No.  10643    *now Pickens*

Name of mother  Nancy Byington    a citizen of   Choctaw   Nation, final enrollment No.  10674

# Applications for Enrollment of Choctaw Newborn
## Act of 1905 Volume XVIII

Caney I.T. Postoffice.

**AFFIDAVIT OF MOTHER**

UNITED STATES OF AMERICA  
   INDIAN TERRITORY  
DISTRICT    Central

*now Pickens*

I    Nancy Bying[sic]    *Deceased* , on oath state that I am   21   years of age and a citizen by   blood   of the   Choctaw   Nation, and as such have been placed upon the final roll of the   Choctaw   Nation, by the Honorable Secretary of the Interior my final enrollment number being   10674   ; that I am the lawful wife of   Jefferson Pickens   , who is a citizen of the   Choctaw   Nation, and as such has been placed upon the final roll of said Nation by the Honorable Secretary of the Interior, his final enrollment number being   10643   and that a   Male   child was born to me on the   $2^d$ day of   February   190 4; that said child has been named   Levi Pickens   , and is now living.

                                 Nancy Pickens  
WITNESSETH:                by Jefferson Pickens

Must be two witnesses { Loring Robinson  
who are citizens        Allen Wright

Subscribed and sworn to before me this, the   $7^{th}$   day of   February   , 190 5

                             A.E. Folsom  
                                     Notary Public.

My Commission Expires:  
     Jan 9- 1909

## *Affidavit of Attending Physician or Midwife*

UNITED STATES OF AMERICA,  
     INDIAN TERRITORY,  
Central      DISTRICT

I,   Austin[sic] Pickens      a      Witness was Present on oath state that I attended on *I was present* Mrs. Nancy Byington now Pickens   wife of Jefferson Pickens   on the   $2^{nd}$   day of February   , 190 4, that there was born to her on said date a   Male   child, that said child is now living, and is said to have been named   Levi Pickens                                   *as witness*

                 *Was Present*   Auston Pickens      M.D.

## Applications for Enrollment of Choctaw Newborn
## Act of 1905   Volume XVIII

Subscribed and sworn to before me this the 7" day of February 1905

A.E. Folsom
Notary Public.

WITNESSETH:
Must be two witnesses who are citizens and know the child. { Loring Robinson
Allen Wright

We hereby certify that we are well acquainted with       Witness Auston Pickens
a ................................... and know ................... to be reputable and of good standing in the community.

*Expires*
*Jan 9-1909*

Must be two citizen witnesses. { Loring Robinson
Allen Wright

---

BIRTH AFFIDAVIT.

### DEPARTMENT OF THE INTERIOR.
### COMMISSION TO THE FIVE CIVILIZED TRIBES.

IN RE APPLICATION FOR ENROLLMENT, as a citizen of the   Choctaw   Nation, of Levi Pickens, born on the 2 day of February , 1904

Name of Father: Jefferson Pickens        a citizen of the   Choctaw   Nation.
Name of Mother: Nancy Pickens (Byington)  a citizen of the   Choctaw   Nation.

Postoffice   Caney, Indian Territory.

Affidavit of Husband of A Deceased Mother.
~~AFFIDAVIT OF MOTHER.~~

UNITED STATES OF AMERICA, Indian Territory,
Central       DISTRICT.

Nancy Pickens     she was
I, Jefferson Pickens, Husband of (Byington Decease , on oath state that ~~I am~~ 21 years of age and a citizen by   blood   , of the   Choctaw   Nation; that ~~I am~~ she was the lawful wife of   (My self) Jefferson Pickens   , who is a citizen, by blood   of the   Choctaw   Nation; that a   Male   child was born to ~~me~~ her on 2 day of   February   1904 , 1.........; that said child has been named   Levi Pickens   , and was living March 4, 1905.

Jefferson Pickens
Husband of Nancy Pickens (Byington) Deceased

Witnesses To Mark:
{

## Applications for Enrollment of Choctaw Newborn
## Act of 1905   Volume XVIII

Subscribed and sworn to before me this 2nd day of   May   , 1905

                                      A Denton Phillips
                                      Notary Public.

### AFFIDAVIT OF ATTENDING PHYSICIAN OR MID-WIFE.

UNITED STATES OF AMERICA, Indian Territory, }
   Central                   DISTRICT. }

                                                            was Present when
I,   Austin Pickens   , a   Midwife, Witness   , on oath state that I ~~attended on~~ Mrs.  Nancy Pickens (Byington)   , wife of  Jefferson Pickens   on the 2nd day of   February 1904   , 1......; that there was born to her on said date a   Male child; that said child was living March 4, 1905, and is said to have been named  Levi Pickens

                                        Auston Pickens

Witnesses To Mark:
   {

Subscribed and sworn to before me this 2  day of   May   , 1905

                                      A Denton Phillips
                                      Notary Public.

*(The affidavit below typed as given.)*

United States of America
    Indian Territory
Central    District

               I, Leering[sic] Robinson upon oath state that I have known Jefferson Pickens for 25 years.  And I, have also known his (Deceased) wife Nancy Pickens (Byington) for a number of years, and also know that she was the lawfull wife of the said Jefferson Pickens, who ~~is~~ *was* both citizens of the Choctaw nation.  There was borned to Mrs Nancy Pickens (Byington) on the 2on day of February 1904. a male child and siad child aws named Levi Pickens and is now living, and I further state that I know of the death of Mrs Nancy Pickens (Byington) her death occured about Five months after the birth of her said child Levi Pickens, I further state that I know Betsie Lewis, a midwife who attended on Mrs Nancy Pickens (Byington) when at the time of the birth of the said Levi Pickens, and the said Betsie Lewis is A-Snake-Indian and has there fore declined to make affidavit to the said child,Birth.
In witness where of I here unto set my hand, This the 2 day of May 1905.

                                      Loring Robinson

# Applications for Enrollment of Choctaw Newborn
## Act of 1905   Volume XVIII

Indian Territory
Central District
    Subscribed abd sworn to be fore me this the 2'' day May 1905.

                                   A Denton Phillips
                                      Notary Public.

                                             7-N.B. 1382.
                            **COPY**
                      Muskogee, Indian Territory, June 1, 1905.

Jefferson Pickens,
    Caney, Indian Territory.

Dear Sir:

    Receipt is hereby acknowledged of your affidavit and the affidavits of Austin Pickens and Loring Robinson to the birth of Levi Pickens, son of Jefferson and Nancy Pickens, deceased, February 2, 1904, and the same have been filed with our records in the matter of the enrollment of said child.

                              Respectfully,
                              SIGNED
                              *T. B. Needles.*
                              Commissioner in Charge.

*Dup -*

                                          7-NB--1382.

                    Muskogee, Indian Territory, June 14, 1905.

Jefferson Pickens,
    Caney, Indian Territory.

Dear Sir:

    Referring to the application for the enrollment of your infant child, Levi Pickens, born February 2, 1904, it appears from the affidavits heretofore filed in this office that Nancy Pickens, the mother of the applicant, is dead. If this is correct, you are requested to have the enclosed proof of death executed and filed in this office in order that this fact may be made a matter of record.

    It also appears from the above mentioned affidavits that Betsy Lewis, a Snake Indian, attended upon your wife at the time of the birth of the applicant and has declined

## Applications for Enrollment of Choctaw Newborn
## Act of 1905   Volume XVIII

to make affidavit as to the birth of the child. The affidavit which you filed in place of the midwife's is executed by Auston Pickens, your brother.

In this event it will be necessary for you to secure the affidavits of two persons who are <u>disinterested</u> and <u>not related</u> to the applicant, who have knowledge of the facts; that the child was born, the date of his birth, that he was living on March 4, 1905, and that Nancy Pickens was his mother, that Betsy Lewis, who is a Snake Indian, attended upon your wife at the time of the time[sic] of the birth of the applicant and has declined to make affidavit to the birth of said child.

This matter should receive your immediate attention as no further action can be taken relative to the enrollment of said child until the can be taken until these affidavits are furnished the Commission.

Respectfully,

SIGNED

*Tams Bixby*
Chairman.

7-NB-1382.

**COPY**

Muskogee, Indian Territory, September 18, 1905.

Jefferson Pickens,
    Caney, Indian Territory.

Dear Sir:

Receipt is hereby acknowledged of your letter of September 11, 1905, in which you request to be informed of the Status of the application for the enrollment of your minor son, Levi Pickens, and to be advised of what evidence is necessary in the matter of the enrollment of said child. You also state therein that you filled out and executed a blank for proof of birth and you are requested to have the same signed and executed before a notary public; care should be taken that said notary public affixes his signature and official seal to same. of death which was forwarded you for the purpose of making proof of the death of your former wife Nancy Pickens.

You are advised that this proof of death has never been received at this office and that it will be necessary that the same be supplied and a blank for that purpose is inclosed herewith.

You are also advised that on June 14, 1905 this office addressed a letter to you advising you that it would be necessary for you to furnish, in the matter of the enrollment of your said son, the affidavits of two persons who are <u>disinterested</u> and not related to the

## Applications for Enrollment of Choctaw Newborn
## Act of 1905   Volume XVIII

applicant, who have knowledge of the circumstances attending the birth of said child, the date when said child was born, the names of his parents and whether or not he wa living on March 4, 1905.

There are on file now with the record in this case relative to the birth of said child two affidavits, the affidavit of Austin Pickens and the affidavit of Loring Robinson.

As requested in the letter of this office dated June 14, 1905, it will be necessary for you to furnish this office the affidavits of two additional disinterested witnesses relative to the birth of said child and you are advised that until the same are supplied nothing further can be done in the matter of the enrollment of the said Levi Pickens as a citizen by blood of the Choctaw Nation.

Respectfully,

Signed   Wm. O. Beall
Acting Commissioner.

D C
Env.

7-NB-1382

**COPY**

Muskogee, Indian Territory, November 9, 1905.

George T. Putty,
    Attorney at Law,
        Marlow, Indian Territory.

Dear Sir:

Receipt is hereby acknowledged of your letter of November 6, 1905, in which you state that there is an Indian child named Levy Pickens, son of Jefferson and Nancy Pickens, who is in charge of one Abel Wade and Mr. Wade desires to know why this child cannot be enrolled or if it can be enrolled what steps are necessary to take in the matter.

In reply to your letter you are advised that on September 18, 1905, a letter was addressed to Jefferson Pickens at Caney, Indian Territory with which was inclosed blank form for proof of the death of his wife Nancy Pickens and he was requested to have the same executed and returned to this office. He was also advised that it would be necessary for him to furnish in the matter of the enrollment of his child Levi Pickens, the affidavits of two persons who are disinterested and not related to the applicant who have knowledge of the circumstances attending his birth, the date of his birth, the names of his parents and

# Applications for Enrollment of Choctaw Newborn
## Act of 1905   Volume XVIII

whether or not he was living on March 4, 1905, but up to this time no response has been received to said letter.

There is inclosed herewith blank form for proof of death which you are requested to have executed showing the death of Nancy Pickens and upon receipt of the affidavits referred to above the matter of the enrollment of Levi Pickens will be given further consideration.

Respectfully,

D.C.

SIGNED

*Tams Bixby*
Commissioner.

---

7-NB-1382

**COPY**

Muskogee, Indian Territory, May 17, 1906.

Jefferson Pickens,
    Kings, Indian Territory.

Dear Sir:

Receipt is hereby acknowledged of the affidavit of Abel Wade to the birth of Levy Pickens, child of Jefferson and Nancy Pickens, February 1, 1904, and this affidavit has been filed in the matter of the application of Levi Pickens as a citizen by blood of the Choctaw Nation. You are advised, however, that it will be necessary for you to forward the affidavit of another disinterested witness who knows of the birth of this child, the date of his birth, and whether or not he is still living. You should also forward evidence of the death of your wife Nancy Pickens as requested in previous letters from this office.

Please give this matter immediate attention.

Respectfully,

Signed    *Wm. O. Beall*
Acting Commissioner.

---

*(The letter above given again but dated May 21, 1906.)*

## Applications for Enrollment of Choctaw Newborn
## Act of 1905  Volume XVIII

*(The affidavit below typed as given.)*

BIRTH AFFIDAVIT.

DEPARTMENT OF THE INTERIOR,
## COMMISSIONER TO THE FIVE CIVILIZED TRIBES.

ENROLLMENT OF MINORS.  ACT OF CONGRESS, APPROVED APRIL 26, 1906.

IN RE APPLICATION FOR ENROLLMENT, as a citizen of the Choctaw Nation, of Levy Picken[sic], born on the 1st day of February, 1904

Name of Father: Jefferson Picken         a citizen of the Choctaw Nation.
Name of Mother: Nancy Picken, nee Byington   a citizen of the Choctaw Nation.

Tribal enrollment of father .......................... Tribal enrollment of mother ..........................

Postoffice    Caney, I.T.

---

AFFIDAVIT OF MOTHER.

UNITED STATES OF AMERICA, Indian Territory,
Southern ---------------------- District.

I, Abel Wade, on oath state that I am 50 years of age and a citizen by blood, of the Choctaw Nation; that I ~~am~~ Nancy Picken, nee Byington the lawful wife of Jefferson Picken, deceased, who ~~is~~ was a citizen, by blood of the Choctaw Nation; that a male child was born to ~~me~~ Nancy Picken on 1st day of February, 1904, that said child has been named Levy Picken, and was living March 4, 1906.

Abel Wade

WITNESSES TO MARK:

Subscribed and sworn to before me this 12th day of May, 1906.

W$^m$ A Proctor
Notary Public.

# Applications for Enrollment of Choctaw Newborn
## Act of 1905   Volume XVIII

*(The affidavit below typed as given.)*

BIRTH AFFIDAVIT.

### DEPARTMENT OF THE INTERIOR,
### COMMISSIONER TO THE FIVE CIVILIZED TRIBES.

ENROLLMENT OF MINORS.   ACT OF CONGRESS, APPROVED APRIL 26, 1906.

IN RE APPLICATION FOR ENROLLMENT, as a citizen of the   Choctaw   Nation, of   Levi Pickens   , born on the   2   day of   Feby   , 1904

Name of Father: Jefferson Pickens          a citizen of the   Choctaw   Nation.
Name of Mother: Nacy Byington Pickens   a citizen of the   Choctaw   Nation.

Tribal enrollment of father   by blood   Tribal enrollment of mother   by blood

Postoffice   Caney I.T.

Affidavit of disenterested witness (Mother deceased)
~~AFFIDAVIT OF MOTHER.~~

UNITED STATES OF AMERICA, Indian Territory, }
   Central            District.   }

I,   Allen Wright   , on oath state that I ~~am~~ was well Acquainted with Nancy Byington, Pickens, (deceased) she was about 21 years of age and a citizen by   blood   , of the   Choctaw   Nation; that I ~~am~~ *she was* the lawful wife of   Jefferson Pickens   , who ~~is~~ was a citizen, by   blood   of the   Choctaw   Nation; that a   male   child was born to ~~me~~ *her* on   2 nd   day of   Febuary   , 1904 , that said child has been named   Levi Pickens   , and was living March 4, 1906.

Allen Wright

WITNESSES TO MARK:
{

Subscribed and sworn to before me this   20<sup>th</sup>   day of   July   , 1906.

A Denton Phillips<br>Notary Public.

## Applications for Enrollment of Choctaw Newborn
## Act of 1905   Volume XVIII

Affidavit of disenterested witness, (Midwife a member of Snake)
~~AFFIDAVIT OF ATTENDING PHYSICIAN OR MID-WIFE.~~

UNITED STATES OF AMERICA, Indian Territory, }
   Central                                District.    }

I,   Loring Robinson       , ~~a~~           , on oath state that I ~~attended on~~   was well acquainted with Nancy Byington Pickens, (deceased)  , wife of Jefferson Pickens   and that   on the  2 nd  day of   Febuary , 1904 ; that there was born to her on said date a   male    child; that said child was living March 4, 1906, and is said to have been named   Levi Pickens

                                            Loring Robinson
WITNESSES TO MARK:
{

Subscribed and sworn to before me this   20th   day of   July  , 1906.

                                        A Denton Phillips
                                          Notary Public.

---

*(The affidavit below typed as given.)*

BIRTH AFFIDAVIT.
### DEPARTMENT OF THE INTERIOR,
## COMMISSIONER TO THE FIVE CIVILIZED TRIBES.

ENROLLMENT OF MINORS.  ACT OF CONGRESS, APPROVED APRIL 26, 1906.

    IN RE APPLICATION FOR ENROLLMENT, as a citizen of the   Choctaw   Nation, of    Levi Pickens       , born on the   1st   day of   February  , 1904

Name of Father:  Jefferson Pickens       a citizen of the   Choctaw   Nation.
Name of Mother: Nancy Byington Pickens   a citizen of the   Choctaw   Nation.

Tribal enrollment of father full blood Choctaw  Tribal enrollment of mother full blood Choctaw

                Postoffice    Unknown

---

                      AFFIDAVIT OF MOTHER.

UNITED STATES OF AMERICA, Indian Territory, }
............................................District. }

    I,......Mother is dead............, on oath state that I am ................. years of age and a citizen by ................. , of the ............................. Nation; that I am the lawful wife of ............................................., who is a citizen, by ......................... of

# Applications for Enrollment of Choctaw Newborn
## Act of 1905  Volume XVIII

the .................................. Nation; that a ..................... child was born to me on ............ day of ......................, 1......, that said child has been named ......................................, and was living March 4, 1906.

.....................................................

WITNESSES TO MARK:
{ ............................................
  ............................................

Subscribed and sworn to before me this .......... day of ............................., 1906.

.....................................................
Notary Public.

---

### AFFIDAVIT OF ATTENDING PHYSICIAN OR MID-WIFE.

UNITED STATES OF AMERICA, Indian Territory,  
Southern ---------------------- District.

I,  Agnes Wade  , a   Midwife   , on oath state that I attended on  Nancy Byington, Pickens  , wife of  Jefferson Pickens  on the 1st day of  February , 1904 ; that there was born to her on said date a  Male  child; that said child was living March 4, 1906, and is said to have been named  Levi Pickens

                  her  
            Agnes x Wade  
WITNESSES TO MARK:          mark  
{ Jefferson Wade  
  Joe Anderson

Subscribed and sworn to before me this  21st  day of  July , 1906.

           T L Wade  
           Notary Public.

---

In re, Application for the enrollment of Levi Pickens, as a member of the Choctaw Nation:

Affidavit of Agnes Wade, Midwife:

Agnes Wade, being first duly sworn, states upon oath, that she is a citizen of the Choctaw Nation or Tribe of Indians, that she is 47 years old, and resides near Marlow postoffice, in the Chickasaw Nation, Indian Territory.

That she formerly lived in the Choctaw Nation, near Caney postoffice, and that she waited upon and nursed Nancy Byington, Pickens, at the birth of her child Levi Pickens,

## Applications for Enrollment of Choctaw Newborn
## Act of 1905   Volume XVIII

that she attended the said Nancy Byington Pickens on and after the first day of February, 1904; and waited on the said Nancy Byington Pickens frequently for a period of about six months after the birth of the said child Levi Pickens; and until her death, about the last of July 1904.

Affiant further states, that after the death of the said Nancy Byington Pickens; the said Jefferson Pickens, father of the said Levi Pickens, gave the said child Levi Pickens, to this affiant, and this affiant Agnes Wade, has had the care and custody of the said child Levi Pickens, continuously since the death of its mother, Nancy Byington Pickens, in the month of July, 1904.

Affiant further states: That she made several efforts to get the said farther, Jefferson Pickens, to have the child enrolled, and that the said Jefferson Pickens has neglected and refused to do so; and, that affiant tried to persuade the grand-father Austin Pickens, to make application for the enrollment of the said child Levi Pickens; but the said Austin Pickens, was a "Snake Indian", and would not sign any application for the enrollment of Indian children.

Wherefore affiant begs to have the accompanying application accepted and that the said Levi Pickens, be enrolled as a citizen of the Choctaw Nation.

Affiant says that the said Levi Pickens, is now and has been in the care and custody of this affiant since the death of his mother, and that she the said Agnes Wade, makes the accompanying application for enrollment as next friend of the said infant Levi Pickens.

This 21st, day of July, 1906.

                                              her
                              Agnes  x  Wade

Witnesses to mark.                    mark
Joe Anderson
Jefferson Wade

Subscribed and sworn to before me this 21st, day of July, 1906.
My commission expires February 27th, 1907.

                                       T L Wade
                                       Notary Public.

## Applications for Enrollment of Choctaw Newborn
## Act of 1905   Volume XVIII

7-NB-1382.

DEPARTMENT OF THE INTERIOR,
COMMISSIONER TO THE FIVE CIVILIZED TRIBES.

- - - - -

In the matter of the application for the enrollment of Levi Pickens as a Choctaw Nation of the Choctaw Nation.

DECISION.

It appears from the record herein that on April 25, 1905, application was made to the Commission to the Five Civilized Tribes for the enrollment of Levi Pickens as a citizen by blood of the Choctaw Nation.

It appears from the record herein and from the records in the possession of this office that the applicant, Levi Pickens, was born February 2[sic], 1904, and is the son of Jefferson Pickens and Nancy Pickens, both of whom are recognized and enrolled citizens by blood of the Choctaw Nation, their names appearing as numbers 10643 and 10647 upon the final roll of citizens by blood of the Choctaw Nation, approved by the Secretary of the Interior February 4, 1903; and that said applicant was living on March 4, 1905.

The Act of Congress approved March 3, 1905 (33 Stats., 1070), provides:

> "That the Commission to the Five Civilized Tribes is authorized for sixty days after the date of the approval of this act to receive and consider applications for enrollment of children born subsequent to September twenty-fifth, nineteen hundred and two, and prior to March fourth, nineteen hundred and five, and who were living on said latter date, to citizens by blood of the Choctaw and Chickasaw tribes of Indians whose enrollment has been approved by the Secretary of the Interior prior to the date of the approval of this act; and to enroll and make allotments to such children."

I am, therefore, of the opinion that Levi Pickens should be enrolled as a citizen by blood of the Choctaw Nation, under the provisions of the Act of Congress above quoted, and it is so ordered.

Tams Bixby    Commissioner.

Muskogee, Indian Territory,
SEP 29 1906

## Applications for Enrollment of Choctaw Newborn
## Act of 1905    Volume XVIII

7-NB-1382                                                                 COPY

Muskogee, Indian Territory, September 29, 1906.

Jefferson Pickens,
    Caney, Indian Territory.

Dear Sir:

    Inclosed herewith you will find a copy of the decision of the Commissioner to the Five Civilized Tribes, rendered September 29, 1906, granting the application for the enrollment of Levi Pickens as a citizen by blood of the Choctaw Nation.

    The attorneys for the Choctaw and Chickasaw Nations have been furnished a copy of the decision and have been allowed fifteen days from the date of this notice within which to file protest against his enrollment. If at the expiration of that time no protest has been filed, the name of Levi Pickens will be placed upon the final roll of citizens by blood of the Choctaw Nation to be submitted to the Secretary of the Interior for his approval.

                           Respectfully,
                             SIGNED
                             *Tams Bixby*
                             Commissioner.

Registered.
Incl. 7-NB-1382

---

7-NB-1382                                                                 COPY

Muskogee, Indian Territory, September 29, 1906.

George T. Putty,
    Attorney at Law,
        Marlow, Indian Territory.

Dear Sir:

    You are hereby notified that the Commissioner to the Five Civilized Tribes, on September 29, 1906, rendered his decision granting the application for the enrollment of Levi Pickens as a citizen by blood of the Choctaw Nation.

    The attorneys for the Choctaw and Chickasaw Nations have been furnished a copy of the decision and have been allowed fifteen days from the date of this notice within which to file protest against his enrollment. If at the expiration of that time no protest has been filed, the name of Levi Pickens will be placed upon the final roll of citizens by blood of the Choctaw Nation to be submitted to the Secretary of the Interior for his approval.

# Applications for Enrollment of Choctaw Newborn
## Act of 1905   Volume XVIII

Respectfully,

SIGNED

*Tams Bixby*
Commissioner.

Registered.

7-NB-1382

**COPY**

Muskogee, Indian Territory, September 29, 1906.

Abel Wade,
    Caddo, Indian Territory.

Dear Sir:

You are hereby notified that the Commissioner to the Five Civilized Tribes, on September 29, 1906, rendered his decision granting the application for the enrollment of Levi Pickens as a citizen by blood of the Choctaw Nation.

The attorneys for the Choctaw and Chickasaw Nations have been furnished a copy of the decision and have been allowed fifteen days from the date of this notice within which to file protest against his enrollment. If at the expiration of that time no protest has been filed, the name of Levi Pickens will be placed upon the final roll of citizens by blood of the Choctaw Nation to be submitted to the Secretary of the Interior for his approval.

Respectfully,

SIGNED

*Tams Bixby*
Commissioner.

Registered.

## Applications for Enrollment of Choctaw Newborn
## Act of 1905   Volume XVIII

7-NB-1382                                                    **COPY**

Muskogee, Indian Territory, September 29, 1906.

Mansfield, McMurray & Cornish,
    Attorneys for Choctaw and Chickasaw Nations,
        McAlester, Indian Territory.

Gentlemen:

    Inclosed herewith you will find a copy of the decision of the Commissioner to the Five Civilized Tribes, rendered September 29, 1906, granting the application for the enrollment of Levi Pickens as a citizen by blood of the Choctaw Nation.

    You are hereby advised that you will be allowed fifteen days from the date of this notice within which to file protest against his enrollment. If at the expiration of that time no protest has been filed, the name of Levi Pickens will be placed upon the final roll of citizens by blood of the Choctaw Nation, to be submitted to the Secretary of the Interior for his approval.

Respectfully,

SIGNED

*Tams Bixby*
Commissioner.

Registered.

    Incl. 7-NB-1382

---

7-NB-1382

Muskogee, Indian Territory, July 28, 1906.

Jefferson Pickens,
    Caney, Indian Territory.

Dear Sir:

    Receipt is hereby acknowledged of your letter, without date, enclosing affidavits of Allen Wright and Loring Robinson to the birth of Levi Pickens, child of Jefferson and Nancy Pickens, February 2, 1904.

    Receipt is also acknowledged of the affidavits of Nellie Perkins and Joseph Wright to the death of Nancy Byington, mother of Levi Pickens, July 25, 1904, and the same have been filed with the record in the matter of the enrollment of Levi Pickens.

# Applications for Enrollment of Choctaw Newborn
## Act of 1905   Volume XVIII

Respectfully,

Commissioner.

---

7-NB-1382

Muskogee, Indian Territory, August 21, 1906.

Abel Wade,
Caddo, Indian Territory.

Dear Sir:-

Receipt is hereby acknowledged of the affidavits of Agnes Wade to the birth of Levi Pickens, child of Jefferson and Nancy Byington Pickens, February 1, 1904.

It appears from the affidavits heretofore forwarded that Levi Pickens was born February 2, 1904. It will be necessary that you furnish a statement showing the correct date of the birth of said child.

Respectfully,

Commissioner.

---

7-NB-1382

Muskogee, Indian Territory, January 10, 1907.

George T. Putty,
Marlow, Indian Territory.

Dear Sir:

Receipt is hereby acknowledged of your letter of December 27, 1906, asking if the enrollment of Levy Pickens has been approved by the Secretary of the Interior.

In reply to your letter you are advised that a decision was rendered granting the application of Levi Pickens as a new born citizen of the Choctaw Nation under the Act of Congress approved March 3, 1905, and his name will be placed upon the next schedule of such citizens prepared for forwarding to the Secretary of the Interior.

Respectfully,

Commissioner.

## Applications for Enrollment of Choctaw Newborn
## Act of 1905  Volume XVIII

Choc. New Born 1383
    Elvin Moran
    (Born Dec. 19, 1904)

                  Department of the Interior,
               Commission to the Five Civilized Tribes.

**BIRTH AFFIDAVIT.**

    ***IN RE-APPLICATION FOR ENROLLMENT,*** as a citizen of the Choctaw Nation, of Elvin Moran, born on the 19 day of December, 190 4

Name of Father: Charles W Moran      a citizen of the Choctaw Nation.
Name of Mother: Fannie Moran      a citizen of the Choctaw Nation.

                Postoffice    Roff, Ind. Ter.

### AFFIDAVIT OF MOTHER.

UNITED STATES OF AMERICA, INDIAN TERRITORY, }
    Southern                    District.

    I, Fannie Moran, on oath state that I am 27 years of age and a citizen by intermarriage, of the Choctaw Nation; that I am the lawful wife of Charles W. Moran, who is a citizen, by blood of the Choctaw Nation; that a male child was born to me on 19 day of December, 1904, that said child has been named Elvin Moran, and is now living. *and was living March 4, 1905.*

                          Fannie Moran

Witnesses To Mark:
{         My Commission Expires Jan. 30, 1907.

Subscribed and sworn to before me this 15 day of April, 1905.

                          J.C. Little
                                Notary Public.

### AFFIDAVIT OF ATTENDING PHYSICIAN OR MID-WIFE.

UNITED STATES OF AMERICA, INDIAN TERRITORY, }
    Southern                    District.

    I, J.W. Gilbert, a Physician, on oath state that I attended on Mrs. Fannie Moran, wife of Charles W Moran on the 19 day of December, 190 4; that there was born to her on said date a male child; that said child is now living *and was living March 4, 1905* and is said to have been named Elvin Moran

## Applications for Enrollment of Choctaw Newborn
## Act of 1905   Volume XVIII

J.W. Gilbert M.D.

Witnesses To Mark:

Subscribed and sworn to before me this 25 day of April , 1905.

My Commission Expires Jan. 30, 1907.

J.C. Little
Notary Public.

---

7 N.B. 1383.

Muskogee, Indian Territory, June 1, 1905.

J. C. Little,
    Attorney at Law,
        Roff, Indian Territory.

Dear Sir:

    Receipt is hereby acknowledged of your letter of May 27, asking what disposition has been made of the application of Elvin Moran for enrollment as a citizen of the Choctaw Nation.

    In reply to your letter you are advised that the affidavits heretofore forwarded have been filed with our records as an application for the enrollment of Elvin Moran, but his name has not yet been placed upon a schedule of citizens by blood of the Choctaw Nation prepared for forwarding to the Secretary of the Interior.

Respectfully,

Commissioner in Charge.

# Applications for Enrollment of Choctaw Newborn
## Act of 1905   Volume XVIII

Choc. New Born 1384
    James Vernon Taliaferro
    (Born Oct. 3, 1903)

**BIRTH AFFIDAVIT.**

## DEPARTMENT OF THE INTERIOR.
## COMMISSION TO THE FIVE CIVILIZED TRIBES.

**IN RE APPLICATION FOR ENROLLMENT,** as a citizen of the Choctaw Nation, of James Vernon Taliaferro, born on the 3 day of October, 1903

Name of Father: James R Taliaferro      a citizen of the Choctaw Nation.
Name of Mother: Minnie A Taliaferro      a citizen of the Choctaw Nation.

    Postoffice    Ardmore Ind. Ter.

### AFFIDAVIT OF MOTHER.

UNITED STATES OF AMERICA, Indian Territory,
Southern      DISTRICT.

    I, Minnie A Taliaferro, on oath state that I am 23 years of age and a citizen by Blood, of the Choctaw Nation; that I am the lawful wife of James R Taliaferro, who is a citizen, by Intermarriage of the Choctaw Nation; that a Male child was born to me on 3 day of October, 1903; that said child has been named James Vernon Taliaferro, and was living March 4, 1905.

                   Minnie A Taliaferro

Witnesses To Mark:

    Subscribed and sworn to before me this 25 day of April, 1905

                   U.T. Rexroat
                         Notary Public.

# Applications for Enrollment of Choctaw Newborn
## Act of 1905   Volume XVIII

**AFFIDAVIT OF ATTENDING PHYSICIAN OR MID-WIFE.**

UNITED STATES OF AMERICA, Indian Territory, }
Southern                                 DISTRICT. }

    I,   Dr Geo. H. Harry  , a  Physician  , on oath state that I attended on Mrs.   Minnie A Taliaferro  , wife of  James R Taliaferro   on the  3  day of October  , 1903; that there was born to her on said date a   Male   child; that said child was living March 4, 1905, and is said to have been named  James Vernon Taliaferro

                                             Geo. H. Harry M.D.

Witnesses To Mark:
{

    Subscribed and sworn to before me this 26  day of  April  , 1905

                                         U.T. Rexroat
                                           Notary Public.

---

Choc. New Born 1385
      Vere Alford
      (Born Dec. 14, 1904)

BIRTH AFFIDAVIT.
## DEPARTMENT OF THE INTERIOR.
## COMMISSION TO THE FIVE CIVILIZED TRIBES.

    **IN RE APPLICATION FOR ENROLLMENT,** as a citizen of the   Choctaw   Nation, of Vere Alford  , born on the  14th  day of  December  , 1904

Name of Father:  Harvey L Alford       a citizen of the United States ~~Nation~~.
Name of Mother:  Docia Alford        a citizen of the   Choctaw   Nation.

                             Postoffice   Antlers, Ind. Ter.

# Applications for Enrollment of Choctaw Newborn
## Act of 1905   Volume XVIII

### AFFIDAVIT OF MOTHER.

UNITED STATES OF AMERICA, Indian Territory, }
Central            DISTRICT.

I,   Docia Alford   , on oath state that I am   24   years of age and a citizen by blood  , of the    Choctaw    Nation; that I am the lawful wife of    Harvey L Alford  , who is a citizen, ~~by~~ ............... of the      United States     ~~Nation~~; that a    female child was born to me on   14th   day of   December    , 1904; that said child has been named   Vere Alford    , and was living March 4, 1905.

Docia Alford

Witnesses To Mark:
{

Subscribed and sworn to before me this  29th  day of   April    , 1905

Wirt Franklin<br>Notary Public.

---

### AFFIDAVIT OF ATTENDING PHYSICIAN OR MID-WIFE.

UNITED STATES OF AMERICA, Indian Territory, }
Central            DISTRICT.

I,   Cora Stammer      , a mid-wife      , on oath state that I attended on Mrs.   Docia Alford      , wife of   Harvey L. Alford      on the  14th   day of   December   , 1904; that there was born to her on said date a    female    child; that said child was living March 4, 1905, and is said to have been named   Vere Alford

Cora Stammer

Witnesses To Mark:
{

Subscribed and sworn to before me this  29th  day of   April    , 1905

Wirt Franklin<br>Notary Public.

# Applications for Enrollment of Choctaw Newborn
## Act of 1905   Volume XVIII

Choc. New Born 1386
    Benjamin Frazier
    (Born Sep. 12, 1904)

BIRTH AFFIDAVIT.

### DEPARTMENT OF THE INTERIOR.
### COMMISSION TO THE FIVE CIVILIZED TRIBES.

IN RE APPLICATION FOR ENROLLMENT, as a citizen of the Choctaw Nation, of Benjamin Frazier, born on the 12th day of September, 1904

Name of Father: Simeon Frazier    a citizen of the Choctaw Nation.
Name of Mother: Lena Frazier    a citizen of the Choctaw Nation.

    Postoffice    Antlers, Ind. Ter.

### AFFIDAVIT OF MOTHER.

UNITED STATES OF AMERICA, Indian Territory, }
    Central      DISTRICT.

I, Lena Frazier, on oath state that I am 26 years of age and a citizen by blood, of the Choctaw Nation; that I am the lawful wife of Simeon Frazier, who is a citizen, by blood of the Choctaw Nation; that a male child was born to me on 12th day of September, 1904; that said child has been named Benjamin Frazier, and was living March 4, 1905.

                                            Lena Frazier

Witnesses To Mark:
{

Subscribed and sworn to before me this 29th day of April, 1905

                                            Wirt Franklin
                                            Notary Public.

### AFFIDAVIT OF ATTENDING PHYSICIAN OR MID-WIFE.

UNITED STATES OF AMERICA, Indian Territory, }
    Central      DISTRICT.

I, Sissie Frazier, a mid-wife, on oath state that I attended on Mrs. Lena Frazier, wife of Simeon Frazier on the 12th day of

# Applications for Enrollment of Choctaw Newborn
## Act of 1905    Volume XVIII

September    , 1904; that there was born to her on said date a    male    child; that said child was living March 4, 1905, and is said to have been named    Benjamin Frazier

Sissie Frazier

Witnesses To Mark:

{

    Subscribed and sworn to before me this    29th    day of    April    , 1905

Wirt Franklin<br>Notary Public.

---

Choctaw NB 1386

Muskogee, Indian Territory, May 29, 1906.

Lena Frazier,
    Hugo, Indian Territory.

Dear Madam:

    Receipt is hereby acknowledged of your letter of May 21, asking the status of the application for the enrollment of your child Benjamin Frazier and in reply you are advised that on August 2, 1905, the Secretary of the Interior approved the enrollment of your child, Benjamin Frazier, as a new born citizen of the Choctaw Nation, and selection of allotment may be made in his behalf under the rules and regulations governing the selection of allotments and the designation of homesteads in the Choctaw and Chickasaw Nations.

Respectfully,

Commissioner.

---

Choc. New Born 1387
    Agbert Wesley
    (Born Feb. 26, 1905)

Applications for Enrollment of Choctaw Newborn
Act of 1905   Volume XVIII

# Department of the Interior,
### COMMISSION TO THE FIVE CIVILIZED TRIBES.

IN RE Application for Enrollment, as a citizen of the Choctaw Nation, of Agbert Wesley , born on the 26 day of February , 1905

Name of Father: Elias Wesley a citizen of the Choctaw Nation.
Name of Mother: Siley Wesley a citizen of the Choctaw Nation.

Post-Office: Cabaniss

### AFFIDAVIT OF MOTHER.

UNITED STATES OF AMERICA,
INDIAN TERRITORY
Central District.

I, Siley Wesley , on oath state that I am 39 years of age and a citizen by Blood , of the Choctaw Nation; that I am the lawful wife of Elias Wesley , who is a citizen, by Blood of the Choctaw Nation; that a child was born to me on the 26 day of February 1905 ; that said child has been named Agbert Wesley , and is now living.

Siley Wesley

Subscribed and sworn to before me this 28 day of April , 1905 .

JH Elliott
Notary Public.
My com exp July 8 1908

### AFFIDAVIT OF ATTENDING PHYSICIAN, OR MID-WIFE.

UNITED STATES OF AMERICA,
INDIAN TERRITORY
Central District.

I, Eliza Ott , a mid wife , on oath state that I attended on Mrs. Siley Wesley , wife of Elias Wesley on the 26 day of February , 1905 ; that there was born to her on said date a male child; that said child is now living and is said to have been named Agbert Wesley

Eliza Ott

# Applications for Enrollment of Choctaw Newborn
## Act of 1905   Volume XVIII

Subscribed and sworn to before me this   28   day of   April   , 1905.

JH Elliott
Notary Public.

My com exp July 8 1908

---

Choc. New Born 1388
     Susan Bacon
     (Born Nov. 2, 1904)
     Ellen Bacon
     (Born Nov. 2, 1904)

Department of the Interior.
Commission to the Five Civilized Tribes.
Muskogee, I. T. July 23, 1904.

. . . . . . . . . . . . . . . . . . . . .

Choctaw 4939.

In the matter of the application of Silly Frazier for enrollment as a citizen by blood of the Choctaw Nation.

LIZZIE ANN BACON, being first duly sworn, testifies as follows:

Examination by the Commission:

Q. What is your name? A. Lizzie Ann Bacon.
Q. How old are you? A. About thirty-five.
Q. What is your Post-Office address? A. Colgate.
Q. Is that in the Choctaw Nation? A. Yes sir.
Q. Were you once then wife of Daniel Bacon? A. Yes sir.
Q. How many children did you have by Daniel Bacon? A. Two.
Q. What were their names? A. Elias Bacon and Ed Bacon.

The witness is identified from original Choctaw enrollment care No. 4939 as Lizzie A. Bacon, Choctaw roll No. 13491.

Q. Are you living with Daniel Bacon at the present time? A. No sir.
Q. Were you divorced from Daniel Bacon?
A. I was married to Daniel Bacon, and we then separated and I married Frazier. After Frazier died I married Bacon again, and we again separated.

# Applications for Enrollment of Choctaw Newborn
## Act of 1905 Volume XVIII

Q. How long did you live with Lewis Frazier? A. Nearly two years.
Q. Were you married to him? A. Yes sir.
Q. Did you have any children by him? A. Yes sir.
Q. How many? A. One.
Q. What was the name of that child? A. Silly Frazier.
Q. Did you ever make application for the enrollment of that child? A. Yes sir.
Q. Where did you make application for the enrollment of that child? A. At Atoka.
Q. Do you know what year it was? A. No sir.
Q. Was the Commission in session at that time at Atoka? A. Yes sir.
Q. Who was with you at the time you made this application? A. Sam A. Ott.
Q. Anybody else? A. Martha Frazier.
Q. Did you make application on a sheet like this blank that is shown you now? (Witness shown regular form of application for enrollment of infant child). A. No sir.
Q. Was Silly Frazier born January 6, 1900? A. Yes sir.
Q. How long after this child was born was it before you sent an application to the Commission for its enrollment?
A. About two years afterwards.
Q. Did you send that application to the Dawes Commission, at Muskogee? A. Yes sir.
Q. Did you get any letter in reply? A. No sir.
Q. Then in November, 1902, you went before the Commission at Atoka and made application at that time? A. Yes sir.

(Witness excused)

SAM A. OTT, being first duly sworn, testifies as follows:

Examination by the Commission:

Q. What is your name? A. Sam A. Ott.
Q. Are you a citizen by blood of the Choctaw Nation? A. Yes sir.
Q. How old are you? A. Thirty-three years old.
Q. What is your Post-Office address? A. Colgate, Choctaw Nation.
Q. Do you know Lizzie Ann Bacon? A. Yes sir.
Q. Do you know her child, Silly Frazier? A. Yes sir.
Q. Do you know when that child was born? A. Yes sir.
Q. When was it born? A. January 6, 1900, in the morning, about half past six o'clock.
Q. How near do you live to Lizzie Ann Bacon? A. Three miles.
Q. Were you present when the child was born?
A. Yes sir, it was born right there in my house.
Q. Who was the midwife, the woman who attended her at the time the child was born?
A. Martha Frazier.
Q. Do you know if Lizzie Ann Bacon ever made a personal application to the Dawes Commission for the enrollment of Silly Frazier?
A. Yes sir.
Q. When did she make that application? A. In November, 1902.
Q. At what place? A. At Atoka, Choctaw Nation.
Q. Were you present at that time? A. Yes sir.

## Applications for Enrollment of Choctaw Newborn
## Act of 1905    Volume XVIII

Q. Did you hear the talk between her and the Commission? A. Yes sir.
Q. Did they give her a blank application like this? (Witness shown regular form of application for enrollment of infant children). A. No sir.
Q. Do you remember if any conversation took place between the Commission and Lizzie Ann Bacon about this child.[sic]   What did they tell her.[sic]   Did they ask her any questions? A. Yes sir - they told her to write to the Commission at Muskogee.
Q. At this time, at Atoka, did you or Lizzie Ann Bacon sign any papers at all? A. Yes sir, I signed a paper.
Q. At Atoka? A. Yes sir, at Atoka.
Q. Was that paper about this child, Silly Frazier? A. Yes sir.
Q. Was that paper left with the Commission? A. Yes sir.
Q. Was it a paper like this I show you? (Showing birth affidavit).
A. Yes sir.
Q. You and Lizzie Ann Bacon did sign a paper something like this, before the Commission, at Atoka, in November, 1902?
A. Yes sir, on November 19, 1902.
Q. After this paper was signed by you and Lizzie Ann Bacon you left it with the Commission? A. Yes sir.
Q. Has Lizzie Ann Bacon selected her allotment of land in the Choctaw Nation?
A. Yes sir.
Q. At the time she made selection of her own allotment did she ask to allot land for Silly Frazier? A. Yes sir.
Q. What did they tell her? A. Told her the name of Silly Frazier was not on the roll.
Q. When did this take place - how long ago? A. Some time in 1903.
Q. Did she write to the Commission at Muskogee to find out about it? A. I don't know.
Q. Did you? A. No sir.
Q. Do you know whether anybody did?
A. No sir.  We tried to find out at South McAlester, from Mansfield & McMurray, attorneys for the Choctaw and Chickasaw Nations.
Q. On November 19, 1902, at Atoka, Indian Territory, at the time you say Lizzie Ann Bacon made application for the enrollment of her child, Silly Frazier, did she make application for the enrollment of any other child? A. It is so long ago I dont[sic]sic] recollect.

(Witness excused).

LIZZIE ANN BACON - Recalled.

Q. Did you make application for the enrollment of Ed Bacon, on November 19, 1902?
A. Yes sir.
Q. Did Martha Frazier sign the paper with you? A. Ye sir.
Q. This was the same day that you made application for the enrollment of Silly Frazier, was it? A. Yes sir.
Q. Did you sign just such a paper for Silly Frazier as you did for Ed Bacon? A. Yes sir.

(Witness excused).

## Applications for Enrollment of Choctaw Newborn
## Act of 1905 Volume XVIII

SAM A. OTT - Recalled.

Q. Do you remember that application was made on the same day for the enrollment of Ed Bacon? A. Yes sir, I was the interpreter.
Q. Did you interpret for her in making the application for Silly Frazier? A. Yes sir.
Q. And you swear positively that application was made upon that day?
A. Yes sir.

..............................

Arthur R. Taylor, being first duly sworn, states that as stenographer to the Commission to the Five Civilized Tribes he reported the proceedings had in the above entitled cause on the 23rd day of July, 1904, and that the above and foregoing is a full, true, and correct transcript of his stenographic notes taken in said cause on said date.

Arthur R Taylor

Subscribed and sworn to before me this 26$^{th}$ day of July, 1904.

Charles H Sawyer
Notary Public.

---

**BIRTH AFFIDAVIT.**
### DEPARTMENT OF THE INTERIOR.
### COMMISSION TO THE FIVE CIVILIZED TRIBES.

---

**IN RE APPLICATION FOR ENROLLMENT,** as a citizen of the Choctaw Nation, of Susan Bacon , born on the 20 day of November , 1904

Name of Father: Daniel Bacon     a citizen of the Choctaw Nation.
Name of Mother: Lizzie A. Bacon     a citizen of the Choctaw Nation.

Postoffice    Cairo I.T.

---

**AFFIDAVIT OF MOTHER.**

UNITED STATES OF AMERICA, Indian Territory, ⎫
    Central           DISTRICT. ⎬

I, Lizzie A. Bacon , on oath state that I am 40 years of age and a citizen by Blood , of the Choctaw Nation; that I am the lawful wife of Daniel Bacon , who is a citizen, by Blood of the Choctaw Nation; that a female *one of Twins* child was born to me on 20 day of November , 1904; that said child has been named Susan Bacon , and was living March 4, 1905.

## Applications for Enrollment of Choctaw Newborn
## Act of 1905  Volume XVIII

                                            her
                                  Lizzie A x Bacon

Witnesses To Mark:                      mark
  { Henry Brock
    Castin Palmer

      Subscribed and sworn to before me this   17 day of     April    , 1905

                                       W.B. Harl
                                            Notary Public.

---

**AFFIDAVIT OF ATTENDING PHYSICIAN OR MID-WIFE.**

UNITED STATES OF AMERICA, Indian Territory, }
   Central                DISTRICT. }

    I,   Martha M<sup>c</sup>Gee   , a mid wife   , on oath state that I attended on Mrs.  Lizzie A Bacon  , wife of  Daniel Bacon  on the 20 day of  November, 1904; that there was born to her on said date a   Female   child; that said child was living March 4, 1905, and is said to have been named  Susan Bacon

                                          her
                                  Martha x M<sup>c</sup>Gee
Witnesses To Mark:                    mark
  { Henry Brock
    Castin Palmer

      Subscribed and sworn to before me this   17 day of     April    , 1905

                                       W.B. Harl
                                            Notary Public.

---

**BIRTH AFFIDAVIT.**
                              **DEPARTMENT OF THE INTERIOR.**
                    **COMMISSION TO THE FIVE CIVILIZED TRIBES.**

      IN RE APPLICATION FOR ENROLLMENT, as a citizen of the    Choctaw    Nation, of Ellen Bacon    , born on the  20 day of Nov  , 1904

Name of Father: Daniel Bacon         a citizen of the  Choctaw    Nation.
Name of Mother: Lizzie A. Bacon      a citizen of the  Choctaw    Nation.

                            Postoffice     Cairo I.T.

# Applications for Enrollment of Choctaw Newborn
# Act of 1905   Volume XVIII

### AFFIDAVIT OF MOTHER.

UNITED STATES OF AMERICA, Indian Territory,  
Central          DISTRICT.

I, Lizzie A. Bacon, on oath state that I am 40 years of age and a citizen by Blood, of the Choctaw Nation; that I am the lawful wife of Daniel Bacon, who is a citizen, by Blood of the Choctaw Nation; that a female *one of Twins* child was born to me on 20 day of November, 1904; that said child has been named Ellen Bacon, and was living March 4, 1905.

                                      her  
                             Lizzie A  x  Bacon  
Witnesses To Mark:          mark  
   { Henry Brock  
    Castin Palmer

Subscribed and sworn to before me this 17 day of April, 1905

                                  W.B. Harl  
                                  Notary Public.

---

### AFFIDAVIT OF ATTENDING PHYSICIAN OR MID-WIFE.

UNITED STATES OF AMERICA, Indian Territory,  
Central          DISTRICT.

I, Martha M$^c$Gee, a mid wife, on oath state that I attended on Mrs. Lizzie A Bacon, wife of Daniel Bacon on the 20 day of November, 1904; that there was born to her on said date a Female child; that said child was living March 4, 1905, and is said to have been named Ellen Bacon

                                      her  
                             Martha  x  M$^c$Gee  
Witnesses To Mark:          mark  
   { Henry Brock  
    Castin Palmer

Subscribed and sworn to before me this 17 day of April, 1905

                                  W.B. Harl  
                                  Notary Public.

# Applications for Enrollment of Choctaw Newborn
## Act of 1905 Volume XVIII

**BIRTH AFFIDAVIT.**

### DEPARTMENT OF THE INTERIOR.
### COMMISSION TO THE FIVE CIVILIZED TRIBES.

---

IN RE APPLICATION FOR ENROLLMENT, as a citizen of the Choctaw Nation, of Ellen Jackson, born on the 20 day of November, 1904

Name of Father: Grandfather Joe Jackson    a citizen of the Choctaw Nation.
Name of Mother: Lizzie A. Bacon    a citizen of the Choctaw Nation.

Postoffice    Coalgate Indian Territory

---

**AFFIDAVIT OF MOTHER.**

UNITED STATES OF AMERICA, Indian Territory, }
Central    DISTRICT.

I, Lizzie A. Bacon, on oath state that I am Forty years of age and a citizen by Blood, of the Choctaw Nation; that I am the lawful wife of Daughter Joe Jackson, who is a citizen, by Blood of the Choctaw Nation; that a Female child was born to me on 20 day of November, 1904; that said child has been named Ellen Jackson, and was living March 4, 1905.

                 her
           Lizzie A Bacon   x
Witnesses To Mark:          mark
{ F.B. Lawrence
{ O.S. Lawrence

Subscribed and sworn to before me this 1 day of May, 1905

         Richard P. Kemp
           Notary Public.
My com exp Dec 17 - 1908

---

**AFFIDAVIT OF ATTENDING PHYSICIAN OR MID-WIFE.**

UNITED STATES OF AMERICA, Indian Territory, }
Central    DISTRICT.

I, Martha Frazier, a Mid-wife, on oath state that I attended on Mrs. Lizzie A Bacon, wife of Daughter of Joe Jackson on the 20 day of November, 1904; that there was born to her on said date a Female child; that said child was living March 4, 1905, and is said to have been named Ellen Bacon

## Applications for Enrollment of Choctaw Newborn
## Act of 1905 Volume XVIII

                                                      her
                                      Martha Frazier  x

Witnesses To Mark:                                  mark
{ F.B. Lawrence
  O.S. Lawrence

Subscribed and sworn to before me this  1  day of    May   , 1905

                                          Richard P. Kemp
                                          Notary Public.
My com exp Dec 17 - 1908

---

**BIRTH AFFIDAVIT.**

## DEPARTMENT OF THE INTERIOR.
## COMMISSION TO THE FIVE CIVILIZED TRIBES.

---

    **IN RE APPLICATION FOR ENROLLMENT,** as a citizen of the    Choctaw    Nation, of Sousin[sic] Jackson    , born on the  20  day of  November  , 1904

Name of Father: Joe Jackson  Grandfather     a citizen of the  Choctaw    Nation.
Name of Mother: Lizzie A. Bacon         a citizen of the  Choctaw    Nation.

                              Postoffice    Coalgate Indian Territory

---

**AFFIDAVIT OF MOTHER.**

**UNITED STATES OF AMERICA, Indian Territory,** }
    Central                    **DISTRICT.**

    I,    Lizzie A. Bacon   , on oath state that I am  Forty   years of age and a citizen by    Blood   , of the    Choctaw    Nation; that I am the lawful wife of   Joe Jackson's Daughter, who is a citizen, by  Blood   of the    Choctaw    Nation; that a Female   child was born to me on  20  day of  November   , 1904; that said child has been named  Sousin Jackson    , and was living March 4, 1905.

                                                her
                                      Lizzie A Bacon  x
Witnesses To Mark:                              mark
{ F.B. Lawrence
  O.S. Lawrence

Subscribed and sworn to before me this  1 th[sic] day of    May   , 1905

                                          Richard P. Kemp
My com exp Dec 17 - 1908                Notary Public.

# Applications for Enrollment of Choctaw Newborn
## Act of 1905   Volume XVIII

### AFFIDAVIT OF ATTENDING PHYSICIAN OR MID-WIFE.

UNITED STATES OF AMERICA, Indian Territory,  
Central   DISTRICT.

I, Martha Frazier, a Mid-wife, on oath state that I attended on Mrs. Lizzie A Bacon, wife of Daughter of Joe Jackson on the 20 day of November, 1904; that there was born to her on said date a Female child; that said child was living March 4, 1905, and is said to have been named Sousin Bacon

                                               her  
Witnesses To Mark:           Martha Frazier x  
   F.B. Lawrence                    mark  
   O.S. Lawrence

Subscribed and sworn to before me this 1th[sic] day of May, 1905

                                   Richard P. Kemp  
                                              Notary Public.  
My commission expires Dec 17 - 1908

---

**BIRTH AFFIDAVIT.**

### DEPARTMENT OF THE INTERIOR.
### COMMISSION TO THE FIVE CIVILIZED TRIBES.

IN RE APPLICATION FOR ENROLLMENT, as a citizen of the Choctaw Nation, of Ellen Bacon, born on the 20 day of November, 1904

Name of Father: Daniel Bacon         a citizen of the Choctaw Nation.  
Name of Mother: Lizzie A. Bacon      a citizen of the Choctaw Nation.

                          Postoffice     ~~Coalgate~~ Ind Ter  
                                        Cairo

---

### AFFIDAVIT OF MOTHER.

UNITED STATES OF AMERICA, Indian Territory,  
Central   DISTRICT.

I, Lizzie A. Bacon, on oath state that I am 40 years of age and a citizen by blood, of the Choctaw Nation; that I am the lawful wife of Daniel Bacon, who is a citizen, by Blood of the Choctaw Nation; that a

## Applications for Enrollment of Choctaw Newborn
## Act of 1905   Volume XVIII

female   child was born to me on   20   day of   November   , 1904; that said child has been named   Ellen Bacon   , and was living March 4, 1905.

                                                    her
                                        Lizzie A  x  Bacon

Witnesses To Mark:                            mark
  { Joseph Wilson
    Henry Brock

Subscribed and sworn to before me this   23  day of    June    , 1905

                                        W.B. Harl
                                              Notary Public.

---

**AFFIDAVIT OF ATTENDING PHYSICIAN OR MID-WIFE.**

UNITED STATES OF AMERICA, Indian Territory, }
   Central               DISTRICT.

I,   Martha M$^c$Gee   , a  mid wife   , on oath state that I attended on Mrs.   Lizzie A Bacon   , wife of  Daniel Bacon   on the 20  day of  November, 1904; that there was born to her on said date a    female    child; that said child was living March 4, 1905, and is said to have been named  Ellen Bacon

                                                her
                                      Martha  x  M$^c$Gee

Witnesses To Mark:                            mark
  { Joseph Wilson
    Henry Brock

Subscribed and sworn to before me this   23  day of    June    , 1905

                                        W.B. Harl
                                           Notary Public.

---

**BIRTH AFFIDAVIT.**
                                  **DEPARTMENT OF THE INTERIOR.**
                         **COMMISSION TO THE FIVE CIVILIZED TRIBES.**

---

    **IN RE APPLICATION FOR ENROLLMENT,** as a citizen of the    Choctaw    Nation, of  Susan Bacon   , born on the  20  day of  November  , 1904

Name of Father: Daniel Bacon                a citizen of the   Choctaw   Nation.
Name of Mother: Lizzie A. Bacon           a citizen of the   Choctaw   Nation.
                              Postoffice    ~~Coalgate~~  Ind Ter
                                           Cairo

# Applications for Enrollment of Choctaw Newborn
## Act of 1905   Volume XVIII

### AFFIDAVIT OF MOTHER.

UNITED STATES OF AMERICA, Indian Territory, }
Central   DISTRICT.

I, Lizzie A. Bacon, on oath state that I am 40 years of age and a citizen by Blood, of the Choctaw Nation; that I am the lawful wife of Daniel Bacon, who is a citizen, by Blood of the Choctaw Nation; that a female child was born to me on 20 day of November, 1904; that said child has been named Susan Bacon, and was living March 4, 1905.

          her
Lizzie A x Bacon
          mark

Witnesses To Mark:
{ Joseph Wilson
  Henry Brock

Subscribed and sworn to before me this 23 day of June, 1905.

W.B. Harl
Notary Public.

### AFFIDAVIT OF ATTENDING PHYSICIAN OR MID-WIFE.

UNITED STATES OF AMERICA, Indian Territory, }
Central   DISTRICT.

I, Martha M$^c$Gee, a Mid wife, on oath state that I attended on Mrs. Lizzie A Bacon, wife of Daniel Bacon on the 20 day of November, 1904; that there was born to her on said date a female child; that said child was living March 4, 1905, and is said to have been named Susan Bacon

          her
Martha x M$^c$Gee
          mark

Witnesses To Mark:
{ Joseph Wilson
  Henry Brock

Subscribed and sworn to before me this 23 day of June, 1905.

W.B. Harl
Notary Public.

## Applications for Enrollment of Choctaw Newborn
## Act of 1905 Volume XVIII

7-4939.

Muskogee, Indian Territory, May 5, 1905.

J. S. Mullen,
    Attorney at Law,
        Ardmore, Indian Territory.

Dear Sir:

    Receipt is hereby acknowledged of your letter of April 19, transmitting the affidavits of Lizzie A. Bacon and Martha McGee to the birth of Susan and Ellen Bacon, twin daughters of David and Lizzie A. Bacon, November 20, 1904, and the same have been filed with our records as applications for the enrollment of said children.

Respectfully,

Commissioner in Charge.

---

7-4937
7 NB 1388

Muskogee, Indian Territory, May 12, 1905.

O. S. Lawrence
    Legal, Indian Territory.

Dear Sir:

    Receipt is hereby acknowledged of your letter of May 1, 1905, enclosing affidavits of Lizzie Bacon and Martha Frazier to the birth of Sousin and Ellen Jackson, November 20, 1904, and the same have been filed with our records as an application for the enrollment of said child.

    Further replying to your letter you are advised that the affidavits heretofore forwarded to the birth of Silly Frazier daughter of Lizzie A. Bacon, have been filed with our records as an application for the enrollment of said child, but her name has not yet been placed upon a schedule of citizens by blood of the Choctaw Nation prepared for forwarding to the Secretary of the Interior.

Respectfully,

Chairman.

## Applications for Enrollment of Choctaw Newborn
## Act of 1905 Volume XVIII

7-NB-1388.

Sub

Muskogee, Indian Territory, May 16, 1905.

Lizzie A. Bacon,
    Coalgate, Indian Territory.

Dear Madam:

    There are enclosed you herewith for execution applications for the enrollment of your infant children, Ellen Bacon and Susan Bacon, born November 20, 1904.

    It is noted from the affidavits heretofore filed with the Commission on May 5, 1905, that you gave the names of the applicants as Susan Bacon and Ellen Bacon stating that Daniel Bacon is their father and that you are his lawful wife. But in the affidavits filed May 11, 1905, you gave their names as Sousin Jackson and Ellen Jackson, without giving their father's name stating, in the place provided for his name, that you are the daughter of Joe Jackson.

    In the enclosed applications the father's name is left blank and the names of the children inserted as Ellen Bacon and Susan Bacon. If Daniel Bacon is their father please insert his name, but if the father is unknown, as the affidavits of May 11, 1905, and Mr. O. S. Lawrence's letter of transmittal of May 1, 1905, suggests, please fill out the blanks accordingly. The surnames of the applicants should follow that of their parents which, in either of the above mentioned cases, would be Bacon.

    In having these affidavits executed care should be exercised to see that all names are written in full, as they appear in the body of the affidavit, and in the event that either of the persons signing the affidavit are unable to write, signatures by mark must be attested by two witnesses. Each affidavit must be executed before a Notary Public and the notarial seal and signature of the officer must be attached to each separate affidavit.

                                          Respectfully,

                                                        Chairman.

V. 16/1.

# Applications for Enrollment of Choctaw Newborn
## Act of 1905   Volume XVIII

7-NB-1388.

Muskogee, Indian Territory, June 15, 1905.

O. S. Lawrence,
    Legal, Indian Territory.

Dear Sir:

    There is enclosed herewith for execution applications for the enrollment of Ellen Bacon and Susan Bacon, born November 20, 1904.

    I regard to the execution of these affidavits your attention is called to the Commission's letter of May 16, 1905, to Lizzie A. Bacon, Coalgate, Indian Territory, which contained affidavits similar to the ones enclosed herewith, and which read in part as follows:

    It is noted in the affidavits heretofore filed with the Commission on May 5, 1905, that you gave the names of the applicants as Susan Bacon and Ellen Bacon stating that Daniel Bacon is their father and that you are his lawful wife. But in the affidavits filed May 11, 1905, you gave their names as Susan Jackson and Ellen Jackson, without giving their father's name stating, in the place provided for is name, that you are the daughter of Joe Jackson.

    In the enclosed applications the father's name is left blank and the names of the children inserted as Ellen Bacon and Susan Bacon. If Daniel Bacon is their father please insert his name, but if the father is unknown, as the affidavits of May 11, 1905, and Mr. O. S. Lawrence's letter of transmittal of May 1, 1905, suggests, please fill out the blanks accordingly. The surnames of the applicants[sic] should follow that of their parents which, in either of the above mentioned cases, would be Bacon.

    There has been no reply to this letter and as no further action can be taken in this matter until the affidavits above referred to are returned to this office properly executed, your attention to this matter will be appreciated.

    In having these affidavits executed care should be exercised to see that all names are written in full, as they appear in the body of the affidavit, and in the event either of the persons signing the affidavit are unable to write, signatures by mark must be attested by two witnesses. Each affidavit must be executed before a Notary Public and the notarial seal and signature of the officer must be attached to each separate affidavit.

                      Respectfully,

                                                 Chairman.

DeB--2/15.

## Applications for Enrollment of Choctaw Newborn
## Act of 1905   Volume XVIII

Choctaw N B 1388

Muskogee, Indian Territory, June 28, 1905.

Lizzie A. Bacon,
    Cairo, Indian Territory.

Dear Madam:

    Receipt is hereby acknowledged of your affidavits and the affidavits of Martha McGee to the birth of Susan and Ellen Bacon, children of Lizzie A. Bacon, November 20, 1904, and the same have been filed with our records in the matter of the enrollment of said child.

Respectfully,

Chairman.

---

7-NB-1388

Muskogee, Indian Territory, October 21, 1905.

Annie McCarty,
    Coalgate, Indian Territory.

Dear Madam:

    Receipt is hereby acknowledged of your letter of October 15, 1905, in which you state that you were appointed administrator of the estate of Susan Bacon, deceased, child of Lizzie Bacon, but that when you went to the land office you were advised, the child's name was not on the Choctaw roll and you could not select her allotment.

    In reply to your letter you are advised that the names of Susan and Ellen Bacon, children of Lizzie A. Bacon appear upon the roll of new born citizens of the Choctaw Nation opposite numbers 1521 and 1522 and that their enrollment was approved by the Secretary of the Interior, September 23, 1905.

Respectfully,

Commissioner.

Applications for Enrollment of Choctaw Newborn
Act of 1905   Volume XVIII

Choc. New Born 1389
    Susan Tonler
    (Born March 5, 1905)

    Cancelled Transferred to
    Choc. Minor Card 779

    Act of Congress approved
    April 26, 1906.

## CHOCTAW 1389

### NEW BORN

ACT OF CONGRESS APPROVED MARCH 30, 1905.

*Susan Tonler*
*(Born March 5, 1905)*

## CANCELLED

*transferred to Choctaw* ~~new born~~ *minor* card 779

ACT OF CONGRESS APPROVED MARCH 30, 1905.

---

Choc. New Born 1390
    Pleas Porter Sexton
    (Born Aug. 15, 1903)

7 13023
**BIRTH AFFIDAVIT.**

### DEPARTMENT OF THE INTERIOR.
### COMMISSION TO THE FIVE CIVILIZED TRIBES.

**IN RE APPLICATION FOR ENROLLMENT,** as a citizen of the Choctaw Nation, of Pleas Porter Sexton, born on the 15 day of August, 1903

Name of Father: Sam Sexton      a citizen of the Choc Nation.
Name of Mother: Isabelle Sexton *nee McKinney* a citizen of the Choc Nation.

289

## Applications for Enrollment of Choctaw Newborn
## Act of 1905   Volume XVIII

Postoffice   Featherston I.T.

---

**AFFIDAVIT OF MOTHER.**

UNITED STATES OF AMERICA, Indian Territory, }
   Central                    DISTRICT. }

I,   Isabelle Sexton   , on oath state that I am   20   years of age and a citizen by   blood   , of the   Choc   Nation; that I am the lawful wife of   Sam Sexton  , who is a *freedman* citizen, by ——— of the   Choctaw   Nation; that a   male   child was born to me on   15   day of   August   , 1903; that said child has been named   Pleas Porter Sexton   , and was living March 4, 1905.

                                        Isabelle Sexton

Witnesses To Mark:
{

   Subscribed and sworn to before me this  29  day of  April   , 1905

                              W.P. M<sup>c</sup>Ginnis
                              Notary Public.

---

**AFFIDAVIT OF ATTENDING PHYSICIAN OR MID-WIFE.**

UNITED STATES OF AMERICA, Indian Territory, }
   Central                    DISTRICT. }

I,   Eliza Sexton   , a   midwife   , on oath state that I attended on Mrs.   Isabelle Sexton   , wife of   Sam Sexton   on the  15  day of  August  , 1903; that there was born to her on said date a   male   child; that said child was living March 4, 1905, and is said to have been named   Pleas Porter Sexton

                                        Eliza Sexton

Witnesses To Mark:
{

   Subscribed and sworn to before me this  29  day of  April   , 1905

                              W.P. M<sup>c</sup>Ginnis
                              Notary Public.

## Applications for Enrollment of Choctaw Newborn
### Act of 1905  Volume XVIII

7-4712.

Muskogee, Indian Territory, May 5, 1905.

Sam Sexton,
    Featherstone, Indian Territory.

Dear Sir:

    Receipt is hereby acknowledged of the affidavits of Isabelle Sexton and Eliza Sexton to the birth of Pleas Porter Sexton, son of Sam and Isabelle Sexton, August 15, 1903, and the same have been filed with our records as an application for the enrollment of said child.

    Respectfully,

Commissioner in Charge.

---

Choc. New Born 1391
    Laura Impson
    (Born Feb. 9, 1904)

# NEW BORN AFFIDAVIT

No ............

## CHOCTAW ENROLLING COMMISSION

IN THE MATTER OF THE APPLICATION FOR ENROLLMENT as a citizen of the Choctaw Nation, of Laura Impson born on the 9th day of March[sic] 190 4

Name of father Thompson J Impson    a citizen of Choctaw Nation, final enrollment No. 158

Name of mother Sadie L Impson    a citizen of Choctaw Nation, final enrollment No. —

Bokchito I.T.      Postoffice.

# Applications for Enrollment of Choctaw Newborn
## Act of 1905   Volume XVIII

### AFFIDAVIT OF MOTHER

UNITED STATES OF AMERICA  
INDIAN TERRITORY  
DISTRICT   Central

I   Sadie L Impson   , on oath state that I am   19   years of age and a cit~~izen by~~ .................. of the ——— Nation, and as such have been placed upon the final roll of the   ———   Nation, by the Honorable Secretary of the Interior my final enrollment number being   ———   ; that I am the lawful wife of   Thompson J Impson   , who is a citizen of the   Choctaw   Nation, and as such has been placed upon the final roll of said Nation by the Honorable Secretary of the Interior, his final enrollment number being   158   and that a   Female   child was born to me on the   9th   day of   March[sic]   190 4; that said child has been named   Laura Impson   , and is now living.

WITNESSETH:                                              Sadie L Impson  
Must be two witnesses { Winnie Impson  
who are citizens          John A M Impson

Subscribed and sworn to before me this, the   4th   day of   February   , 190 5

W.C. Caudill  
Notary Public.

My Commission Expires:   Nov 3 1907

---

## *Affidavit of Attending Physician or Midwife*

UNITED STATES OF AMERICA,  
INDIAN TERRITORY,  
Central   DISTRICT

I,   N. J. Hamilton   a   Practicing Physician on oath state that I attended on Mrs. Sadie L ~~Hamilton~~ Impson   wife of   Thompson J Impson   on the   9th   day of March[sic]   , 190 4, that there was born to her on said date a   Female   child, that said child is now living, and is said to have been named   Laura Impson

N.J. Hamilton        M. D.

Subscribed and sworn to before me this the   14th   day of   February   1905

W.C. Caudill  
Notary Public.

WITNESSETH:  
Must be two witnesses { Winnie Impson  
who are citizens and  
know the child.          John A.M Impson

## Applications for Enrollment of Choctaw Newborn
## Act of 1905 Volume XVIII

We hereby certify that we are well acquainted with N.J. Hamilton a Physician and know him to be reputable and of good standing in the community.

Must be two citizen witnesses. { Winnie Impson
John A M Impson

**BIRTH AFFIDAVIT.**

### DEPARTMENT OF THE INTERIOR.
### COMMISSION TO THE FIVE CIVILIZED TRIBES.

**IN RE APPLICATION FOR ENROLLMENT,** as a citizen of the Choctaw Nation, of Laura Impson, born on the 9th day of February, 1904

Name of Father: Thomas J Impson    a citizen of the Choctaw Nation.
Name of Mother: Sada[sic] Impson    a citizen of the Choctaw Nation.

Postoffice    Bokchito I.T

**AFFIDAVIT OF MOTHER.**

UNITED STATES OF AMERICA, Indian Territory, Central DISTRICT.

I, Sada Impson, on oath state that I am 20 years of age and a citizen by intermarriage, of the Choctaw Nation; that I am the lawful wife of Thomas J Impson, who is a citizen, by Blood of the Choctaw Nation; that a Female child was born to me on 9th day of February, 1904; that said child has been named Laura Impson, and was living March 4, 1905.

Sada Impson

Witnesses To Mark:
{

Subscribed and sworn to before me this 29th day of April, 1905

WC Caudill
Notary Public.

# Applications for Enrollment of Choctaw Newborn
## Act of 1905   Volume XVIII

### AFFIDAVIT OF ATTENDING PHYSICIAN OR MID-WIFE.

UNITED STATES OF AMERICA, Indian Territory, }
Central                          DISTRICT.

I,   N. J. Hamilton   , a   Physician   , on oath state that I attended on Mrs.   Sada Impson   , wife of   Thomas J Impson   on the   9th   day of February   , 1904; that there was born to her on said date a   Female   child; that said child was living March 4, 1905, and is said to have been named   Laura Impson

N.J. Hamilton

Witnesses To Mark:
{

Subscribed and sworn to before me this   29th   day of   April   , 1905

WC Caudill<br>Notary Public.

---

**BIRTH AFFIDAVIT.**

### DEPARTMENT OF THE INTERIOR.
### COMMISSION TO THE FIVE CIVILIZED TRIBES.

---

IN RE APPLICATION FOR ENROLLMENT, as a citizen of the   Choctaw   Nation, of Laura Impson   , born on the   9th   day of   March   , 1904
Roll 10626

Name of Father: Thompson J Impson       a citizen of the   Choctaw   Nation.
Name of Mother: Sada[sic] Impson         a citizen of the   Choctaw   Nation.

Postoffice   Bokchito I.T

---

### AFFIDAVIT OF MOTHER.

UNITED STATES OF AMERICA, Indian Territory, }
Central                          DISTRICT.

I,   Sada Impson   , on oath state that I am 20   years of age and a citizen ~~by~~ .................... , of the   United States   Nation; that I am the lawful wife of Thompson J Impson   , who is a citizen, by blood   of the   Choctaw   Nation; that a   female   child was born to me on   9th   day of   March   , 1904; that said child has been named   Laura Impson   , and was living March 4, 1905.

Sada Impson

Witnesses To Mark:
{

## Applications for Enrollment of Choctaw Newborn
## Act of 1905   Volume XVIII

Subscribed and sworn to before me this 9th day of June, 1905

> WC Caudill
> Notary Public.

---

### AFFIDAVIT OF ATTENDING PHYSICIAN OR MID-WIFE.

UNITED STATES OF AMERICA, Indian Territory,
Central   DISTRICT.

I, N. J. Hamilton, a physician, on oath state that I attended on Mrs. Sada Impson, wife of Thompson J Impson on the 9th day of March, 1904; that there was born to her on said date a female child; that said child was living March 4, 1905, and is said to have been named Laura Impson

> N.J. Hamilton MD

Witnesses To Mark:

Subscribed and sworn to before me this 9th day of June, 1905

> WC Caudill
> Notary Public.

---

140

Blue County,
  ss
Choctaw Nation

This is to certify that on the 18th day of February 1903 I united in the bonds of matrimony Thompson J Impson and Miss Sadie Lester according to the law of the Choctaw Nation.

Given under my hand this the 7th day of July, 1905

> C.M. Pimby
> County and Probate
> Judge, Blue County
> Choctaw Nation.

Recorded this 7th day of July 1905 on page 392 Record Book for Blue Co C.N.
> C.P. Intolubbe
> Clerk Blue Co C.N.

# Applications for Enrollment of Choctaw Newborn
## Act of 1905   Volume XVIII

---

7--3762.

Muskogee, Indian Territory, May 5, 1905.

Thomas J. Impson,
  Bokchito, Indian Territory.

Dear Sir:

Receipt is hereby acknowledged of the affidavits of Sada Impson and N. J. Hamilton to the birth of Laura Impson, daughter of Thomas J. and Sada Impson, February 9, 1904, and the same have been filed with our records as an application for the enrollment of said child.

Respectfully,

Chair[sic]

---

7--NB--1391

Muskogee, Indian Territory, June 3, 1905.

Thomas J. Impson,
  Bokchito, Indian Territory.

Dear Sir:

There is enclosed you herewith for execution application for the enrollment of your infant child, Laura Impson.

In the affidavits executed February 14, 1905, the date of the applicant's birth is given as March 9, 1904, while in the affidavits executed April 29, 1905, this date is given as February 9, 1904. In the enclosed affidavits the date of birth has been left blank. You are requested to insert correct date and when the affidavits have been properly executed return to this office.

In having these affidavits executed care should be exercised to see that all names are written in full, as they appear in the body of the affidavit, and in the event that either of the persons signing the affidavit are unable to write, signatures by mark must be attested by two witnesses. Each affidavit must be executed before a Notary Public and the notarial seal and signature of the officer must be attached to each separate affidavit.

It is noted from the affidavits heretofore filed in support of the application for the enrollment of this child that the applicant claims through you.

# Applications for Enrollment of Choctaw Newborn
## Act of 1905   Volume XVIII

In this event it will be necessary that you file in this office, either the original or a certified copy of the license and certificate of your marriage to the mother of the applicant, Sarah[sic] Impson.

This matter should receive your immediate attention as no further action can be taken relative to the enrollment of said child until the Commission has been furnished this evidence.

                        Respectfully,

Enc-FVK-21

---

7 NB 1391

Muskogee, Indian Territory, June 13, 1905.

Thompson J. Impson,
    Bokchito, Indian Territory.

Dear Sir:

Receipt is hereby acknowledged of your letter of June 9, 1905, transmitting the affidavits of Sada Impson and N. J. Hamilton M. D. to the birth of Laura Impson, daughter of Thompson J. and Sada Impson, March 9, 1904, and the same have been filed in the matter of the enrollment of said child.

                        Respectfully,

                                      Chairman.

---

7-NB-1391.

Muskogee, Indian Territory, June 14, 1905.

Thomas J. Impson,
    Bokchito, Indian Territory.

Dear Sir:

Referring to the application for the enrollment of your child, Laura Impson, born March 9, 1904, your attention is called to the Commission's letter of June 3, 1905, in which you were requested to furnish evidence of your marriage to the applicant's mother, Sada Impson.

# Applications for Enrollment of Choctaw Newborn
## Act of 1905   Volume XVIII

Before this matter can be finally disposed of it will be necessary that you file with the Commission either the original or a certified copy of the license and certificate of this marriage.

Please give this matter your immediate attention.

Respectfully,

Chairman.

---

7-NB-1491[sic]

Muskogee, Indian Territory, July 25, 1905.

Thomas J. Impson,
    Bokchito, Indian Territory.

Dear Sir:

Receipt is hereby acknowledged of your letter of July 19, 1905, enclosing the marriage certificate between yourself and Sadie Lester which you offer in support of the application for the enrollment of your child Laura Impson as a citizen by blood of the Choctaw Nation and the same has been filed with the record in this case.

Respectfully,

Commissioner.

---

Choc. New Born 1392
    Charley Laflore[sic]
    (Born Nov. 28, 1904)

Applications for Enrollment of Choctaw Newborn
Act of 1905   Volume XVIII

BIRTH AFFIDAVIT.

## DEPARTMENT OF THE INTERIOR.
## COMMISSION TO THE FIVE CIVILIZED TRIBES.

IN RE APPLICATION FOR ENROLLMENT, as a citizen of the   Choctaw   Nation, of Charley Laflore   , born on the  28  day of  Nov  , 1904

Name of Father: Osborn[sic] Laflore   a citizen of the  Choctaw  Nation.
Name of Mother: Elle Laflore   a citizen of the  Choctaw  Nation.

Postoffice   Spencerville Ind. Ter.

### AFFIDAVIT OF MOTHER.

UNITED STATES OF AMERICA, Indian Territory, }
    Central   DISTRICT.

I,  Elle Laflore  , on oath state that I am  20  years of age and a citizen by Blood  , of the  Choctaw  Nation; that I am the lawful wife of  Osborn Laflore  , who is a citizen, by Blood  of the  Choctaw  Nation; that a  male  child was born to me on  28  day of  Nov  , 1904; that said child has been named  Charley Laflore  , and was living March 4, 1905.

                    her
                Elle x Laflore
Witnesses To Mark:      mark
  { Thos Fennell
    Osborne Laflore

Subscribed and sworn to before me this 21th[sic] day of  March  , 1905

                Thomas Fennell
                Notary Public.

### AFFIDAVIT OF ATTENDING PHYSICIAN OR MID-WIFE.

UNITED STATES OF AMERICA, Indian Territory, }
    Central   DISTRICT.

I,  Osborn Laflore  , a  Physician  , on oath state that I attended on Mrs.  Elle Laflore  , wife of  Osborn Laflore  on the  28  day of  Nov  , 1904; that there was born to her on said date a  male  child; that said child was living March 4, 1905, and is said to have been named  Charley Laflore

                Osborne Laflore

# Applications for Enrollment of Choctaw Newborn
## Act of 1905   Volume XVIII

Witnesses To Mark:

{

    Subscribed and sworn to before me this  28   day of    March         , 1905

                                    Thomas Fennell
                                    Notary Public.

---

*(The letter below typed as given.)*

                        Muskogee, Indian Territory, March 25, 1905.

Osborn LeFlore,
    Spencerville, Indian Territory.

Dear Sir:

    Receipt is hereby acknowledged of the affidavits of Elle LeFlore and Osborn LeFlore to the birth of Charley LeFlore, son of Osblrn and Elle LeFlore, November 28, 1904.

    It is stated in the affidavit of the mother that she is a citizen by blood of the Choctaw Nation. If this is correct you are requested to state the names of her parents, and the name under which she was listed for enrollment. This matter should receive your immediate attention.

                      Respectfully,

                                                      Chairman.

*Madin name Elle Payne*
*Lettie Payne Mother*
*Forbis Payne Father*
*if this (illegible) satisfy. Let me now (illegible) send her scertif No of her alotment*

                                      *Yours truly,*
                                      *Osborn Leflore*

Applications for Enrollment of Choctaw Newborn
Act of 1905   Volume XVIII

Choc. New Born 1393
    Willie Wade
    (Born June 8, 1903)

**NEW-BORN AFFIDAVIT.**

Number..................

## Choctaw Enrolling Commission.

IN THE MATTER OF THE APPLICATION FOR ENROLLMENT, as a citizen of the Choctaw Nation, of Willie Wade

born on the 8th day of June 190 3

Name of father  Alex Wade          a citizen of   Choctaw
Nation final enrollment No   5260
Name of mother  Agnes Wade         a citizen of   Choctaw
Nation final enrollment No   5261

Postoffice   Boswell Ind Ter

**AFFIDAVIT OF MOTHER.**

UNITED STATES OF AMERICA,
   INDIAN TERRITORY,
Central       DISTRICT

I            Agnes Wade            on oath state that I am 25 years of age and a citizen by blood of the Choctaw Nation, and as such have been placed upon the final roll of the Choctaw Nation, by the Honorable Secretary of the Interior my final enrollment number being 5261 ; that I am the lawful wife of Alex Wade , who is a citizen of the Choctaw Nation, and as such has been placed upon the final roll of said Nation by the Honorable Secretary of the Interior, his final enrollment number being 5260 and that a Male child was born to me on the 8 day of June 190 3 ; that said child has been named Willie Wade , and is now living.

                                            her
                                  Agnes x Wade
WITNESSETH:                         mark
  Must be two   ⎫  Daniel F Wade
  Witnesses who ⎬
  are Citizens. ⎭  Sampson Scott

Subscribed and sworn to before me this   21   day of   January   190 5

                          SH Downing
                                    Notary Public.

My commission expires   March 14th 1908

# Applications for Enrollment of Choctaw Newborn
## Act of 1905   Volume XVIII

### *Affidavit of Attending Physician or Midwife*

UNITED STATES OF AMERICA,  
   INDIAN TERRITORY,  
  Central    DISTRICT

I, Elisa Bacon a Midwife on oath state that I attended on Mrs. Agnes Wade wife of Alex Wade on the 8th day of June, 1903, that there was born to her on said date a male child, that said child is now living, and is said to have been named Willie Wade

                            her  
                  Elisa x Bacon          M. D.  
                        mark

Subscribed and sworn to before me this the 21 day of January 1905

                          SH Downing  
                              Notary Public.

**WITNESSETH:**  
Must be two witnesses who are citizens and know the child. { Daniel F. Wade  
Sampson Scott

We hereby certify that we are well acquainted with Elisa Bacon a Mid-wife and know her to be reputable and of good standing in the community.

                Must be two citizen witnesses. { Daniel F Wade  
                                      Sampson Scott

**BIRTH AFFIDAVIT.**

### DEPARTMENT OF THE INTERIOR.
### COMMISSION TO THE FIVE CIVILIZED TRIBES.

IN RE APPLICATION FOR ENROLLMENT, as a citizen of the Choctaw Nation, of Willie Wade, born on the 8th day of June, 1903

Name of Father: Alex Wade   *Roll 5260*   a citizen of the Choctaw Nation.  
Name of Mother: Agnes Wade   " *5261*   a citizen of the Choctaw Nation.

                      Postoffice    Boswell Ind. Ter.

# Applications for Enrollment of Choctaw Newborn
# Act of 1905   Volume XVIII

**AFFIDAVIT OF MOTHER.**

UNITED STATES OF AMERICA, Indian Territory, }
  Central                    DISTRICT.       }

I, Agnes Wade, on oath state that I am 25 years of age and a citizen by blood, of the Choctaw Nation; that I am the lawful wife of Alex Wade, who is a citizen, by blood of the Choctaw Nation; that a male child was born to me on 8$^{th}$ day of June, 1903; that said child has been named Willie Wade, and was living March 4, 1905.

                                               her
                                       Agnes  x  Wade
Witnesses To Mark:                 mark
  { Alfred B. Morris
  { Isaac Leflore

Subscribed and sworn to before me this 10" day of June, 1905

                                       SH Downing
                                             Notary Public.

---

**AFFIDAVIT OF ATTENDING PHYSICIAN OR MID-WIFE.**

UNITED STATES OF AMERICA, Indian Territory, }
  Central                    DISTRICT.       }

I, Elisa Bacon, a midwife, on oath state that I attended on Mrs. Agnes Wade, wife of Alex Wade on the 8$^{th}$ day of June, 1903; that there was born to her on said date a male child; that said child was living March 4, 1905, and is said to have been named Willie Wade

                                       her
                                   Elisa  x  Bacon
Witnesses To Mark:               mark
  { Alfred B. Morris
  { Isaac Leflore

Subscribed and sworn to before me this 10" day of June, 1905

                                       SH Downing
                                           Notary Public.

# Applications for Enrollment of Choctaw Newborn
## Act of 1905   Volume XVIII

*(The letter below does not belong with the current applicant.)*

7-1764.

Muskogee, Indian Territory, May 4, 1905.

David R. Swink,
  Swink, Indian Territory.

Dear Sir:

  Receipt is hereby acknowledged of the affidavits of Lena B. Swink and Mrs. Lizzie Petty to the birth of William L. Swink, son of David R. and Lena B. Swink, November 8, 1902, and the same have been filed with our records as an application for the enrollment of said child.

                    Respectfully,

                                        Chairman.

---

7--NB--1393

Muskogee, Indian Territory, June 1, 1905.

Alex Wade,
  Boswell, Indian Territory.

Dear Sir:

  There is enclosed you herewith for execution application for the enrollment of your infant child, Willie Wade, born June 8, 1903.

  The affidavits heretofore filed with the Commission show the child was living on January 21, 1905. It is necessary, for the child to be enrolled, that he was living on March 4, 1905.

  In having these affidavits executed care should be exercised to see that all names are written in full, as they appear in the body of the affidavit, and in the event that either of the persons signing the affidavit are unable to write, signatures by mark must be attested by two witnesses. Each affidavit must be executed before a Notary Public and the notarial seal and signature of the officer must be attached to each separate affidavit.

                    Respectfully,

                                        Chairman.

Enc. FVK-16

# Applications for Enrollment of Choctaw Newborn
## Act of 1905   Volume XVIII

7 NB 1393

Muskogee, Indian Territory, June 14, 1905.

Alex Wade,
    Boswell, Indian Territory.

Dear Sir:

    Receipt is hereby acknowledged of the affidavits of Agnes Wade and Elisa Bacon to the birth of Willie Wade, son of Alex and Agnes Wade, June 8, 1903, and the same have been filed in the matter of the enrollment of said child.

Respectfully,

Chairman.

---

Choc. New Born 1394
    David Butter[sic]
    (Born Feb. 5, 1903)

**BIRTH AFFIDAVIT.**

**DEPARTMENT OF THE INTERIOR.**
**COMMISSION TO THE FIVE CIVILIZED TRIBES.**

**IN RE APPLICATION FOR ENROLLMENT,** as a citizen of the   Choctaw   Nation, of David Butler   , born on the   $5^{th}$   day of   Feb   , 1903
*deceased*

Name of Father: Able Butler       a citizen of the   Choctaw   Nation.
Name of Mother: Elie M<sup>c</sup>Kinney *nee Butler*   a citizen of the   Choctaw   Nation.

Postoffice   Goodwater I.T.

**AFFIDAVIT OF MOTHER.**

UNITED STATES OF AMERICA, Indian Territory,  }
    Central   DISTRICT.  }

    I,   Elie M<sup>c</sup>Kinney   , on oath state that I am   43   years of age and a citizen by   Blood   , of the   Choctaw   Nation; that I ~~am~~ *was* the lawful wife of   Able

## Applications for Enrollment of Choctaw Newborn
## Act of 1905   Volume XVIII

Butler *deceased*, who ~~is~~ *was* a citizen, by Blood of the Choctaw Nation; that a male child was born to me on 5$^{th}$ day of February, 1903; that said child has been named David Butler, and was living March 4, 1905.

                                                her
                                   Elie x M$^c$Kinney
Witnesses To Mark:               mark
  { LG Battiest
    Nelson Kemp

Subscribed and sworn to before me this 10$^{th}$ day of April, 1905

                                     *(Name Illegible)*
                                        Notary Public.

---

**AFFIDAVIT OF ATTENDING PHYSICIAN OR MID-WIFE.**

UNITED STATES OF AMERICA, Indian Territory, }
    Central                DISTRICT. }

                                                                         *saw*

I, Edward Jones, a neighbor, on oath state that I ~~attended on~~ Mrs. Elie M$^c$Kinney, wife of Able Butler *within 8 days after the child was born and she was nursing the child and said that* on the 5$^{th}$ day of February, 1903; that there was born to her on said date a male child; that said child was living March 4, 1905, and is said to have been named David Butler

                                          Edward Jones

Witnesses To Mark:
  {

Subscribed and sworn to before me this 10$^{th}$ day of April, 1905

                                    *(Name Illegible)*
                                    Notary Public.

# Applications for Enrollment of Choctaw Newborn
## Act of 1905   Volume XVIII

*(The affidavit below typed as given.)*

W. J. WHITEMAN.

## WHITEMAN MERCANTILE CO.,
DEALERS IN
## GENERAL MERCHANDISE

Commission to the Five Civilized Tribes,   GOODWATER, I. T., _____July 6th,_____ 1905
Muskogee, Indian Territory.
\-\-\-\-\-\-\-\-\-\-\-\-\-\-\-\-\-\-\-   7-NB-1394.

I   Dixon J M$^c$Clure   on oath state that I am   38   years old, that I am a citizen by blood of the Choctaw Nation, my PostOffice address is Goodwater I.T.
I am personally acquainted with Alec.McKenney and know her to be a citizen by blood of the Choctaw Nation, and that on the 5th,day of February,1903. there was born to her a male child and said child has been named David.Butler, and was living on the 4th, day of March1905. and is living on this date,

Signed   Dixon J M$^c$Clure

Subscribed and sworn to before me this  6th,day of   July   1905.

WJ Whiteman
Notary Public.

---

BIRTH AFFIDAVIT.
### DEPARTMENT OF THE INTERIOR.
### COMMISSION TO THE FIVE CIVILIZED TRIBES.

**IN RE APPLICATION FOR ENROLLMENT,** as a citizen of the   Choctaw   Nation, of David Butter[sic]   , born on the   5   day of   Feb  , 1903

Name of Father:   Able Butter           a citizen of the   Choc   Nation.
Name of Mother:   Aly[sic] M$^c$Kinney nee Butter  a citizen of the   Choctaw   Nation.

Postoffice   Goodwater, Ind Ter

## Applications for Enrollment of Choctaw Newborn
## Act of 1905   Volume XVIII

### AFFIDAVIT OF MOTHER.

UNITED STATES OF AMERICA, Indian Territory, }
................................................................... DISTRICT. }

I, Aly M$^c$Kinney nee Butter , on oath state that I am 43 years of age and a citizen by blood , of the Choctaw Nation; that I ~~am~~ was the lawful wife of Able Butter , who is a citizen, by blood of the Choctaw Nation; that a male child was born to me on 5$^{th}$ day of February , 1903; that said child has been named David Butter , and was living March 4, 1905.

                                                                         her
                                            Aly x M$^c$Kenney[sic] nee Butter

Witnesses To Mark:                               mark
{ WJ Whiteman
{ W.H. M$^c$Brayer

Subscribed and sworn to before me this 19$^{th}$ day of Aug , 1905

                                                WJ Whiteman
                                                Notary Public.

---

*Acquaintances*
### AFFIDAVIT OF ~~ATTENDING PHYSICIAN OR MID-WIFE~~.

UNITED STATES OF AMERICA, Indian Territory, }
................................................................... DISTRICT. }

*We*                                                             *we are acquainted with*
~~I~~, Edward Jones and Dixon J McClure , on oath state that ~~I attended on~~ Mrs. Aly M$^c$Kinney *who was the* , wife of Able Butter (deceased) on the 5$^{th}$ day of February , 1905; that there was born to her on said date a male child; that said child was living March 4, 1905, and ~~is said to have~~ *has* been named David Butter

                                                Edward Jones
Witnesses To Mark:
{                                           Dixon J M$^c$Clure

Subscribed and sworn to before me this 19$^{th}$ day of Aug , 1905

                                                WJ Whiteman
                                               Notary Public.

# Applications for Enrollment of Choctaw Newborn
## Act of 1905  Volume XVIII

**AFFIDAVIT OF ATTENDING PHYSICIAN OR MID-WIFE.**

UNITED STATES OF AMERICA, Indian Territory,}
Central   DISTRICT.

I, Winey Colbert, a disinterested witness, on oath state that I ~~attended on~~ am acquainted with Mrs. Aly Butler, wife of Abel Butler ~~that~~ on the 5<sup>th</sup> day of Feby, 1903; that there was born to her on said date a male child; that said child was living March 4, 190**6**, and is said to have been named David Butler

                                                          her
                                            Winey x Colbert

Witnesses To Mark:                      mark
  { W.P. Covington
    J.W. Homer

Subscribed and sworn to before me this 6<sup>th</sup> day of May, 190**6**

                                    Lacey P. Bobo
                                      Notary Public.

---

**BIRTH AFFIDAVIT.**

**DEPARTMENT OF THE INTERIOR.**
## COMMISSION TO THE FIVE CIVILIZED TRIBES.

IN RE APPLICATION FOR ENROLLMENT, as a citizen of the Choctaw Nation, of David Butler, born on the 5<sup>th</sup> day of Feby, 1903

Name of Father: Abel Butler  (A. 2945)   a citizen of the Choctaw Nation.
Name of Mother: Aley Butler (A-2946)   a citizen of the    "   Nation.

                      Postoffice   Goodwater, I.T.

---

**AFFIDAVIT OF MOTHER.**

UNITED STATES OF AMERICA, Indian Territory,}
Central   DISTRICT.

I, Aly Butler, on oath state that I am 45± years of age and a citizen by blood, of the Choctaw Nation; that I ~~am~~ was the lawful wife of Abel Butler, who is a citizen, by blood of the Choctaw Nation; that a male child was born to me on 5<sup>th</sup> day of February, 1903; that said child has been named David Butler, and was living March 4, 1905.

## Applications for Enrollment of Choctaw Newborn
## Act of 1905   Volume XVIII

                                                                   her
                                              Aly  x  Butler
                                                  mark

Witnesses To Mark:
{ W.P. Covington
{ J.W. Homer

    Subscribed and sworn to before me this   6<sup>th</sup>   day of   May   , 1906

                                      Lacey P. Bobo
                                      Notary Public.

---

### AFFIDAVIT OF ATTENDING PHYSICIAN OR MID-WIFE.

UNITED STATES OF AMERICA, Indian Territory, }
    Central           DISTRICT.  }

                                                        *know that*

    I,   Joel Logan   , a disinterested witness   , on oath state that I ~~attended on~~
Mrs.   Aly Butler   , wife of   Abel butler   on the  5<sup>th</sup>   day of   Feby   , 1903; ~~that there was born to her on~~ *gave birth on*  said date ~~a~~  *to a*   male   child; that said child was living March 4, 1906, and is said to have been named   David Butler

                                          his
                                     Joel x Logan
Witnesses To Mark:              mark
{ W.P. Covington
{ J.W. Homer

    Subscribed and sworn to before me this   6<sup>th</sup>   day of   May   , 1906

                                    Lacey P. Bobo
                                    Notary Public.

        *Child appeared*
             *L.P.B.*

# Applications for Enrollment of Choctaw Newborn
## Act of 1905   Volume XVIII

Muskogee, Indian Territory, April 19, 1905.

Elie McKinney,
    Goodwater, Indian Territory.

Dear Madam:

    Receipt is hereby acknowledged of the affidavits of Elie McKinney and Edward Jones to the birth of David Butler, son of Able Butler and Elie McKinney, February 5, 1903.

    It is stated in your affidavit that you are a citizen by blood of the Choctaw Nation. If this is correct you are requested to state under what name you were enrolled, the names of your parents, and if you have selected an allotment of the lands of the Choctaw and Chickasaw Nations please give your roll number as it appears upon your allotment certificate.

                      Respectfully,

        *Goodwater IT*                                            Chairman.
        *4/29/05*                *(Copy.)*
        *Aly Butler*
            *Choctaw By Blood Roll # 2946 from all Choctaw certificate # 10750*
        *Able Butler Roll #2945 now dead*
        *Aly Butler has* (the remainder illegible)

---

                                                                  7-NB-1394.

Muskogee, Indian Territory, June 3, 1905.

Elie McKinney,
    Goodwater, Indian Territory.

Dear Madam:

    Referring to the application for the enrollment of your infant child, David Butler, born February 5, 1903, it is noted that in place of the affidavit of the attending physician or midwife that of Edward Jones has been filed.

    Please secure the affidavit of the physician who attended you at the time of birth of the applicant, but in the event that there was no one in attendance it will be necessary that the affidavits of two persons, who are disinterested and not related to the applicant, who have actual knowledge of the facts that the child was born, the date of his birth; that he was living on March 4, 1905, and that you are his mother, be filed in this office.

## Applications for Enrollment of Choctaw Newborn
## Act of 1905   Volume XVIII

    The affidavit of Edward Jones, above referred to, to these facts is on file. It will, therefore, be necessary that you secure a similar affidavit from another person.

    This matter should receive your immediate attention, as no further action can be taken until this affidavit is filed with the Commission.

                              Respectfully,

                                          Commissioner in Charge.

---

7-NB-1394

                          Muskogee, Indian Territory, August 4, 1905.

Aly McKinney,
    Goodwater, Indian Territory.

Dear Madam:

    There is inclosed you herewith for execution application for the enrollment of your infant child, born February 5, 1903.

    It is noted from the affidavits heretofore filed in this office that the surname of the parents of the child is given as "Butler, while it appears from the records of this office, that you and your former husband are enrolled under the surname of "Butter".

    The inclosed application is prepared to cover the case. Please have the affidavits properly executed and return immediately, as no further action can be taken relative to the enrollment of your infant child, David, until the affidavits in due form are filed in this office.

                            Respectfully,

LM 6/4                                       Commissioner.

## Applications for Enrollment of Choctaw Newborn
## Act of 1905 Volume XVIII

7-NB-1394

Muskogee, Indian Territory, August 23, 1905.

Aly McKinney,
    Goodwater, Indian Territory.

Dear Madam:

    Receipt is hereby acknowledged of your affidavit and the joint affidavit of Edward Jones and Dixon J. McClure to the birth of David Butter, February 5, 1903, and the same have been filed in the matter of the enrollment of said child.

        Respectfully,

                Commissioner.

---

<u>Choc. New Born 1395</u>
    Robert E. Adams
    (Born March 7, 1903)

**BIRTH AFFIDAVIT.**

### DEPARTMENT OF THE INTERIOR.
### COMMISSION TO THE FIVE CIVILIZED TRIBES.

**IN RE APPLICATION FOR ENROLLMENT,** as a citizen of the Choctaw Nation, of Robert E. Adams, born on the 7 day of March, 1903

Name of Father: James Adams      a citizen of the Choctaw Nation.
Name of Mother: Lilly Adams nee Going      a citizen of the Choctaw Nation.

        Postoffice     LeFlore, I.T.

**AFFIDAVIT OF MOTHER.**

UNITED STATES OF AMERICA, Indian Territory, }
    Central                     DISTRICT. }

    I, Lilly Adams nee Going, on oath state that I am 24 years of age and a citizen by blood, of the Choctaw Nation; that I am the lawful wife of

## Applications for Enrollment of Choctaw Newborn
## Act of 1905   Volume XVIII

James Adams    , who is a citizen, by blood   of the   Choctaw   Nation; that a   male    child was born to me on   7   day of   March   , 1903; that said child has been named   Robert E. Adams    , and was living March 4, 1905.

Lilly Adams, nee Going

Witnesses To Mark:
{

Subscribed and sworn to before me this   29   day of   March   , 1905

Robert E Lee

*My com expires Jan 11-1906*                              Notary Public.

---

**AFFIDAVIT OF ATTENDING PHYSICIAN OR MID-WIFE.**

UNITED STATES OF AMERICA, Indian Territory, }
    Central                    DISTRICT. }

I,   Sarah Adams    , a   midwife    , on oath state that I attended on Mrs.   Lilly Adams, nee Going    , wife of   James Adams    on the   7   day of March   , 1903; that there was born to her on said date a   male   child; that said child was living March 4, 1905, and is said to have been named   Robert E Adams

her<br>Sarah x Adams

Witnesses To Mark:                              mark
{ Thomas Adams
  *(Name Illegible)*

Subscribed and sworn to before me this   29   day of   March   , 1905

Robert E Lee

*My com expires Jan 11-1906*                              Notary Public.

---

DEPARTMENT OF THE INTERIOR,
COMMISSIONER TO THE FIVE CIVILIZED TRIBES.
CHICKASAW LAND OFFICE
ARDMORE, I. T.
OCTOBER 12, 1905.

In the matter of the selection of an allotment and designation of a homestead for Robert E. Adams, Choctaw New Born, Card number 1395, approved Roll number 1220.

James Adams, after being duly sworn by John H. Carlock, notary public, testified as follows:

# Applications for Enrollment of Choctaw Newborn
## Act of 1905 Volume XVIII

Q What is your name? A James Adams.
Q What is your post office address? A Leflore.
Q What is your age? A Twenty-six.
Q What is the name of your mother? A Sillen Adams.
Q What is the name of your father? A Sam Adams.
Q Are your[sic] married? A Yes sir.
Q What is the name of your wife? A Lilly
Q Were you ever married prior to your marriage to Lilly Adams? A Yes.
Q What was your former wife's name? A Sallie Jackson.
Q Were you divorced from Sallie Jackson? A Yes.

"Sallie Jackson is identified on Choctaw Field Card number 3007, as Sallie Adams, approved Roll number 8812".

Q When were you divorced from Sallie Adams?
A When divorced -- lets[sic] see - about four years now.
Q Did you secure a decree of divorce from the Indian Court? A Yes.
Q Did you secure that decree of divorce or did she?
A I got it.

Q When were you married to Lilly Adams, your present wife?
A I married about three years now, three years ago.
q What was the name of her father? A Wilson Going.
Q What was the name of her mother? A Susian[sic] Amos.
Q Was Lilly Going married prior to the time she married you.[sic]
A Yes.
Q What was the name of her husband? A Thomas McCurtain.
Q When was Lilly Going divorced from Thomas McCurtain?
A I don't know.
Q Did she secure a decree of divorce from the Indian Court, do you know whether she did or not? A Yes, I know.

Q Was that prior to the time she married you? A Yes.
Q Have you any children? A Yes.
Q What are their names? A Robert.
Q Is Robert E. Adams your child? A Yes.
Q Is he the only child you have? A Yes.
Q What is his mother's name? A Lilly Adams.
Q When were you married to Lilly Adams[sic]
A First of March, 1902.
Q Did you secure a marriage license from the Indian Court? A Yes.
Q Have you a copy of that marriage license? A At home
Q Who were you married by? A Arbus Cobb
Q Was he an ordained minister of the gospel? A Yes.
Q Where did that ceremony take place? A At my home.
Q What was your place of residence at that time? A Near Leflore.

## Applications for Enrollment of Choctaw Newborn
## Act of 1905 Volume XVIII

Helen A Smith, being duly sworn as Stenographer to the Commissioner to the Five Civilized Tribes, states that she reported the above proceedings on the 12th day of October, 1905, and he same is a true and perfect transcript of her stenographic notes.

Helen A Smith

Subscribed and sworn to before me this 12th day of October, 1905.

J.H. Carlock
NOTARY PUBLIC.

---

7--3035.

Muskogee, Indian Territory, May 5, 1905.

James Adams,
    Leflore, Indian Territory.

Dear Sir:

Receipt is hereby acknowledged of the affidavits of Lilly Adams, nee Going and Sarah Adams to the birth of Robert E. Adams, son of James and Lilly Adams, March 7, 1903, and the same have been filed with our records as an application for the enrollment of said child.

Respectfully,

Commissioner in Charge.

---

7-NB-1395

Muskogee, Indian Territory, October 30, 1905.

Chief Clerk,
    Choctaw Land Office,
        Atoka, Indian Territory.

Dear Sir:

Referring to Choctaw roll card NB 1395, Robert E. Adams, you are advised that the card has been corrected to show "father's roll" No. 8811 and "for father's enrollment see Choctaw roll card" No. 3007.

You are therefore directed to make like changes upon duplicate Choctaw card of the same number in the possession of your office.

Applications for Enrollment of Choctaw Newborn
Act of 1905   Volume XVIII

Respectfully,

Commissioner.

Choc. New Born 1396
    Solmon[sic] Adams
    (Born Jan. 28, 1903)

# NEW BORN AFFIDAVIT

No

## CHOCTAW ENROLLING COMMISSION

IN THE MATTER OF THE APPLICATION FOR ENROLLMENT as a citizen of the Choctaw Nation, of Solomon[sic] Adams born on the 28 day of January 190 3

Name of father Thomas Adams   a citizen of Choctaw Nation, final enrollment No. 8909   *D.?.* Thomas
Name of mother Lorinda Adams ^   a citizen of Choctaw Nation, final enrollment No. 8664

Leflore I.T.   Postoffice.

**AFFIDAVIT OF MOTHER**

UNITED STATES OF AMERICA }
    INDIAN TERRITORY
DISTRICT   Central

I   Lorinda Adams   , on oath state that I am   25   years of age and a citizen by   blood   of the   Choctaw   Nation, and as such have been placed upon the final roll of the   Choctaw   Nation, by the Honorable Secretary of the Interior my final enrollment number being   8664   ; that I am the lawful wife of   Thomas Adams   , who is a citizen of the   Choctaw   Nation, and as such has been placed

## Applications for Enrollment of Choctaw Newborn
## Act of 1905 Volume XVIII

upon the final roll of said Nation by the Honorable Secretary of the Interior, his final enrollment number being 8909 and that a Male child was born to me on the 28 day of January 190 3; that said child has been named Soloman Adams, and is now living.

her
Lorinda x Adams
mark

WITNESSETH:

Must be two witnesses who are citizens { Ned Sockey
Willy Blue

Subscribed and sworn to before me this, the 17 day of February , 190 5

James Bower
Notary Public.

My Commission Expires:
Sept 23 - 1907

---

### *Affidavit of Attending Physician or Midwife*

UNITED STATES OF AMERICA,
INDIAN TERRITORY,
Central DISTRICT

I, Sallie Pusley a midwife on oath state that I attended on Mrs. Lorinda Adams wife of Thomas Adams on the 28 day of January , 190 3, that there was born to her on said date a Male child, that said child is now living, and is said to have been named Soloman Adams

Sallie Pusley    midwife

Subscribed and sworn to before me this the 25 day of February 1905

Geo M Goodwin
Notary Public.

WITNESSETH:

Must be two witnesses who are citizens and know the child. { Ned Sockey
Willy Blue

We hereby certify that we are well acquainted with Sallie Pusley a midwife and know her to be reputable and of good standing in the community.

Must be two citizen witnesses. { Ned Sockey
Willy Blue

## Applications for Enrollment of Choctaw Newborn
## Act of 1905   Volume XVIII

BIRTH AFFIDAVIT.

### DEPARTMENT OF THE INTERIOR.
### COMMISSION TO THE FIVE CIVILIZED TRIBES.

IN RE APPLICATION FOR ENROLLMENT, as a citizen of the   Choctaw   Nation, of Salman[sic] Adams   , born on the   28   day of   Jan   , 1903

Name of Father: James Adams   No 8909   a citizen of the   Choctaw   Nation.
Name of Mother: Lauinte Adams   No 8664   a citizen of the   Choctaw   Nation.

Postoffice   Leflore Ind Ter

### AFFIDAVIT OF MOTHER.

UNITED STATES OF AMERICA, Indian Territory, }
Central                           DISTRICT.   }

I,   Lauinte Adams   , on oath state that I am   28   years of age and a citizen by   Blood   , of the   Choctaw   Nation; that I am the lawful wife of   Thomas Adams   , who is a citizen, by   Blood   of the   Choctaw   Nation; that a male   child was born to me on   28   day of   January   , 1903; that said child has been named   Salman Adams   , and was living March 4, 1905.

                                        her
                              Lauinte Adams   x
Witnesses To Mark:                           mark
  { Lillie Dixon
  { Woodson Lewis

Subscribed and sworn to before me this   26   day of   April   , 1905.

                              L N Hunt
My com expires Jan 9- 1908               Notary Public.

### AFFIDAVIT OF ATTENDING PHYSICIAN OR MID-WIFE.

UNITED STATES OF AMERICA, Indian Territory, }
Central District                  DISTRICT. }

I,   Sallie Pusley   , a   midwife   , on oath state that I attended on Mrs.   Lauinte Adams   , wife of   Thomas Adams   on the   28   day of   Jan   , 1903; that there was born to her on said date a   male   child; that said child was living March 4, 1905, and is said to have been named   Salman Adams

                              Sally Pusly[sic]

319

# Applications for Enrollment of Choctaw Newborn
## Act of 1905   Volume XVIII

Witnesses To Mark:

{

    Subscribed and sworn to before me this 27  day of     April     , 1905

                                      Geo M Goodwin
                                      Notary Public.

                                                  7-2944.

                        Muskogee, Indian Territory, May 5, 1905.

Thomas Adams,
    Leflore, Indian Territory.

Dear Sir:

    Receipt is hereby acknowledged of the affidavits of Lauinte Adams and Sally Pusly to the birth of Salman Adams, son of Thomas and Lauinte Adams, January 28, 1903, and the same have been filed with our records as an application for the enrollment of said child.

                        Respectfully,

                                          Commissioner in Charge.

---

<u>Choc. New Born 1397</u>
    Mattie Frazier
    (Born Nov. 6, 1903)

# Applications for Enrollment of Choctaw Newborn
## Act of 1905  Volume XVIII

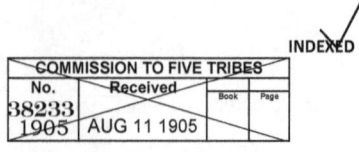

Frazier, Dixon,
Wesley, I.T.
Choctaw Nation,
Aug. 10, 1905

Transmits certificate of marriage
of Dixon Frazier to Rhoda Leader.

CHOCTAW ENROLLMENT COMMISSION

*Marriage Certificate*

In accordance to the Law and the Laws of God. This man named Dixon Frazier, and this woman named Rhoda Leader came before me and were joined in the bonds of matrimony on this Day Aug 3$^{rd}$ 1899. Jacksfork County. Choc Nation.

Ceremony performed by
(signed)                    Rev. Benjamin Baker
Sam Jones, Witness

BIRTH AFFIDAVIT.

### DEPARTMENT OF THE INTERIOR.
### COMMISSION TO THE FIVE CIVILIZED TRIBES.

IN RE APPLICATION FOR ENROLLMENT, as a citizen of the Choctaw Nation, of Mattie Frazier, born on the 6$^{th}$ day of Nov, 1903

Name of Father: Dixon Frazier         a citizen of the Choctaw Nation.
Name of Mother: Rhoda "   (nee Leader)   a citizen of the Choctaw Nation.

Postoffice    Wesley IT

## Applications for Enrollment of Choctaw Newborn
## Act of 1905 Volume XVIII

### AFFIDAVIT OF MOTHER.

UNITED STATES OF AMERICA, Indian Territory,  
Central DISTRICT.

I, Rhoda Frazier *(nee Rhoda Leader)*, on oath state that I am 35 years of age and a citizen by blood, of the Choctaw Nation; that I am the lawful wife of Dixon Frazier, who is a citizen, by blood of the Choctaw Nation; that a female child was born to me on $6^{th}$ day of November, 1903; that said child has been named Mattie Frazier, and was living March 4, 1905.

                         her  
                         Rhoda x Frazier

Witnesses To Mark:            mark
- WHMartin
- William G Cunningham

Subscribed and sworn to before me this $1^{st}$ day of May, 1905

                     W.H. Angell  
                         Notary Public.

### AFFIDAVIT OF ATTENDING PHYSICIAN OR MID-WIFE.

UNITED STATES OF AMERICA, Indian Territory,  
Central DISTRICT.

I, Sokey Impson, a midwife, on oath state that I attended on Mrs. Rhoda Frazier, wife of Dixon Frazier on the 6 day of Nov, 1903; that there was born to her on said date a Female child; that said child was living March 4, 1905, and is said to have been named Mattie

                     Sokey Impson

Witnesses To Mark:

Subscribed and sworn to before me this 5 day of May, 1905

                     Lark Sadler  
                       Notary Public.

## Applications for Enrollment of Choctaw Newborn
## Act of 1905   Volume XVIII

7-N.B. 1397.

Muskogee, Indian Territory, May 15, 1905.

Dixon Frazier,
    Wesley, Indian Territory.

Dear Sir:

    Receipt is hereby acknowledged of the affidavit of Sokey Impson to the birth of Mattie Frazier, daughter of Dixon and Rhoda Frazier, November 6, 1903, and the same is filed with our records in the matter of the enrollment of said child.

Respectfully,

Chairman.

———————

7-NB-1397.

Muskogee, Indian Territory, June 15, 1905.

Dixon Frazier,
    Wesley, Indian Territory.

Dear Sir:

    Referring to the application for the enrollment of your infant child, Mattie Frazier, born November 6, 1903, it is noted in the affidavits heretofore filed in this office that your wife claims to be a citizen by blood of the Choctaw Nation.

    If this is correct you are requested to state when, where and under what name she were listed for enrollment, the names of her parents and other members of her family for whom application was made at the same time, and if she has selected an allotment of land, give her roll number as the same appears upon her allotment certificate, and if she was married before her marriage to you, please give the name of her former husband and the names and dates of birth of her children, if any, by such former marriage.

    This matter should receive your immediate attention as no further action can be taken until this information is furnished the Commission.

Respectfully,

Chairman.

## Applications for Enrollment of Choctaw Newborn
## Act of 1905   Volume XVIII

*(The letter below typed as given.)*

Stringtown I. T. June 22 1905.

The Hon. Dawes Commission

Gentlemen

I received you Notice in Regards to my Infant Child Born Nov 6, 1903 In Reply will say she is my Daughter Name Mattie Frazier Her Mothers Name before Marriage to me Was Rhoda Leader Choctaw by Blood married 2nd Time to Simon Frazier She is now Dead he was Half Blood Choctaw I Think My Wife does not know what her Mother's Name was before she married Thomas Leader.
Do not know whether my Wife has made Application for Enrollment. Think she is not on the Roll. Through Neglect of her Stepfather Simon Frazier. She has Two Children by Simon Frazier but she was not married to him. There Names Frank Frazier about 15 yrs Old and Ben Frazier Died about 6 yrs ago.

                     Yours Respectfully,
                           Dixon Frazier.

---

Choctaw N B 1397

Muskogee, Indian Territory, June 27, 1905.

Dixon Frazier,
     Stringtown, Indian Territory.

Dear Sir:

     Receipt is hereby acknowledged [sic] your letter of June 22, in the matter of the enrollment of your child, Mattie Frazier, in which you state that your wife, Rhoda Frazier, was Rhoda Leader before her marriage to you. You give the names of her parents, but state you do not think she was ever enrolled.

     You are advised that we are still unable to identify Rhoda Leader or Frazier upon our records as an applicant for enrollment in the Choctaw Nation, and you should at once forward the original or a certified copy of the marriage certificate between yourself and Rhoda Leader, or the affidavits of witnesses who were present at your marriage, in order that the application for the enrollment of your child, Mattie Frazier, may receive consideration.

                     Respectfully,

                           Chairman.

## Applications for Enrollment of Choctaw Newborn
## Act of 1905   Volume XVIII

7-NB-1397

Muskogee, Indian Territory, August 14, 1905.

Hicks & Frazier,
    Wesley, Indian Territory.

Gentlemen:

    Receipt is hereby acknowledged of your letter of August 10, 1905, inclosing marriage certificate between Dixon Frazier and Rhoda Leader and the same has been filed in the matter of the enrollment of their child Mattie Frazier as a citizen by blood of the Choctaw Nation.

    Respectfully,

    Acting Commissioner.

7-NB-1397

Muskogee, Indian Territory, August 25, 1905.

Chief Clerk,
    Choctaw Land Office,
        Atoka, Indian Territory.

Dear Sir:

    There is inclosed herewith what purports to be marriage certificate in the Choctaw language which you are requested to have translated and have returned to this office as early as practicable.

    Respectfully,

    Commissioner

EB 2-25

# Index

ADAMS
  Arthur .......................... 90,91
  James ............. 313,314,315,316,319
  Lauinte .......................... 319,320
  Lilly ............................ 313,314,315,316
  Lorinda .......................... 317,318
  Robert ........................... 315
  Robert E ......................... 313,314,315,316
  Sallie ........................... 315
  Salman ........................... 319,320
  Sam .............................. 315
  Sarah ............................ 314,316
  Sillen ........................... 315
  Solmon ........................... 317
  Soloman .......................... 318
  Solomon .......................... 317
  Thomas ........... 314,317,318,319,320
ALBERSON
  Ben .............................. 31,33
ALFORD
  Docia ............................ 269,270
  Harvey L ......................... 269,270
  Vere ............................. 269,270
ALLEN
  D ................................ 108,109
  Dr T J ........................... 44
  Jessie ........................... 109
  M L .............................. 109
  T J .............................. 43,45,46
  T J, MD .......................... 43,45
AMOS
  Susian ........................... 315
ANDERSON
  Charles .......... 73,74,75,76,77,78,79,80,
    81,82,83,85,86
  Charley ..... 71,72,73,76,77,79,80,84,85
  Eva .............................. 72,75
  Ever ............................. 81
  Joe .............................. 259,260
  Liley ............................ 81
  Liliy ............................ 81
  Lillie ........................... 72,75
  Lou .............................. 81,86
  Lucinda .......................... 73
  Lue ......... 71,72,73,77,78,79,80,82,83,
    84,85,87
  Pearl ......... 71,72,73,74,75,78,79,80,81,
    82,83,84,86,87
  Robert ........................... 49,57,58
  Rodgers .......................... 73
  Tobias ........................... 50,51
ANGELL
  W H ..... 82,98,99,102,103,104,181,322
ARCHER
  Arthur O ......................... 102,103,104
ARMSTRONG
  J H .............................. 195,197,199
  J H, MD .......................... 195,197
ARNOTE
  A J .............................. 209
AUSTIN
  Ida .............................. 15
AVERY
  C M .............................. 242,243
BACON
  Daniel ......... 274,277,278,279,282,283,
    284,286,287
  David ............................ 285
  Ed ............................... 274,276,277
  Elias ............................ 274
  Elisa ............................ 302,303,305
  Ellen .... 274,278,279,280,282,283,285,
    286,287,288,302
  Lizzie ........................... 285,288
  Lizzie A ...... 274,277,278,279,280,281,
    282,283,284,285,286,287,288
  Lizzie Ann ....................... 274,275,276
  Sousin ........................... 282
  Susan .......... 274,277,278,283,284,285,
    286,287,288
BAILEY
  David A .......................... 92
BAKER
  Benjamin, Rev .................... 321
BALDWIN
  George W ......................... 32
  Henry ............................ 31
  Katie ............................ 31
  Mary ............................. 28,29,30,31,32
  Mary J ........................... 27
BARNES
  John ............................. 93
  Miss M L ......................... 93,94
BARNHILL

# Index

Henry .................. 25,26,27,29,30,33,34
Henry F ............................. 27,28,30,31
Katie .... 25,26,27,28,29,30,31,32,33,34
Mary ................................ 28,29,30,33
Mary J ...................................... 25,26,33
BARTON
   B H .............................................................. 2
BASCOMB
   Charles ........................ 117,118,119,120
   Cornelius .................... 117,118,119,120
   Jincy ................................... 118,119,120
BATTIEST
   Frank ......................... 200,201,202,203
   L G ................................................... 306
BATTLES
   Frank ................................................. 93
   Mattie ........................ 191,192,193,194
BAYS
   Emma ............................ 42,43,44,45,46
   Harold J ........................ 42,43,44,45,46
   James ................................................ 45
   John .............................. 42,43,44,45,46
BEALL
   Wm O .................................. 85,254,255
BECKETT
   A L ................................................. 123
BELL
   Thos M ............................. 101,104,105
BENHAM
   Mildred .................................... 209,210
BENTON
   John ........................................... 213,214
BERNARD
   Polly L ............................... 241,242,244
BICKLE
   James H ................................... 245,246
BILLINGTON
   D S ........... 40,41,160,161,162,163,165,
   218,220
   D S, MD ......................... 40,160,218
   Dr D S ............................. 41,42,161,220
   H A ........................................... 162,163
BIXBY
   Commissioner ............................... 236
   Tams ........ 54,81,136,140,141,230,234,
   253,255,261,262,263,264
BLAIR

   M C ................................................. 181
BLAKE
   Thedia D ....................................... 237
BLUE
   Willy .............................................. 318
BOBO
   Lacey P ................. 53,137,233,309,310
BOHART
   J A ................................................. 121
BOND
   Henry J ..................................... 100,101
   Sampson ....... 99,100,101,102,103,104,
   105,106
   Silway ... 100,101,102,103,104,105,106
   Simeon .. 100,101,102,103,104,105,106
BOSSON
   Thos M ......................................... 134
BOTTOMS
   Beatrice ......................................... 237
BOWER
   James .......... 11,18,23,113,155,212,318
BOYDSTUN
   Alfred E ........................................ 65,66
   George A ...................................... 65,66
   Lucetta ......................................... 65,66
BQRNHILL
   Katie ............................................... 33
BRIDGES
   D A ............................................... 149
BROCK
   Henry ......................... 278,279,283,284
BROWNING
   Nellie B ........................................... 63
BRUTON
   J 92
BULLARD
   Andrew C ............................... 245,246
   A C ................................................. 120
BUTLER
   Abel .................................... 306,309,310
   Able .......................................... 305,311
   Aley ............................................... 309
   Aly ....................................... 309,310,311
   David .... 305,306,307,309,310,311,312
   Elie ................................................ 305
BUTTER
   Able ........................................ 307,308

Aly .................................................. 307,308
David .................. 305,307,308,312,313
BYING
   Nancy ............................................ 249
BYINGTON
   Nancy ......... 244,245,246,248,249,250,
   251,256,264
   Silas ............................................... 101
CAIN
   P L ..................................... 151,152,153
CAMPBELL
   Nanie ....................................... 121,122
CARLOCK
   J H .................................................. 316
   John H .......................................... 314
CARNEY
   Millie .............................................. 120
   Milly .................................... 118,119,120
CARR
   Alma ............ 135,136,137,138,140,142
   Jim Walter ......... 135,137,138,139,140,
   141,142
   John M ......... 135,136,137,142,143,144
   William M ................. 139,141,142,143
   William Madison ..................... 137,144
   Wm M ....................... 135,136,138,140
   Wm O .............................................. 111
CARR & ROGERS ............................. 21
CASS
   Eliza ..................................... 22,23,24,25
   Maurice N ......................................... 22
   N Osborne ............................... 23,24,25
   Norris .................................. 21,22,23,24,25
   Osborne ...................................... 22,23
CAUDILL
   W C ..................... 292,293,294,295
CHAPPELL
   Walter W .......................................... 81
CHRISTY
   Wilson ............................................... 23
   Joshua ............................................... 24
   Sallie ........................................ 23,24,25
   Wilson ............................................... 24
CLARK
   Batton ............................................. 134
   W P ............................................. 88,89
CLIFTON

W F, BSMD .................................. 157
W F, MD ....................................... 157
COBB
   Arbus .............................................. 315
COCKE
   John .................................................. 47
COLBERT
   Bill ............................................. 189,191
   Dave ............................................ 18,19
   Winey ............................................. 309
COLEY
   David ................. 223,224,225,226,227
   Louvina ........................................... 227
   Lovina .................................. 223,224,225
   Nora ................... 223,224,225,226,227
COLLIER
   Martha .............................. 39,40,41,42
   Oliver ................................ 39,40,41,42
   Thomas Scruggs ............... 39,40,41,42
CONNELL
   J V ........................................... 114,115
COOPER
   Lucinda ........................... 224,225,227
COPLEN
   Lemm Joseph ................... 110,111,112
   Myrtle Palmer .................. 110,111,112
   Ollie May ......................... 110,111,112
CORNELIUS
   C C .................................................... 41
COSTON
   Lina ............................................. 58,59
COTTON
   C S .................................................... 95
COVINGTON
   W P ............................. 53,233,309,310
CROSS
   John H .......................................... 107
CROWDER
   Martin B ......................................... 59
   P C ................................................. 116
CUDGINGTON
   William B ...................................... 134
   William B, MD .............................. 134
CULBERSON
   James ......................................... 98,99
CUNNINGHAM
   William G ...................................... 322

# Index

William H .................. 102,103,104
CURLEY
   James ........................ 17,18,19,20,21
   Lee ................................................ 17,18
   Lewie ...................... 17,19,20,21
   Louie ................................................... 21
   Rhoda .............................. 19,20,21
   Roady ................................................ 21
   Roda ............................................. 17,18
CURRY
   Guy A ......... 118,119,120,245,246,247
DAMRON
   M A ............................................. 113,114
DANA
   Charles ............................................ 95
   Charles A ................................... 94,95
   Eliza ............................................ 94,95
   Vester M .................................. 94,95,96
DANIELS
   John Thomas ..................... 58,59,60,61
   Lina .................................... 58,59,60,61
   W N .................................................... 61
   William ............................ 58,59,60,61
DAVIS
   Floy E ............................................. 237
   Mr ...................................................... 80
   Oscar ............................................ 18,19
   W M ............................................. 76,79
DEARING
   H G ..................................... 213,214
DEENENT
   Maude ........................................ 217,222
DENISON
   C A ................................................. 184
DIFENDAFER
   Chas T ............................. 13,19,27,38
DIXON
   Lillie ............................................. 319
DOWNING
   S H ..................... 148,149,301,302,303
DUNLAP
   John W ............................................ 18
DURANT
   Elizabeth ........................ 148,149,150
DYER
   Celia ............................................ 145,146
   David ..................... 132,133,145,146

Dixon ................................................ 145,146
ELLIOTT
   J H ........................... 130,273,274
FENNEL
   Jack ..................................... 89,90,91
   Louisa ................................. 89,90,91
   Louisia ............................................. 91
   Vannie Elizabeth ................... 89,90,91
FENNELL
   Thomas ........................ 62,63,299,300
   Thos ............................................... 299
FIZER
   James ...................................... 39,40
FOBB
   Insey ...................................... 132,133
   Lee ....................................... 132,133
   Phillis ................................... 132,133
   Vicey .............................. 1,2,3,4,6,7,9
FOLSOM
   A E . 43,65,66,97,187,200,202,249,250
   I A ................................................... 180
   Ida ........................................ 10,11,12
FOWLER
   H L .................................................. 14
FRANKLIN
   Wirt ..... 48,49,57,58,60,71,72,84,88,89,
210,270,271,272
FRAZIER
   Batsey ......................................... 180
   Ben ............................................... 324
   Benjamin ............................. 271,272
   Dixon .................. 321,322,323,324,325
   Frank ........................................... 324
   James ..................................... 47,48
   Lena ..................................... 271,272
   Lewis ........................................... 275
   Lizzie A ...................................... 274
   Martha ......... 275,276,280,281,282,285
   Mattie .......... 320,321,322,323,324,325
   Rhoda ...................... 321,322,323,324
   Silly ......................... 275,276,277,285
   Simeon ....................................... 271
   Simon .......................................... 324
   Sissie .................................... 271,272
   W E ............................................. 184
FRONTERHOUSE
   William ................................. 197,198

## Index

FULLER
  E E ................... 213,214,215
FULSOM
  Mr ................................. 32
GARDNER
  E J ........................... 14,15,16
  Elba .............................. 208,209
  Jeff ..................... 132,133,145,146
GARLAND
  Ward, Jr .......................... 22
GIBSON
  Elizen ............................. 4,5
  Laisen ............................. 1,2
GILBERT
  J W ............................... 266
  J W, MD ........................... 267
GILLIUM
  Ben F ........................ 128,129
GOING
  Frank .............. 227,228,229,230,231, 232,233,234,235,236,237,238,239
  Lesina ..................... 230,231,232
  Lilly ................... 313,314,315,316
  Lizzie .... 228,229,230,231,232,233,236
  Osborne .......................... 229
  Peter ........... 228,229,230,231,232,233, 234,236,238,239
  Sophia ............................ 231
  Vinson ............................ 229
  Wilson ............................ 315
GOINS
  Elizabeth ..................... 147,150
  H W ........................... 147,148
  Jim ............................... 150
GOODWIN
  Geo M ........................ 318,320
GRAHAM
  T 134
GRAVES
  B F ............................... 220
  J H ............................... 220
GREGG
  Allen C ......................... 35,36
GRIFFIN
  J F ............................... 123
GUESS
  Billy ............................ 88,89

  Dicy ............................ 88,89
  Sophia .......................... 88,89
HALL
  R R ........................... 172,173
HAMILTON
  N J ............... 292,293,294,295,296
  N J, MD .............. 292,295,297
HAMLET
  Dr W H ........................... 86
  W H .......................... 71,72,84
HAMMER
  George .............. 74,75,76,77,78,80
HARDAGE
  Andrew C ..................... 151,152
  William W .................... 151,152
HARKINS
  Alice ....................... 13,14,15,17
  Allice ............................. 14
  Isaac .................... 13,14,15,16,17
  James ............................ 62,63
  Levicy .................. 13,14,15,16,17
  Richard .......................... 62,63
  Viney ............................ 62,63
  William M ..................... 113,114
HARL
  W B .................. 278,279,283,284
HARRIS
  Eliza ............................. 59
  Paul C ........................... 47,48
  W L .............................. 20
HARRISON
  J M ............................... 43
HARRY
  Geo H, Dr ........................ 269
  Geo H, MD ....................... 269
HART
  C K .............................. 158
HAYNES
  Sarah ............................. 49
  Sarah J ......................... 47,48
HEFLIN
  J McC ............................ 44
HENDERSON
  Lillie ............................. 237
HENRY
  Mathew ........................... 23
HICKS & FRAZIER ................. 325

## Index

HIERONYMUS
  S C .................................................. 95
HOGAN
  Sidney G ............................... 156,157
HOKLOTUBBE
  Stanley .................................. 118,119
HOKUBY
  Petter ......................................... 180
HOMER
  Adeline ..................................... 98,99
  J W ......................................... 309,310
  Jacob ........................................ 51,232
  Paul ............................................ 50,51
  Sol J ................................. 169,170,173
  Sylphie ......................................... 97
HOMMA
  Isabel ......................................... 146
HOPSON
  E W ......................................... 14,15,17
  Esa, MD ..................................... 14
HULSEY
  Wm J ..................................... 192,215
HULSEY & PATTERSON ... 193,194,216
HUMPHREYS
  J M .......................................... 189
HUNT
  L N .......................................... 319
HUNTER
  Dicy ........................................... 89
HUTCHINSON
  Albert Jerry ............................... 154
  Clare Gertrue ............................ 154
  Jim ........................................ 154,155
  Lewis S .................................. 154,155
  Lillie .......................................... 155
  Lillie Lee ............................... 154,155
  Matilda .................... 151,152,153,154
  Ollie ......................... 151,152,153,154
  Willia A ..................................... 152
  Willie A ..................................... 151
  Willie Alexander ....... 151,152,153,154
HUTCHISON
  Albert Jerry ........................... 156,157
  Jim ........................................ 157,158
  L S ........................................ 156,157
  Lillie .................................. 156,157,158
  Louis S .................................. 157,158

IMPSON
  Dennis .................................. 208,209
  John A M ............................... 292,293
  Laura ..... 291,292,293,294,295,296,297
  Sada .................... 293,294,295,296,297
  Sadie L .................................. 291,292
  Sarah ......................................... 297
  Sokey .................................... 322,323
  Thomas J ............ 293,294,296,297,298
  Thompson J ........ 291,292,294,295,297
  Winnie .................................. 292,293
INTOLUBBE
  C P ........................................... 295
ISAAC
  Tom .......................................... 237
JACKSON
  Belle Z ...................... 124,125,126,127
  Ellen ......................... 280,285,286,287
  Green .............................. 124,126,127
  Greenwood .............. 124,125,126,127
  Joe ..................... 280,281,282,286,287
  Robert .................................. 195,196
  Sallie ......................................... 315
  Simon C .......................... 124,125,127
  Sousan ..................................... 237
  Sousin .............................. 281,285,286
  Susan ....................................... 287
JACOB
  Austin ........................................ 97
  Eastmon ................................... 180
JAMES
  Allen ................................. 2,3,4,5,6,7
  Allen W ............................. 1,2,4,6,7,8,9
  Martin A ..................... 1,2,3,4,5,6,7,8,9
  Vicey .................................... 4,6,7
  A W ........................................... 3,8
JOHNSON
  Mores ....................................... 116
  O L ....................... 12,13,19,27,38,130
JONES
  Allington .................................... 171
  C C ......................................... 22,24
  Cham ....................................... 116
  Charles W ................ 65,66,67,68,69,70
  Cleo .................................... 63,64,69
  Dora .................................. 128,129,130
  Edward ............... 306,308,311,312,313

Fred R .................. 66,67,69,70
Freddierica .......... 63,64,65,66,68,69,70
Ida ........................ 10,11,12
J W ....................... 179,180
Lucetta ................. 65,66,67,68,69,70
Rebecca ............... 38
Rosanna ............... 10,11
Rosie Ann ............ 10,12
Rred R .................. 67
Sam ....................... 321
W E ...................... 107
Willie ................... 10,11,12
KELLER
   T C ....................... 113
KEMP
   Benjamin ............ 34,35,36,37,38
   Martin .................. 35,36,37,38
   Nelson .................. 306
   Rebecca ............... 35,36,37,38
   Richard P ............ 280,281,282
KENNEDY
   D S ....................... 100,101,104,105
KILLEBREW
   James T ............... 161
KING
   Arlington ............. 182,183
   Viney ................... 237
KINKADE
   Tennessee ........... 11
KINKAID
   Tennessee ........... 12
LAFLORE
   Charley ................ 298,299
   Elle ....................... 299
   Osborn ................. 299
   Osborne ............... 299
LANCE
   S W ...................... 44
LARECY
   W E ...................... 59,61
LARRABEE
   C F ....................... 236
LATHAM
   T B ....................... 86
LAWRENCE
   F B ....................... 280,281,282
   O S ....................... 280,281,282,285,286,287

LEADER
   Rhoda .................. 321,322,324,325
   Thomas ................ 324
LEDBETTER & BLEDSOE ............. 9
LEE
   Robert E .............. 314
LEFLORE
   Charley ................ 300
   Elle ....................... 300
   Isaac ..................... 303
   L C ....................... 43
   Osblrn .................. 300
   Osborn ................. 300
LENTZ
   John M ................ 40,41,159,160,161,162, 163,218,219,220
LESTER
   C L ....................... 4,5,229,231,232,233
   Laura .................... 298
   Sadie .................... 295,298
LEWIS
   Betsie ................... 251
   Betsy .................... 252,253
   Calvin .................. 179,223,224
   J A ....................... 95,171
   Sallie .................... 171
LINDSAY
   W T ...................... 207
LINDSEY
   Dr W T ................ 204,205,206
   W T ...................... 204,205,206
   W T, MD .............. 201,202
LINSEY
   Dr W T ................ 201,203
   W T ...................... 201,202
LITTLE
   J C ....................... 266,267
LOGAN
   Joel ...................... 310
LONG
   Frances R ............ 32
   Maggie ................ 26,28
   Magie ................... 26
LOUIS
   Sallie .................... 95
LUCAS
   Phoebe ................. 15

# Index

MANSFIELD & MCMURRAY ......... 276
MANSFIELD, MCMURRAY &
   CORNISH .................... 141,235,238,264
MARTIN
   W H .............................................. 322
MATOY
   Albert ..................... 200,201,202,203
MAXEY
   Katie ............................................... 78
MAYSEY
   Samuel A ...................................... 93
MCAFEE
   Frank ..................................... 182,183
MCBRAYER
   W H .............................................. 308
MCBRIAN
   C A ............................................... 116
MCCARTY
   Annie ........................................... 288
MCCLURE
   Dixon J ........................... 307,308,313
MCCOY
   Wesly ..................................... 223,224
MCCURTAIN
   Thomas ....................................... 315
MCDANIELS
   Lina ................................................ 59
MCGEE
   Harrison ............................... 1,2,3,4,5
   Martha ........ 278,279,283,284,285,288
   Sisey ......................................... 2,3,6
   Sissy ............................................ 4,7
   Swinney ...................................... 241
MCGILBERRY
   Turner .......................................... 217
MCGINNIS
   W P .............................................. 290
MCGUIRE
   E A ............................................... 142
   E O ............................................... 139
MCINTOSH
   Justin ........................................... 101
MCKENNEY
   Alec ............................................. 307
   Aly ............................................... 308
MCKENZIE
   T A ............................................... 134

MCKINNEY
   Aly ............................ 307,308,312,313
   Elie .................................. 305,306,311
   Isabelle ........................................ 289
MCMURTREY
   Joseph B .................................. 91,92
   Minnie L ................................... 91,92
   Thomas Walter .......................... 91,92
MCMURTRY
   J B .................................................. 93
   J D .................................................. 94
   Joseph B ....................................... 94
   Thomas Walter ............................. 94
MERRY
   G G .............................................. 184
MILLER
   J S ............................................. 90,91
   J S, MD ......................................... 90
MISHAMAHTABBIE
   Winie ............................................. 37
MISHAMAHTUBBIE
   Dave .............................................. 37
   Winie ............................................. 37
MITCHELL
   William H .................................... 237
MONCRIEF
   Clinton ........................................ 134
   Mrs W L ...................................... 134
   Walter L ...................................... 134
MOON
   Mr .................................................. 75
MOORE
   C D .............................................. 105
   Christopher D ......................... 102,105
   D C .............................................. 104
   Elizabeth ..................................... 121
   Emma ............................... 96,97,98,99
   Fannie .............................. 96,97,98,99
   H M .............................................. 217
   James E ....................................... 121
   James Lillian Theresa .............. 121,122
   Pennie ....................... 107,108,109,110
   Willie ......................................... 96,97
   Willis ............................................. 98
MORAN
   Charles W ................................... 266
   Elvin ..................................... 266,267

# Index

Fannie ............................................ 266
**MORRIS**
  Alfred B ...................................... 303
  James .......................................... 237
**MOSES**
  Ben ........................................186,187
  Charles ..................................188,191
**MOUSER**
  Noah .....................................162,163
**MULLEN**
  J S .............................................. 285
**MULLENS**
  M G .............................................. 108
**MUNCRIEF**
  Clinton ..................................133,134
  Olivia .....................................133,134
  Walter Lee ...........................133,134
**NAIL**
  Dick ............................................ 117
  E J .........................................155,156
  Joe .............................................59,60
  Joel ........................................116,117
  Nicholas J ................................10,11
  Richard .................................116,117
  Salina ....................................116,117
  Saline .......................................... 117
**NANCE**
  J M .............................................. 158
**NASLIT**
  Sissie ........................................... 229
**NEAL**
  Susan ....................................159,160
**NEEDLES**
  T B .........................................226,252
**NELSON**
  Eastmon ....................................... 93
  Isham ....................................147,148
  Molsey ......................................... 58
**NEVINS**
  Floyd ........................................... 241
**NEWMAN**
  E A ........................................188,189,191
**NIGERS**
  J W .............................................. 217
**NOAH**
  Anna .....................................102,105
**NOLLET**

Tom ................................................ 54
**O RILEY**
  Catharine .................................... 115
**OAKES**
  Edward ........................................ 167
  T J ............................................59,60
**O'DONBY**
  W J ..........................135,136,138,139
**O'RILEY**
  Catherine ..................................... 115
**ORPHAN**
  Levi ................................26,27,30,33
  Rena ..................................26,27,33
**OTT**
  Eliza ............................................ 273
  Mack ............................................ 167
  Mattie ...........................192,193,194
  Sam A ....................................275,277
  Stephen ...............................192,193
**PAISLEY**
  Mary .............................................. 36
**PALMER**
  Adeline ....................................... 111
  Castin ...................................278,279
  Frank ........................................... 111
  Myrtle .......................................... 111
**PARKE**
  Frank E .................................242,243
  Roy ........................................242,243
**PAYNE**
  Elle .............................................. 300
  Forbis ......................................... 300
  Lettie ........................................... 300
**PEARSON**
  T F ................................................ 41
**PERKINS**
  Laura ......................168,174,175,176
  Lena ................170,171,174,175,177
  Lena Bell ...........168,169,172,173,174,
  176,177,178
  Lena Belle .........................173,174,175
  N A ............................................. 171
  Nellie .... 169,170,171,172,173,174,177
  Noah ........... 169,170,171,172,173,174,
  175,176,177,178
  Nosh ............................................ 176
  Serena ................ 169,170,172,174,177

## Index

PERRY
  Allen............10,11
PETER
  Harriet............179,180,181
  Sara............179
  Sarah............179,180,181
  Thompson............179,180,181
PETTY
  Lizzie............304
PHILLIPS
  A Denton............171,195,196,251,252,257,258
PICKEN
  Jefferson............256
  Levy............256
  Nancy............256
PICKENS
  Austin............249,251,252,254,260
  Auston............250,251,253
  Jefferson............248,249,250,251,252,253,254,255,257,258,259,260,261,262,264,265
  Levi............248,249,250,251,252,253,254,255,257,258,259,260,261,262,263,264,265
  Levy............254,255
  Nacy Byington............257
  Nancy............248,249,250,251,252,253,254,255,261,264
  Nancy Byington............257,258,259,260,265
PIERCE
  Leroy............46,47,48,49
  Maude M............46,47
  Maudie May............48,49
  Robert L............46,47,48,49
PINBY
  C M............295
PLATO
  Claudia A............237
PLATT
  B F............208,209,210
  Beulah V............208
  Beulah Viola............209,210
  Bulah V............208,209
  Bulah Viola............211
  Elizabeth F............208,209,210,211
POPE
  Noel............118,119
PROCTOR
  Wm A............256
PUSLEY
  John............128,129
  Mary............37
  Nannie............128,129
  Sallie............318,319
PUSLY
  Sally............319,320
PUTTY
  George T............254,262,265
PYLE
  Cora A............237
RAMSEY
  Mary Ann............116,117
RAPPOLEE
  Dr............65
  H E............65,67,68,69,70
  H E, MD............65
  J L............67,68,69
REED
  Arlee............112,113,114,115
  Catherine............112,113,114,115
  Lizzie............245,246,247
  M F............112,113,114,115
REID
  M............101
RENFIELD
  Orrin M............122
REXROAT
  U T............268,269
RIDDLE
  Coleman............244,245,246,248
  Elizabeth............147,148,149,150
  L A............147,148
  Lena............147,148,149,150
  Lorin A............150
  Lorrin............148,149,150
  Louisa............244,245,246,248
  Nancy............244,245,246,247
RILEY
  Catharine O............115
ROBERTSON
  Coleman............247
  David............240,241,242,243,244
  Fredie............240,241,242,243,244

Irene .......................... 240,241,242,244
Louisa ............................................ 247
Mrs Coleman ............................... 247
ROBINSON
   C D ..................................... 113,114
   Jesse ................................... 155,156
   Leering ..................................... 251
   Loring ............... 171,249,250,251,252, 254,258,264
ROCKETT
   H B ........................................... 134
RODGERS
   Geo D ........................................ 238
ROFF
   Andrew V ........... 106,107,108,109,110
   Joseph David ...... 106,107,108,109,110
   Pearl .................... 106,107,108,109,110
ROGERS
   Jas A ............................................ 241
ROSE
   Vester ..................................... 49,57,58
   Vester W ................................. 32,88,89
ROSS
   Emma J ............... 212,213,214,215,216
SADDLEFIELD
   Eliza Jane .................................... 72
   J B .................................................. 72
SADLER
   Lark ............................................. 322
SAMUELS
   John ............................................... 75
   Lee ................................................. 75
SAWYER
   Charles H .................................... 277
SCOTT
   Sampson .................................. 301,302
SCROGGINS
   George ............... 194,196,197,198,199
   George Lee ................................. 197
   George W .................................. 195
   Georgie Lee ........ 194,196,197,198,199
   Gorgie Lee ............................ 194,195
   Lucinda ............... 194,195,196,197,199
SEELEY
   G W ....................................... 212,213
SETTLE
   J M ......................................... 125,127

SEXTON
   Eliza ..................................... 290,291
   Isabelle ............................ 289,290,291
   Pleas Porter ..................... 289,290,291
   Sam .................................. 289,290,291
SHANAFELT
   Richard ...................................... 181
SHAW
   Bessie ............................. 183,184,185
   Keith ....................... 182,183,184,185
   Rena ........................ 182,183,184,185
   Sena ................................... 183,184
   Send ......................................... 184
SHEALDS
   Jack .................................... 186,187
   Nancy ................................. 186,187
   Rosie Lee ........................... 186,187
SHIELD
   Jack ............................... 188,189,190
   Nancy ................................. 188,189
   Rosie Lee .................... 186,188,189
SHIELDS
   Jack ............................... 188,189,191
   Nancy ............................ 188,189,191
   Rosa Lee ................................... 188
   Rosie Lee ........................... 190,191
SHONEY
   W A .................................. 14,59,183
SIMON
   Johan .................................. 156,157
SISK
   Dr A R ..................................... 18,19
   A R, MD ...................................... 18
SITTEL
   Edward D ............................ 26,28,29
   Edward O ................................... 32
SMITH
   Dora ......................... 128,129,130,131
   G S ............................................ 129
   Georgeann ............................ 130,131
   Helen A ................................... 316
   J H P ............ 201,202,203,204,205,206
   Jack ....................................... 35,36
   Jemmie .................................... 131
   Jimmie ...................... 127,129,130,131
   Jimmie Lee .......................... 128,129
   Louisa ........................................ 20

## Index

Mrs G S .......... 129
W H .......... 20
Will .......... 128,129
William .......... 129,130,131
SOCKEY
　Ned .......... 318
SPEARS
　D A .......... 125,126,127
SPRING
　J B .......... 100
SQUARE
　Lucinda .......... 73
STALLING
　Carrie M .......... 215
STALLINGS
　Carrie M .......... 211,212,213,214,215,216
　Carrie Maye .......... 212
　Jared A .......... 211,212,213,214,215,216
　Oweta .......... 211,212,213,214,215,216
STAMMER
　Cora .......... 270
STEPHENS
　L K .......... 111,112
　L K, MD .......... 111
STILES
　Harvey .......... 191,192
　Lena .......... 193,194
　Lilia .......... 191,192
　Mattie .......... 191,192,193
STOBER
　B W .......... 158
STOVER
　B W .......... 155
　B W, MD .......... 155
SULLIVAN
　T M .......... 117
SUMTER
　Robt O .......... 195,196
SUTTLE
　J M .......... 125
SWINK
　David R .......... 304
　Lena B .......... 304
　William L .......... 304
　William W .......... 14
TALBERT
　Jno E .......... 50

TALIAFERRO
　James R .......... 268,269
　James Vernon .......... 268,269
　Minnie A .......... 268,269
TAYLOR
　Arthur R .......... 277
　General .......... 221
　John .......... 217,218,219,220,221,222
　Mary (Allen) .......... 221
　Maud .......... 218,219,220
　Maude .......... 218,219,222
　Viola Etna .......... 218,219,221
　Virla Etna .......... 217,219,220,221,222
THOMAS
　Elbina .......... 51,52,53,54,55,56
　Emma .......... 49,50,51,52,53,54,55,56
　Josiah .......... 49,50,51,52,53,54,55,56
　Melvina .......... 49,50,51,53
　Mrs Josiah .......... 50
THOMPSON
　Green .......... 114,115
　Sena .......... 182,183,184,185
TOBB
　Vicey .......... 6
　Vicy .......... 6
TOLBERT
　John E .......... 51
TOM
　Jesse .......... 52
　Sallie .......... 52
TONLER
　Susan .......... 289
TROY
　Dr .......... 32
TUEY
　L C .......... 224
TURNER
　T B .......... 123
UNDERWOOD
　Abbin .......... 57,58
　Alexander .......... 57,58
　Patsy .......... 57,58
WADE
　Abel .......... 254,255,256,263,265
　Agnes .......... 259,260,265,301,302,303,305
　Alex .......... 301,302,303,304,305
　Daniel F .......... 301,302

Eastman ........................... 192,193
  J A ........................................ 171
  Jefferson ........................... 259,260
  Sarah ................................. 192,193
  T L ..................................... 259,260
  Willie .................. 301,302,303,304,305
**WALKER**
  Hannah ........................... 152,153,154
**WALL**
  Bennie ..................................... 158
**WALLACE**
  Dr W M ................................. 59,60
  John ................................... 107,108
  W M ......................................... 61
  W M, MD .................................... 59
**WALLS**
  Bennie ............... 159,160,161,162,163, 164,165,166
  Danie ...................................... 164
  Jess ..................... 39,40,166,218,219
  Jesse ............................... 163,164,165
  Jessie ................. 159,160,161,162,163
  Jessy ...................................... 164
  Pink ............ 159,160,161,162,163,165
  T J ............................ 159,160,218,219
**WASHINGTON**
  Marcus ..................................... 171
**WEINER**
  W G ..................................... 30,31
**WELLS**
  A J ..................................... 136,138,142
  A J, MD .............................. 136,138
**WESLEY**
  Agbert ................................. 272,273
  Elias ....................................... 273
  Siley ...................................... 273
**WHITEMAN**
  W J ..................................... 307,308
**WILKINS**
  J H ......................................... 86
**WILLIAMS**
  J E ......................................... 110
  John .................................... 75,76
**WILLIS**
  A W .................................. 156,157
**WILSON**
  E M ................................... 212,213

  Eddie ................................. 186,187
  Jesse E ..................................... 237
  Joseph ............................... 283,284
  Kitsy .................................. 180,181
  Ola ................................... 126,127
**WINLOCK**
  Rufus .................................. 35,36
**WINSHIP**
  Mela ...................................... 133
**WOLLRIDGE**
  Adeline ................................... 123
  Nicholas .................................. 123
**WOOD**
  J R ......................................... 43
**WOODSON**
  Lewis ..................................... 319
**WOOLEY**
  Clara ...................................... 130
**WOOLRIDGE**
  Adeline ............................ 122,123,124
  Boyd Tinner .............................. 124
  Boyd Turner .......................... 122,123
  Nicholas ............................. 122,123
**WRIGHT**
  Allen ......................... 249,250,257,264
  S T ......................................... 80
**ZION**
  Floyd ...... 199,201,202,204,205,206,207
  Roy ..................... 199,200,201,203,204
  Susan ................. 200,201,202,203,204, 205,206,207
  W E ................... 200,201,202,203,204, 205,206,207

www.ingramcontent.com/pod-product-compliance
Lightning Source LLC
Chambersburg PA
CBHW020243030426
42336CB00010B/587